Praise for Anne Applebaum and

Between East and West

"Achieves both specificity and readability."

—*The New York Times*

"Ms. Applebaum offers us windows into the lives of the men and sometimes women who constructed the police states of Eastern Europe. She gives us a glimpse of those who resisted. But she also gives us a harrowing portrait of the rest—the majority of Eastern Europe's population, who, having been caught up in the continent's conflicts time and time again, now found themselves pawns in a global one."

—*The Wall Street Journal*

"Applebaum wants to give flesh to a concept." —*The New Yorker*

"She is a terrific writer, rare among regional experts. . . . Applebaum possesses an overarching vision of what occurred in Eastern Europe."

—*The Christian Science Monitor*

"Her researches have led her radically to reappraise some of the most basic historical assumptions made in the West."

—*London Evening Standard*

"Applebaum [has the] ability to take a dense and complex subject, replete with communist acronyms and impenetrable jargon, and make it not only informative but enjoyable—and even occasionally witty."

—*The Telegraph* (London)

Anne Applebaum

Between East and West

Anne Applebaum is a columnist for *The Washington Post* and the author of several history books, including *Gulag*, which won the Pulitzer Prize for Nonfiction, and *Iron Curtain*, which was a National Book Award finalist. She is a former visiting professor at the London School of Economics, a former member of *The Washington Post* editorial board, a former deputy editor of *The Spectator* magazine, and a former Warsaw correspondent of *The Economist*. Her essays appear in *The New York Review of Books*, *The New Republic*, *Foreign Policy*, and *Foreign Affairs*.

www.anneapplebaum.com

Between East and West

ANNE APPLEBAUM

Between East and West

Across the Borderlands of Europe

ANCHOR BOOKS
A Division of Penguin Random House LLC
New York

FIRST ANCHOR BOOKS EDITION, JUNE 2017

Copyright © 1994, 2015 by Anne Applebaum
Map of Eastern Europe © Anita Karl & James Kemp
Chapter-opening maps © John Flower

Grateful acknowledgement is made to following for permission to reprint previously
published material: *CCP/Belwin, Inc.*: Excerpts from "Theme from New York, New
York," words by Fred Ebb, music by John Kander, copyright © 1977 by United
Artists Corporation c/o EMI Unart Catalog Inc. International copyright secured.
Made in USA. All rights reserved. Worldwide print rights controlled by CCP/Belwin,
Inc., Miami, FL. Used by permission. *Farrar, Straus & Giroux, Inc.*: Excerpts from
Prussian Nights by Alexander Solzhenitsyn, translated by Robert Conquest,
translation copyright © 1977 by Robert Conquest. Reprinted by permission of
Farrar, Straus & Giroux, Inc. *Vera Rich*: Excerpts from *Song Out of Darkness* by
Taras Shevchenko, translated by Vera Rich, copyright © 1961 by Vera Rich.
Reprinted by permission of Vera Rich.

The Library of Congress has cataloged the Pantheon edition as follows:
Applebaum, Anne, 1964–
Between East and West : across the borderlands of Europe /
Anne Applebaum.
p. cm.
1. Europe, Eastern—Description and travel.   2. Applebaum, Anne,
1964——Journeys—Europe, Eastern.   I. Title.
DJK19.A66 1994   914.704—dc20   94-5091   CIP

Anchor Books Trade Paperback ISBN: 978-0-525-43318-7
eBook ISBN: 978-0-525-43319-4

Author photograph © James Kegley
Book design by Chris Welch

www.anchorbooks.com

Printed in the United States of America

For Radek

Contents

CONTENTS

Introduction to the 2015 Edition

Between East and West was first published in 1994, and very soon after that it began to seem out of date. The book describes a journey I made from Kaliningrad to Odessa – from the Baltic to the Black Sea, across the borderlands of Europe – in the autumn of 1991, with a few scenes added from other trips in 1992. Almost immediately afterward, all of the places that I had visited plunged into an era of convulsive change. All of the people that I had met would have been profoundly affected.

The republics of Lithuania, Belarus, Ukraine, and Moldova, still part of the Soviet Union when I first visited, all became independent states. Longstanding institutions – the Communist Party, the collective farms – vanished or transformed themselves beyond recognition. New politicians replaced the old, and were themselves replaced in turn. More importantly, the strange state of suspended animation which I discovered in the early 1990s – the sense that the Soviet empire had ended, but nothing else had yet replaced it – was rudely overturned by the arrival of global culture, bitter political struggle, and revolutionary economic tumult. The meandering discussions of history and identity that seemed so important in 1991 or 1992 also began to feel irrelevant as the new states in the region took very different paths.

And yet – if my descriptions of L'viv or Uzhgorod weren't of much use to the analysts trying to understand the region five years later, twenty years later they have another kind of significance, not as journalism but as history. I myself have belatedly realized that to read *Between East and West* now is to encounter a world that no longer exists.

Nowadays, the isolated village of Bieniakonie, where I met a man who spoke in verse, has its own website. But when I turned up there in 1991, people stopped in the street to stare at me. In Chernovtsy, I was the first American that a pair of university English professors had ever met. In L'viv, I had no way of calling home – there were no mobile phones of course, and the regular lines barely functioned. When I was driving across the Carpathian Mountains with a pair of grumpy Hungarians, we saw no restaurants, no shops, no hotels. Although we weren't far from the border, there was no sense that we were anywhere near 'Europe', or that the 'West' was anything but a mythological construction. This isolation, and the accompanying desolation, were the result of decades of war, ethnic cleansing, and totalitarian rule.

Twenty years later, the isolation has been lifted. But despite a transition process which has succeeded in some places and failed almost entirely in others, the impact of those multiple tragedies can still be felt all across the region. As it turned out, it was not possible to start from scratch in 1991. History did not simply fade away. Many people in the region were disoriented by the collapse of the USSR, not invigorated by the end of communism, and confused or angered by what followed. They felt no attachment to the new states in which they suddenly found themselves to be living, and no responsibility to their new governments. They longed for more stable identities: to be Polish, to be Russian, to emigrate. They certainly felt no special connection to their new fellow citizens, and in this they resembled most of the other inhabitants of all of the other post-Soviet republics. Even Russians themselves often felt no allegiance to their 'new' country, or to their new countrymen.

But with no sense of allegiance, no public spirit, and no national feeling, it was difficult to make democracy work, let alone the rule of law. The people who eventually came to lead independent Ukraine failed to build Ukraine's institutions. Instead, they built their own fortunes. I saw the beginnings of that process in L'viv, where I met a Canadian woman, an émigré Ukrainian, whose attempt to renovate a hotel failed when her Ukrainian partner stole it. Her story, described in this book, now looks like a harbinger of what was to come.

At the national level, a succession of leaders, culminating in

President Viktor Yanukovych, looted the state, dismantled Ukraine's army, eviscerated its bureaucracy, and destroyed both the public and private sectors, all the while increasing their own personal wealth. Ukraine's oligarchs – the real beneficiaries of two decades of independence – never necessarily felt any loyalty to their countrymen either. Some have sided with 'Ukraine' or 'Europe' in the current political conflict, but others side with 'Russia.' Their decisions have nothing to do with the welfare of ordinary Ukrainians at all.

In Belarus, the literary nationalists whom I met in Minsk proved to be a tiny minority. They never had the support to transform their country into a modern democracy, or even to give it the self-confidence to pursue its own policies. Instead, Alexander Lukashenka, an old-fashioned fascist, took charge of the security services, the only functioning arm of the state, and set up a new dictatorship which answers to Moscow. In Moldova, those who wanted to bring the country closer to Europe were flummoxed by an ongoing struggle against the breakaway province of Transdniestria – a strange place in 1991, as I discovered, and stranger now – which today remains a zone of lawlessness and arms dealing. Politics remains deeply divided between a Communist Party which became a de facto pro-Russian force and a motley group of Westernizers.

Of the states that I described at the time, only Lithuania can be said to have achieved any kind of stability. Thanks to the fierce drive for independence, and thanks to memories of a pre-Communist past that had not been snuffed out, Lithuania pushed itself to meet the standards to join the European Union and NATO. But even now, the situation of the Poles in Lithuania has not normalized itself, and Polish-Lithuanian relations remain surprisingly uneasy. The voices of the Lithuanians who told me in 1991 that the Poles stole their culture have an echo in the politics of today.

In the past two decades the region has certainly changed – but so have I. Odd though it may sound, I probably wouldn't have the presumption to write a first-person travel narrative now, and I'm not even sure I still approve of the genre. If I were to write this book again, I would probably be more cautious about pronouncing judgment. I would certainly remove myself from the story. Indeed, when re-reading this book now, I have the constant urge to edit, to correct, to fact-check, even though I know it can't be done: my notebooks from this trip have long since vanished in a series of transatlantic and cross-European moves.

And maybe that's just as well. For if this book still has a value, it's as a record of a experience that can never happen again. The people I met on that trip are doubtless more worldly, more busy, maybe more confident, maybe more cynical than when I met them. They would no longer treat me like an emissary from another world, and I would no longer perceive them, as I did then, as exotic and strange. But in 1991, this is what I was, and this is what they were. So I leave the book for the readers to enjoy exactly as it was written.

Introduction

For a thousand years, the geography of the borderlands dictated their fate.

The borderlands lie in a flat plain, crushed between the civilizations of Europe – and those of Asia. East of Poland, west of Russia, their lack of mountains, seas, deserts, and canyons has always made the borderlands easy to conquer. Five centuries ago, an army on horseback could march from a castle on the Baltic to a fort on the Black Sea without meeting a physical obstacle greater than a fast-running river or a wide forest. Even now, a spy running east from Warsaw to Kiev would find nothing natural to obstruct him. Distances are great, but messages to the King or the Khan or the Grand Duke or the Czar have always been easier to send here than in the more mountainous parts of Europe, because so little stands in the way of the messenger.

The borderlands' featurelessness attracted invaders, and the most celebrated – the most threatening – always came from the East. Long after the Mongol invasion of the thirteenth century, the name of the Golden Horde was still uttered in whispers, and the fame of the Turks, who attacked again and again from the sixteenth century to the eighteenth, has persisted as well. From the North came the most destructive invaders – the rapacious Swedes, who destroyed the region utterly in the Great Deluge of 1655, and the Muscovites, who began their incursions into the borderlands at about the same time. The least expected invaders came from the South, where Moldovan princes rose up to claim more territory in the sixteenth century, and Cossacks rebelled, setting fire to villages, in the seventeenth. Those who ruled the longest always came from the West. From the twelfth century onward, Poles and Lithuanians administered vast regions of the borderlands, while the Teutonic Knights controlled the northern Baltic corner, reigning for so long that their descendants, the Germans, came to believe that East Prussia would belong to them in perpetuity.

The invasions came and subsided, each time leaving traces: ideas about architecture and literature and religion, words and idioms, boys with black eyes or girls with blond hair. The pagan, Lithuanian names for rivers and forests stuck; so did the love of Turkish carpets and German tools. Sometimes there were larger changes. By the end of the eighteenth century, many of the Lithuanian, Belarusian, and Ukrainian nobility had abandoned their older languages in favor of Polish. In the thirteenth century, the Teutonic Knights completed the region's first holocaust, destroying the indigenous people of Prussia and replacing them with Germans.

But most of the time, the Polonizations and Prussifications and Russifications, the drives to win Catholic converts, the crusades to build Orthodox churches, the plans to change churches into mosques, all failed to unify the region. The borderlands were simply too wide and too empty, it was too difficult for any invading nation to maintain permanent rule. Instead of uniformity, the waves of invasion created odd hybrids: the cathedral with a minaret in Kamenets Podolsky, or the town of Trakai, where five religions (Catholic, Orthodox, Jewish, Moslem, Karaim) once set up their houses of worship around a single lake. Throughout most of the borderlands' history, the borderland peoples – the peasants and the woodsmen and even the nobility – remained various. From town to town the local legends changed; from village to village the people sang different folk tunes with different melodies.

Because of the invaders' failure to impose uniform standards, it could even be said that there were, until recently, no nations in the borderlands – or at least no nation-states in the sense that we know them now. There were the nobility and the invaders – the Poles and Russians and Germans and Tartars and Turks – who sometimes changed roles, defeating one another, only to be defeated in turn. There were the peasants: the Estonians and the Livonians who spoke Baltic tongues, the Mazurians and Kashubians who had Baltic languages all their own, the many descendants of the Slavic tribes – Volhinians,

Podolians, Polesians, Galicians, Braclavians, now known as Ukrainians or Belarusians – who had similar words for sun, sky, and earth, but used the word *chai* for tea, if they lived in the East, and called the same beverage *herbata* if they lived in the West. In the cities and the villages there were Jews, more Jews than were found anywhere else in the world: Jewish merchants and tailors, poor Jews and rich Jews, Jews whose Yiddish dialects and religious customs differed from region to region along with those of their Slavic neighbors. Scattered among all of these peoples there were others: colonies of Armenians, Greeks, and Hungarians, Tartars and Karaims, the descendants of war prisoners or merchants or heretics or criminals. For a thousand years the peoples of the borderlands spoke their dialects and worshiped their gods, while the waves of invaders washed over them, mingled, receded, and washed over them again.

With the nineteenth century came the first intimations of change. New ideas about nations and nationhood began filtering east, first from Napoleonic France, then from newly unified Germany, eroding older traditions, causing even those who were not noble to place themselves in national categories. In the eighteenth century, if a borderland peasant were asked about his nationality, he would probably have replied 'Catholic' or 'Orthodox' or perhaps simply used the Polish word *tutejszy* – it means 'one of the people from here.' But in the nineteenth century, the children of the *tutejszy*, whatever dialect they spoke, began moving to cities, where they became Polish, Russian, German, Lithuanian, Ukrainian, or Belarusian. The numbers of *tutejszy*, people without a nation, began slowly to diminish.

This process might have gone on for quite some time but for the unexpected collapse of three borderland empires – czarist Russia, Austro-Hungary, and Prussia – at the end of the First World War. In the subsequent vacuum, a handful of brand-new states, together with a clutch of ancient states that had long been ruled by others, issued proclamations of independence: Czechoslovakia and Yugoslavia, Hungary and Poland, Lithuania, Latvia, Estonia, and Soviet Russia. None of these states had set borders, all had claims on their neighbors' territory. 'The war of the giants has ended,' wrote Churchill, 'the war of the pygmies begins.'

At the peace conference that followed, the established nations of the West took it upon themselves to help redraw the borders of the region according to what, at the time, were held to be rational principles. Peoples with sufficient national consciousness were to be recognized; those without were to be incorporated into others. Rules were drawn up, plebiscites held, exceptions made for history or expedience.

But in the end, borders in the borderlands were drawn by force. During the five-year course of the Russian civil war, no less than eleven armies – from the forces of the independent Ukrainian Republic to the White Russians to the Bolsheviks to the Poles – fought for possession of Ukraine. During the 1919–20 war between newly independent Poland and newly established Soviet Russia, a million men marched back and forth across a thousand miles of territory, and at the final battle – the last grand cavalry battle in European history – twenty thousand horsemen charged back and forth at one another, sabers flashing.

The borders that emerged from the battles and the negotiations hardly satisfied anyone. The Germans disliked the strip of Poland that lay between East Prussia and Germany proper; the Lithuanians were furious that the Poles had claimed Wilno, their Vilnius. The Ukrainians still wanted their own state, and a handful of Belarusians felt the same way. Some of these grievances helped fuel the Second World War: territorial ambitions led Germany to invade first Czechoslovakia, then Poland. Rather than banding together to fight Germany, Poles, Lithuanians, and Czechs quarreled and argued throughout the 1930s, and failed to come to one another's assistance during the war itself.

Because border disputes and national incompatibilities had provided Hitler with an excuse to start the war, they remained in the minds of the Allied leaders as it drew to a close. Rationality and drawing borders by treaty hadn't worked, they told themselves; territorial wars were no longer acceptable. Better, neater solutions had to be found; the messy parts of Eastern Europe had to be made clean. When they first met in Tehran in 1943, Roosevelt, Churchill, and Stalin began to discuss the problem, sometimes obliquely. There was a precedent they all knew about: after the First World War, the Turks had transferred more than a million Greeks out of Turkish territory, while the Greeks deported the same number of Turks. Greeks, Turks, cows, and chickens had traveled across Europe in packed trains. 'While this is a harsh procedure,' noted Harry Hopkins, one of Roosevelt's advisers, 'it is the only way to maintain peace.'

Quietly, Churchill agreed. As for Stalin, he had already tried the same methods on Russia's ethnic Germans, on the Tartars, and on the Karelian Finns, among others, and he came up with the plan: he simply proposed to keep those territories he had acquired in 1939 and 1940 – the Baltic states and eastern Poland, as well as the Ruthenian province of Czechoslovakia and the Bukovyna and Bessarabian provinces of Romania – and to deport anyone who no longer belonged. Although those were lands acquired by invasion and collusion – according to the secret Molotov-Ribbentrop pact between the Soviet Union and Nazi Germany – America and Britain agreed to let Stalin have what he wanted.

At Potsdam, in 1945, Stalin claimed Königsberg and the northern half of East Prussia, too: no Germans, he lied, were left in East Prussia anyway. All had fled. Russia needed a warm-water port on the Baltic, and, after the long war, the Soviet people deserved to own a little bit of Germany, as it would make them feel like they had won a true victory. The other Allied leaders agreed. So the Baltic coast became his, too – although millions of Germans were still there, although Königsberg Bay does, in fact, freeze in winter – and the Soviet Union had pushed itself as far west as possible.

By 1945, the job of reordering the borderland peoples was already half completed. Hitler had already murdered most of the borderland Jews. Occupying Soviet officers had already sent over a million Polish officials, landowners, and soldiers to Siberia and Central Asia, along with over half a million West Ukrainians and half a million Balts. After the war, the deportations continued, grew, and developed into the largest mass movement of people in recorded history. The Poles remaining in southern Lithuania, western Belarus, and Ukraine – several million of them – were sent to the German lands in Silesia, Pomerania, and southern East Prussia. Germans from those territories were then evacuated to West Germany. Balts and West Ukrainians and Moldovans who objected to Soviet rule were moved to Siberia. Germans and Romanians were removed from the Bukovyna; Ruthenian nationalists were shipped out of Ruthenia, the eastern province of Czechoslovakia.

During the years that followed, Russian became the language of administration in those territories, and Russian Orthodoxy became the only, barely tolerated, religion. Russian settlers were moved in, wherever population levels had dropped, to take the place of those who had been deported. Soviet historians wrote Poles and Germans out of history books, as if they had never been there at all. Königsberg became Kaliningrad, streets changed their names, and so did people. Romanians in Moldova became Moldovans and learned to write in Cyrillic. The Latin alphabet was banned.

The idea was simple, beautifully clear. Gradually, all of the subtle dialects that had been spoken in the borderlands, all of the national variations and differences in costume and taste, all would be submerged in an onslaught of Russification. Difference would be destroyed: Stalin planned for the borderlands to disappear into Soviet Russia. Call it ethnic cleansing, to use a phrase coined later in another context, or call it cultural genocide. Either way, it was very successful. The West turned its face away and did not notice while the crescent of land stretching from Königsberg on the Baltic to Moldova and Odessa on the Black Sea was altered beyond recognition.

The region had been conquered before, but the Soviet empire cast a deeper shadow than any of its predecessors. Whole nations were forgotten: within a few decades the West no longer remembered that anything other than 'Russia' lay beyond the Polish border. Kiev was thought to be a Russian city. Lithuania was considered by many to be a Russian province; it was as if the many and various peoples of the region had simply dissolved into the colorless Pripet Marshes, the vast, muddy Belarusian swamp. The national identity of these lands could no longer be clearly defined. In London and Paris, the history of the borderlands was consigned to dusty bookshops, the languages of the borderlands were banished to small magazines, the borderland émigrés retreated into small clubs and churches. After forty years, even the memory of the many-colored, multiethnic borderlands had faded away.

It was during a hot summer, just at the end of what later came to be called the Soviet 'years of stagnation,' when I first saw the borderlands. For a night and half a day, the train I had boarded in Leningrad had been heading south across Russia and Ukraine, stopping from time to time in small towns, each with a down-at-heel railway station, a grimy platform, and a kiosk where one could buy sweet soft drinks and dry biscuits. I remember feeling happy and very free: I was going out, going home, going away from Leningrad, leaving behind the rules and restrictions that had governed the two months I had spent there as a student. But I also remember the frustration one always felt traveling in the Soviet Union. At that time, foreigners were consigned to certain cities, special roads, restricted train journeys. Sipping tea from a glass, I stared out the window, wanting to know more about the flat, unkempt countryside that lay just beyond the train tracks. To me it was forbidden territory, as inaccessible as the moon.

Then, quite unexpectedly, my wish was granted. The train pulled into a much larger station. We had arrived in the city of L'viv, in southwestern Ukraine, and a surprise announcement came over the loudspeakers: repairs had to be made, the train would stop for five hours. Passengers were allowed to disembark. It was as if someone had told me that it was possible to walk into a picture frame: I jumped out of the carriage and ran across the train station, into the forbidden landscape.

A few hours later, I was standing in a cemetery. The rain threatened by the summer heat had started to fall, and it was growing dark. All around me, laid haphazardly one beside the other, were a thousand monuments to L'viv's confused history. I pushed the weeds away from the face of one ponderous tombstone and saw the symbol K & K – it meant *Kaiserlich und Königlich*, imperial and royal, the symbol of Austro-Hungary – carved beneath the epitaph. Nearby, white marble graves inscribed in a lovely Polish script leaned against one another, as if in penance for some forgotten crime. Some of the tombs were Ukrainian, marked by the Greek Catholic cross; these often featured a small portrait of the deceased as well. There were also newer, Soviet graves, topped by a red star, and old stones too worn to be read. So many nations, one buried on top of the other, so many different people jostling one another for space – the cemetery, it seemed to me then, contained the secret history that the dull Soviet landscape and boring regulations had concealed. I returned to the train, and woke up the next morning in Hungary, gazing out the window at a field of yellow sunflowers, still holding the passport that the border police had demanded, scrutinized, and wordlessly returned the night before.

Although I left Europe a few days later, L'viv continued to bother me. L'viv, or Lvov, or Lwów: it was Soviet but it was also Ukrainian, or Polish, or sometimes Jewish, depending upon whom one asked. I knew of no other places like that – except possibly Kobrin, where my father's grandfather was born. As a child, I was sometimes told that he came from Poland, sometimes that he came from Russia. When I looked at his town on a map, however, it sat inside a country called Belarus. Only in between, and earlier, was the town in Poland, and only in the nineteenth century was it called Russia. That was a surprise: I would not have expected my stable, settled family to be linked to a place with a shifty, uncertain identity. Much later, in 1989, I moved to Warsaw, where I lived through hyperinflation, the first democratic elections, and four changes of government in as many years: I watched almost as many prime ministers come to power as I could remember American presidents. Warsaw gave me a taste for instability, and as soon as I could, I went back to L'viv.

On my first trip, in the spring of 1990, I found the city much the same. The cemetery was still there, along with the cobbled streets, the ancient houses, and the neat market square that I remembered from my brief visit. But this time, in the center of the main park, old women stood beneath the blue and yellow Ukrainian flag, discussing the fate of Stepan Bandera – the guerrilla leader who fought for Ukrainian independence in the 1930s and 1940s – and selling metal pins shaped like a trident, Ukraine's national symbol. Young men, with rough skin and long hair, laughed and joked and hawked smudged newspapers with titles like *Free Ukraine* and *Democratic Ukraine*. In front of the opera house, a group of men were furiously chipping away at the base of a statue of Lenin. When I returned the following day, Lenin was gone. The dull Soviet landscape that I had once watched through a train window had been altered forever.

In the West, what was happening in L'viv was already described as a 'nationalist wave' that was said to be 'sweeping' Eastern Europe and the former Soviet Union. A clutch of columnists were already editorializing about the dangers of national revival in places like Ukraine and Lithuania, whose last semi-independent leaders had been puppets of Nazi Germany and whose borders would be disputed. Politicians were already claiming that independence for the non-Russian Soviet republics would lead to a destabilizing collapse of the Soviet Union and the creation of an angry, revanchist Russia. George Bush, visiting Kiev in the summer of 1991, sang the praises of Soviet leader Mikhail Gorbachev and told the Ukrainians to abandon these dangerous nationalist tendencies: 'Long live the Soviet Union,' he said. Still, against his wishes, and against the wishes of the American State Department, the British Foreign Office, and almost everyone else in Western Europe, Ukraine became independent anyway a few weeks later, along with the Baltic republics, Belarus, the Caucasian republics, and Central Asia.

Post-Soviet nationalism certainly would prove to be dangerous, destabilizing, and uncomfortable for diplomats. But there were other things to say about it as well. After all, what some called nationalism others called patriotism, and still others called freedom: the stability so beloved of international statesmen had also been a prison. In the nineteenth century, nationalism had been considered a part of liberalism, intimately and inextricably connected to democracy. Nationalists were considered democratic heroes, the embodiment of all that was progressive and just. In the former Soviet Union in the years following 1989, nationalism was still popularly believed to be progressive; nationalist leaders were still believed, at least in the beginning, to speak for the many people whose voices had been suppressed in the past. After all, each period of 'thaw' in the Soviet Union – the 1920s and the 1960s – had been accompanied by national revivals. Nationalism in the era following the Soviet collapse also included cultural revival: freedom to speak native languages, to read native literature, to discover the truth about national history.

Anyone who believed in democracy and economic reform also knew that post-Soviet nationalism was a practical necessity. Alexis de Tocqueville wrote that rational patriotism emerges when 'a man understands the influence which his country's well-being has on his own; he knows the law allows him to contribute to the production of this well-being, and he takes an interest in his country's prosperity, first as a thing useful to him and then as something he has created.' In order for democracy to take hold in the post-Soviet world after many decades (or centuries) of tyranny, people had to identify with their governments, they had to believe that their country's well-being would bring about their own well-being. Citizens of the post-Soviet republics had to vote for local and national leaders who they believed would represent them, not distant Russians in Moscow; in order for new parliaments and new legal systems to win credibility, they could not merely be Soviet institutions with new names.

Anyone who wanted to see peace in the nations of the post-Soviet Union also knew that nationalism, in its more benign forms, was necessary. While it was true that the republics of the Soviet Union had ostensibly been at peace with one another, that peace also had been a fiction, enforced by terror, lies, and the traditional Russian belief in 'divide and rule.' Make little nations hate one another, the Russian argument went, and they will have less energy to rebel against a large one; make minorities resent the majority and they will be unable to join together to rebel against Russian rule. Undoing the terror, setting straight the lies, re-integrating the minorities into the mainstream required precisely the sort of re-examination of history that the nationalists were calling for. Leaving the Russians to run things as they had before would not have solved any national conflicts, but merely allowed them to fester.

It was equally true, of course, that the Soviet era could not be erased: however artificial, hatreds implanted in both the Russian colonizers and the non-Russian colonies during the seventy years of Soviet power remained. Russians who have been moved, sometimes by force and sometimes by choice, to Estonia or Latvia cannot be wished away or deported. In most cases, a man who has lived in a given town for forty years feels he has as much right to it as a man whose family lived in the same town for a thousand years, but has lived elsewhere for forty.

Dangerous, liberating, or perhaps both: the nationalist leaders who brought down the Soviet Union wore double-faced masks in more senses than one. They looked back to the past, sometimes the very ancient past, to justify their actions and legitimize their claims; they also looked toward the future, hoping that by means of education or repression, democracy or war, they would be able to create new states out of old nations. They could work good or evil, create havoc or peace; but finally, it was to see how their new ideas affected the people whom they claimed to represent – the people who had once called themselves *tutejszy* – that I went back. In the days of waning Soviet power, not long after such trips first became possible, I traveled from the Baltic to the Black Sea, from Kaliningrad to Odessa, along the western border of what had been the Soviet Union, across East Prussia, western Belarus, and western Ukraine, through sub-Carpathian Ruthenia, the Bukovyna, Bessarabia.

It was not an effortless journey. There are no guidebooks to this region, no signposts, and no obvious tourist attractions. Most of the beautiful buildings and houses have suffered from at least a century of neglect. Travel here demands a forensic passion, not merely a love of art or architecture or natural beauty; there are many layers of civilization in the borderlands, and they do not lie neatly on top of one another. A ruined medieval church sits on the site of a pagan temple, not far from a mass grave surrounded by a modern town. There is a castle on the hill and a Catholic church at its foot and an Orthodox church beside a ruined synagogue. A traveler can meet a man born in Poland, brought up in the Soviet Union, who now lives in Belarus – and he has never left his village. To sift through the layers, one needs to practice a kind of visual and aural archaeology, to imagine what the town looked like before the Lenin statue was placed in the square, before the church was converted into a factory and the main street renamed. In a conversation, one must listen to the overtones, guess what the speaker might have said fifty years ago on the same subject, understand that his nationality might then have been different – know, even, that he might have used another language.

By the time I got there, the region had lain for more than forty years under the ice of Soviet rule, and it still seemed, at times, as if the past were crushing the present. There were days when it seemed as if no one could talk of anything that was not tragic, as if no one could remember anything without bitterness. But then there were other days, days when I would, quite unexpectedly, meet someone who saw the past not as a burden but as a forgotten story, now due to be retold; there were days when I would find an old house, or old church, or something unexpected like the cemetery in L'viv, which suddenly revealed the secret history of a place or a nation. That was part of what I was looking for: evidence that things of beauty had survived war, communism, and Russification; proof that difference and variety can outlast an imposed homogeneity; testimony, in fact, that people can survive any attempt to uproot them.

Prelude

Oddly enough, I could find no simple way to reach Kaliningrad from the west.

I stared at the maps. Kaliningrad lies just north of the Polish border, and the old road from Warsaw was still marked. But the road was useless; no civilian traffic had been allowed through the border checkpoint since the war. The trains that once plied the route to and from Berlin had stopped long ago. Nor could one fly; at that time, only military planes had permission to land in the Kaliningrad District.

For four decades there had been no sea access, either, not even from Gdańsk, the port that gazes at Kaliningrad across their shared corner of the Baltic like a jealous twin sister. Since the Second World War, Kaliningrad had been a closed city, a naval base that excluded foreigners, even Poles. As a Russian-speaking enclave between Poland and Lithuania, the Kaliningrad District – the northern half of what was once called East Prussia – grew famous for its strategic listening posts, high security, and high concentration of naval officers. Kaliningrad had considered Polish Gdańsk, with its noisy trade unions, free-thinking dissidents, and black market trade, a suspicious neighbor. I assumed that sea links between the cities had vanished forever, and began planning to start my journey backward, by flying east to Moscow or Vilnius and then talking a train west, to Kaliningrad.

In fact, there was another way. The very name 'Kaliningrad' had hardly been mentioned for forty years, so secretive were the city's military bases; and then one day, just after the ban on foreign visitors was lifted in the summer of 1991, a small tin kiosk advertising tourist day trips had simply appeared in the port.

'Agh,' said the Polish ticket salesman, shrugging his shoulders by way of explanation. He was an older man, with eyes full of ill temper. 'Some German did some deal.' He thrust his thumb in the direction of the bay. 'Some German did some deal with some Russian. *Jakaś Komuna* – some Commie.'

He hadn't meant to insult. It was just the way things were. If a Pole owned a business and it had something to do with Russians, then he must have good connections, and so much the better for him.

'What does the trip cost?'

'Fifty marks.'

'Can I pay in Polish *zlotys*?'

'Fifty marks.'

'What about dollars?'

'Fifty marks,' he repeated for the third time, his vocal tone unchanged.

'Why charge Deutschemarks on a trip from Poland to Russia?'

The ticket salesman shrugged again.

Perhaps it was historical justice: after all, Gdańsk was once a German-speaking city called Danzig, and Kaliningrad was once a German-speaking city called Königsberg. I paid the fifty marks. The ship was due to leave the following evening at midnight.

From behind, the two travelers were indistinguishable. Both wore leather jackets, dark-colored jeans, thin wool jerseys. They had neatly shaved the backs of their necks, and cut their blond hair short to a crisp frizz. Only when they turned toward me could I see that she wore two silver earrings, while he wore only one: sexual difference was preserved.

'We left our kayaks at the port,' he told me, speaking clipped English. 'I hope nothing will happen to them.'

We were standing on the deck, watching the shoreline recede. It was dark, but the lights of the docked ships cast a faint glow on the water. Over the tops of the quayside warehouses the great cranes of the Gdańsk and Gdynia shipyards stood silhouetted against the sky like prehistoric birds.

'Did you have relatives in Königsberg?' I asked the girl, using the city's prewar name.

She shook her head and replied quickly, 'No, no, we are from Munich,' as if she had been accused of something. They had watched a documentary about the history of Königsberg, she said, and they wanted to see it for themselves.

She had learned nothing of Königsberg in school, only that there were once Germans on the Baltic coast and that there were none anymore. Why there were none – what fate had befallen millions of people – no one had ever told her, only hinted. And she did not want to know, or anyway she told me that she did not want to know, too much about what had happened.

'You see, to talk about it too much – people might think we were revanchists,' she said earnestly. 'We do not want to be accused of being revanchists.'

I laughed. But there was no joke intended. The German couple glanced at one another, faintly shocked. The girl turned from me to her boyfriend.

'Don't worry,' she comforted him, 'the kayaks will be fine.'

I wandered back inside.

The ship was an old Soviet vessel, but the interior had been redesigned according to a Polish idea of what German tourists would like. Plastic ship models and plastic starfish lay strewn about the room. Oversized beer mugs, a glass unicorn horn, a miniature life preserver painted in cheerful orange, and a few shreds of fishing net stood on a table in the center. Proud little flags from Polish and German cities hung from the heavily lacquered wooden walls: Katowice, Kraków, Hamburg, Braunschweig, Łódź, Essen, Bad Kreuznach.

One of the officials, decked out in the uniform of a Polish border guard, was busy registering the passports of the passengers. The origins of his methodology lay in both the Communist work ethic and the post-Communist disrespect for security arrangements. He picked up each passport in his big, meaty hands and gazed halfheartedly at the photographs. He flipped through the pages. Sometimes he stopped to look at a place of birth or an unusual visa. Every so often, when he found a nice, blank page, he put a large stamp on it, gaining evident satisfaction out of the loud noise made when ink hit paper. Stamped or unstamped, he tossed all the passports into a cardboard box.

The Russian captain stood beside him, fingering his jaunty new cap with pride. Occasionally he whispered something into the ear of the customs official that seemed to be very funny. The customs official threw his head back, opened his great jowls, and laughed and laughed. The two looked pleased with themselves, as if they were up to something very lucrative. It occurred to me that the ship would make an excellent front for smugglers.

The other passengers, Germans, Poles, and Russians, sat in national groups, as far apart from one another as possible. The Poles stood hunched over the 'bar,' a long wooden table with a handful of bottles grouped together at one end. The Germans clustered together in a tight circle, talking to one another in quiet, earnest voices.

There were only two Russians. Both were men, both were leaning against the side wall, both were dressed in identical tracksuits. 'We are not tourists,' one of them said. 'We are sportsmen from Krasnoyarsk.' Proudly he showed me a leather case full of fencing foils.

Germans, Poles, and Russians: ever since the Teutonic Knights laid the first stone of the Königsberg city wall, these three nations had been fighting for control of the Baltic coast and the lands that spread south and east from there.

Over the centuries, all three countries lost men, wealth, and national energy by trying to dominate this one stretch of land. Both Poland's and Germany's attempts to rule over all the borderlands led to defeat and partition, and Russia's imperial overreach backfired as well.

But, for the moment, none of my fellow passengers seemed likely to play much of a role in any great national struggle, either now or at any time in the future. I lay down on a bench and fitfully slept out the overnight journey.

In the morning I awoke abruptly, disoriented. Gray light filtered through the ship's round windows. I found my way to the deck. The wind was blowing, but the air was warm and smelled of salt.

We were about to enter Kaliningrad Bay, a long body of water protected from the Baltic by a narrow spit of sandy land; to the right lay a tiny island. A lighthouse stood in its center, with holes in its red-tiled roof like missing teeth. Moss grew along its base, as if no one had touched it for years. The Germans, now clustered against the railing, began talking and laughing. These were prewar ruins; they must be traces of Prussia! More islands followed, nearly every one graced by a ruined house, an old dock, or a bit of sea wall.

Gradually the roar of the engines grew duller, the ship slowed, and the passengers fell silent. We had turned down a narrow channel, and now beheld an extraordinary sight. All along the banks floated dozens, perhaps hundreds, of naval ships, each with its forest of gun mounts, its bristling radar dishes, its rusted rudder, its wilted red flag and Soviet naval insignia painted on the side of its seaweed-covered hull. Some were still floating listlessly in the stagnant water. Others were beached, leaning on their sides like bloated fish. Still others were pulled farther upshore, where they had been mounted on wooden scaffolds like museum exhibits. There were amphibious landing vessels designed for the coasts of the northern NATO states, as well as gunboats, destroyers, and little outboard motorboats for the coast guard.

We passed a sailor hosing down one of the piers, and farther down the bank, the tinny noise of a hammer on metal echoed from inside a hull. But no one else was about. Where a merchant port would have echoed with the noise of cranes, packing crates, and trucks, these docks were lifeless. The ships seemed to be on display, as if they were not meant for any real purpose at all. Not a single one had ever carried useful goods, not a single one had ever earned its keep, not a single one had even fought a war. Hidden from the world like treasured concubines, the ships would leave the Kaliningrad docks only when they were finally hauled away to be melted back down into scrap metal.

Russia's greatest strength has always lain in the size of her armies, her ability to fight wars on land. Perhaps that was why her attempts to garner sea power often appeared useless in the past. The Marquis de Custine, a snide French aristocrat who visited Russia in 1839, was shocked when told that the entire Russian navy served no purpose beyond vanity and the amusement of the czar:

'The view of the naval power of Russia . . . has thus caused me only a painful impression. The vessels which will be inevitably lost in a few winters, without having rendered any service, suggest to my mind images – not of the power of a great country, but of the useless toils to which the poor unfortunate seamen are condemned.'

How efficiently the Russians had transplanted their nineteenth-century habits onto the acquired soil of East Prussia! The need of the young Soviet nation to demonstrate its size and strength through vast numbers of useless ships – so little had changed.

Beside me, the male half of the Munich couple lifted his camera to photograph an especially rusty destroyer.

'Don't,' cautioned his female companion. 'It is not allowed to photograph military objects. They will arrest you.' The man glanced around surreptitiously. The only people who could see him were fellow passengers. He hesitated for a few seconds and then, obediently, he lowered his camera, twisted the lens cap firmly, and tucked the camera away in his bag.

The fear of Russia was already upon him. His girlfriend nodded her head, approving.

Without warning, the ship lurched. Everyone stumbled sideways. We had arrived.

'It is the first private dock in the Soviet Union,' declared the captain, speaking to no one in particular.

As we drew closer, a crudely lettered sign rose above the shore:
WILKOMMEN IM KÖNIGSBERG
WELCOME IN KÖNIGSBERG
BIENVENUE À KÖNIGSBERG

The ship hit the sea wall with a vengeance, and everyone stumbled sideways again as the boat began to rock, violently.

'*Ja, ja!*' shouted a squat Russian on the shore. 'This way, this way!' and he pointed to a tin-roofed kiosk, just like the one we had left behind in Gdańsk. We would have to pay a landing fee.

'Fifty marks, fifty marks!' he shouted, waving and smiling happily: the German couple, the Polish smugglers, and the Russian fencers fumbled for their wallets as they filed down the gangplank, making an odd parade.

I made my way through customs and out into the empty square.

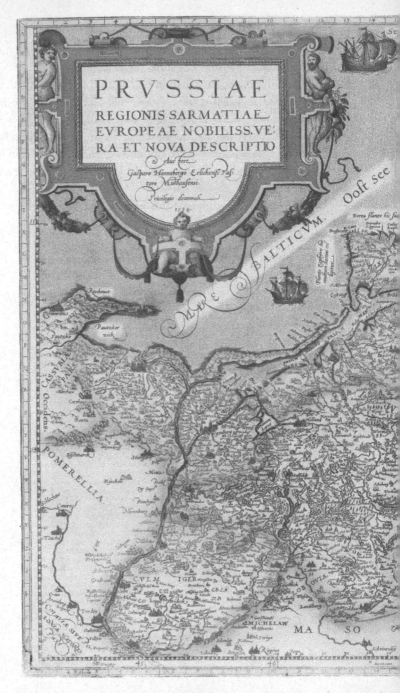

Abraham Ortelius, 'Prussiae Regionis Sarmatiae Europeae Nobiliss. Vera Et Nova
www.raremaps.com)

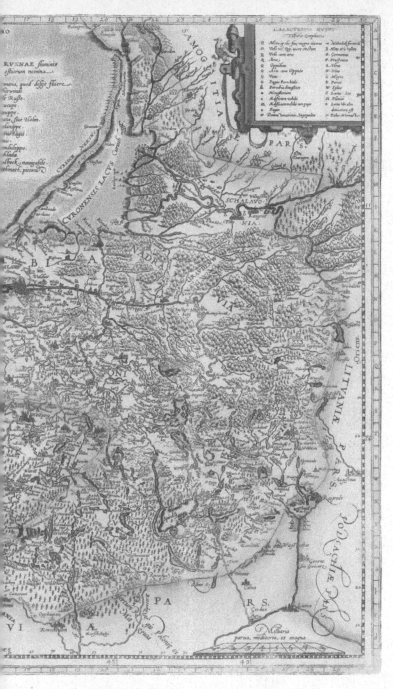

Descriptio', 1584. (Map image courtesy of Barry Lawrence Ruderman Antique Maps

PART ONE
Germans

Germanization is making satisfactory progress ... by which we do not mean the dissemination of the German language, but that of German morality and culture, the upright administration of justice, the elevation of the peasant, the prosperity of towns ...

— Prince Otto von Bismarck, 1869

The new Reich must again set itself on the march along the road of the German Knights of old, to obtain, by the German sword, soil for the German plow and daily bread for the nation.

— Adolf Hitler, Mein Kampf, *1925*

The term 'ethnic cleansing' is a recent one, but what it describes has existed for many centuries. Rome did it to Carthage, and the Teutonic Knights did it to the indigenous people of the region that was later called Prussia.

The story begins in 1226, when Konrad, the Polish Duke of Mazovia, invited Hermann von Salza, Grand Master of the Teutonic Order of the Most Holy Virgin, to come to his aid: the pagan Prus clans were burning villages in his duchy and stealing Polish women. He was unable to defeat them on his own. Surely, the duke wrote to the Grand Master, the Order – which had made its name fighting the Turks in Jerusalem – would not want to deny itself the satisfaction of saving yet another part of the earth for Christianity. Converting the Prus, Konrad reckoned, would add greater glory to the Crusaders' legend, and help the Poles breathe easier at the same time.

They were a difficult people to deal with, the marauding Prus. Their language was not one of the Slavic tongues, but closely related to the very ancient tongue of the equally perplexing Lithuanians. They had neither spices nor soft beds. They drank to excess. They lived in the northern Baltic forests, worshiped trees, and believed that no noble should go to the burial ground without his wife, his dogs, his falcons, his weapons, his servants. They did not abide by laws and other rules of civilization – they were forest nomads. They believed white horses to be bad luck. Being polygamous, they faced a perpetual shortage of women; hence the raids on Duke Konrad's territory.

The Duke of Mazovia must have been confused by the pagan woodsmen, and rather preoccupied, because not long afterward, the Teutonic Grand Master presented the Pope with a copy of the Kruszwica Act, a document that Konrad was said to have signed in 1230. On behalf of the Poles, the Kruszwica Act granted all of Prus to the Teutonic Order, in perpetuity, and retracted all Polish claims to the land. The Poles protested when the copy appeared, claiming that Konrad had never signed it, that the lands had never been granted to anyone. The Teutonic Knights, they said, had no right to be there, they were illegal occupiers.

Somehow, no one could find the original document.

The Pope took the side of Von Salza and blessed the soon-to-be Christian lands. The German presence on the far Baltic coast was assured, presumably in perpetuity. The Polish conflict with eastward-moving Germans had begun.

The Teutonic Knights changed the region forever. In the Holy Land, the Order had won a reputation among other Crusaders for dour, unsmiling efficiency. In the dark forests of Prus, their gloom deepened into fanaticism. A brother was required to eat his meals in silence, to sleep in the same room as his fellows, to own nothing – not his horses, weapons, or servants – and to avoid the company of all women, including his mother and sisters. Doing battle against the pagans, the Knights wore a white mantle marked with a black cross.

The Prus were no match for them. Within a few decades, the Teutonic Knights had conquered and converted all the lands up and down the coast. They built heavy, charmless, Gothic castles, and forbade the Prus to speak any language other than that of their conquerors. They taught them – at swordpoint – to worship Christ, and brutally murdered those who refused. The Order destroyed pagan temples, and the pagan rites soon disappeared. The Order gave German names to rivers and towns, and the old ones were forgotten. The indigenous people disappeared, their blood mingling with German blood or spilling on the ground, and they were almost forgotten.

But the fame of the Baltic crusade spread. Even Chaucer's Knight had sat at the head of the Knights' table in Prussia, and had traveled in Lithuania and Ukraine – then called 'Rus' or 'Ruce':

> *Ful ofte tyme he hadde the bord bigonne*
> *Aboven alle nacions in Pruce;*
> *In Lettow hadde he reysed, and in Ruce ...*

Slowly, even the name of the land – 'Prussia' – came to refer to the conquerors of the coast rather than its original inhabitants.

In the centuries subsequent, Prussia grew stronger. The city of Königsberg, founded in 1255, grew from a fortress to a garrison town, eventually to become the City of the German Enlightenment. Kant, Herder, and Hamann taught at the university; Frederick the Great was the city's patron. In the nineteenth century, Prussia rose alongside Königsberg, expanding to include parts of Poland and Lithuania, dominating united Germany, which arose later on. Along the way, Prussia evolved the strongest army in Europe and spawned some of the greatest kings. The Junkers, Prussia's warrior class, grew rich and powerful. As time went on, it seemed inconceivable to imagine Königsberg as anything but a German city, and even more difficult to imagine East Prussia belonging to anyone but Germans.

Looking back from the complacent safety of the nineteenth century, it even seemed to many Germans that the Teutonic Knights' thirteenth-century invasion of the Baltic coast had been an inevitable event. History has a purpose, they said to themselves, there are no accidents: as the seasons changed, as the earth turned, so had the civilized Germans gravitated toward the barbaric East.

The Germans of this time – historians like Heinrich von Treitschke and Johannes Voigt, politicians like Bismarck – remembered the Teutonic Knights within the context of the great German eastern migration, that mostly peaceful movement of farmers and traders across the Vistula, over the Carpathians, toward Danzig and the Banat, which began in the Middle Ages and continued right up until the last war. Sometimes invited, sometimes taking the decision themselves, the migrating Germans seldom went back. Instead, they founded their own villages, tilled new fields, opened shops, and remained German, even when they no longer spoke their own language, even when their neighbors were Serbs or Moldovans or Poles or Russians. So many of them moved eastward that it even seemed to the Germans as if the motion itself, the very activity of walking toward the sunrise, had been preordained, as if, in the words of the historian Michael Burleigh, civilization was always meant to flow down a 'cultural gradient' from the higher West to the lower East, from German to Slav, replacing barbarism with sophistication. German thinkers used metaphors from nature or biology to explain the phenomenon; German writers called the migration organic, comparing it to the migration of birds or the change of seasons. The Teutonic Knights were an important element of the story because they had started the process. The Knights had been a 'breakwater' in the 'wave-tossed sea of the Eastern peoples.' The Knights had set a standard for others to follow.

These images were particularly powerful in the second half of the nineteenth century, when Germany was struggling both to unify itself and to subsume newly acquired lands in western Poland and the Baltic. Racial pride was to be found in the memory of civilized German colonists settling Eastern lands, of civilized Germanic warriors conquering the Baltic coast, of educated German entrepreneurs and technicians bringing trade and science to the barbarian Slavs. All Germans could be proud of the *Drang nach Osten*, the drive to the East, that had made their nation great. The memory filled the imperial imagination and provoked the colonial instinct. While Germany had no African or Asian colonies to speak of, Germans did have a national duty to civilize the Slavic East; it was a mission. Every schoolchild, von Treitschke felt, should know 'of the most stupendous and fruitful occurrence of the later Middle Ages – the northward and eastward rush of the German spirit and the formidable activities of our people as conqueror, teacher, discipliner of its neighbors.'

Germany's defeat in the First World War quieted some of this passion for colonization but did not eliminate it. Even the mapmakers who redrew Germany's borders at Versailles could not bring themselves to make East Prussia anything but German. They were willing to take away some of the Polish lands that Prussia had captured, they were willing to reduce Germany's size and strength, but rather than give East Prussia to anyone else, they simply left the country divided. On interwar maps, one can see East Prussia, separated from Germany proper by a narrow strip of Poland, and still perched up in its northern corner of the Baltic.

It is true that in that odd, interwar time, East Prussia was just as archaic and uncomfortable as it appears on the maps. It was northern and coastal where most of Germany was central and landlocked. Its inhabitants were suspect Easterners, not quite in the same league as Bavarians or Rhinelanders. In the 1930s, East Prussia was poorer, more agrarian, and more primitive than the rest of Germany, and it was isolated: to get there, trains to Berlin had to cross a hostile strip of Polish territory. But however peculiar or nonsensical, Königsberg was an ancient city made of stone and brick; Königsberg did not seem accidental, its sturdy houses did not seem fragile.

To Hitler, East Prussia was a symbol – as it had been for nineteenth-century historians – of the heroic German past; to Hitler, the story of the Teutonic Knights seemed the greatest and best example of the *Drang nach Osten*. The Teutonic Knights had accomplished what none of the other German migrations, earlier or later, had managed: the Teutonic Knights had removed an entire nation from the Baltic coast, and replaced them with Germans. Celebrating their glory, Hitler held torchlight rallies in Teutonic castles. He turned the fortress at Marienburg into a school for elite Nazi youth. He called on the Germans to set out eastward once again, to emulate their forebears, to conquer the lower races in the name of spreading German culture and, eventually, 'to make sure that only people of true German blood dwell in the East.' He named his invasion of the Soviet Union Operation Barbarossa, after the empire-building medieval German emperor. The black cross of the Teutonic Knights adorned his ships and planes, as it had adorned German ships and planes during the First World War. Armed with the memory of the Teutonic Knights' triumphs, he set out to conquer the East.

But the 'wildly agitated, restless Slav and semi-Slav flood' did, in the end, have its revenge on those who believed that Germans were destined to rule the Eastern peoples forever.

On April 6, 1945, Soviet troops entered Königsberg after a short and – some would later say – foolhardy defense. Until the last moment, Nazi commanders had forbidden civilians to leave the city, so many witnesses remained to see it fall. The pagan Prussians, being a people without a written language, never recorded the end of their civilization. The German Prussians, being a people obsessed with history, did so many times over.

In May 1945 Graf Hans von Lehndorff, a Junker aristocrat who was working as a doctor in the city, took a walk through Königsberg. Slowly, systematically, Soviet soldiers were blowing holes in the streets, wrecking churches, burning houses, raping women. The scale of the destruction is difficult to imagine. The idea was not simply to defeat Königsberg, but to destroy its history. Not only were people killed, but their architectural monuments were burned so they might more easily be forgotten:

'Up the Königstrasse, over the Rossgartenmarkt and beyond, up to the Castle, wound an enormous coil of incoming troops, in which we now became engulfed. I pinched my thigh hard to convince myself that all this was reality and no dream. "Königsberg in 1945," I told myself repeatedly.'

The doctor turned a corner, looked at the ruins, and gave a yelp of recognition:

'Of course there used to be houses standing here: just about here was where our dentist used to live. He worked up there – in the air. Perhaps in those days he may sometimes have looked out of the window at the peaceful street below, as though he were waiting for something. Now, between flaming ruins, a wildly yelling throng, without beginning or end, was pushing its way along the same street.'

Karl Potrek, a civilian from Königsberg, sought refuge in the countryside:

'In the farmyard further down the road stood a cart, to which four naked women were nailed through their hands in a cruciform position ... parallel to the road stood a barn and to each of its doors a naked woman was nailed through the hands ... In the dwellings we found a total of seventy-two women, including children, and one old man, all dead, all murdered in a bestial manner, except only for a few who had bullet holes in their necks. Some babies had their heads bashed in . . . All the women, as well as the girls from eight to twelve years and even the woman of eighty-four years, had been raped.'

Josefine Schleiter of Osterode in East Prussia was trekking west:

'Suddenly a motorcar stopped and three very tall fellows surrounded and seized hold of me, and threw me into their car. My cries could not be heard in the snowstorm. The car started off and I was standing in it, being gazed at by one of the Russians. I was ice-cold. Since mid-day I had been without food and had nothing but what was on my body. One of the fellows, who was covered up in rugs, grinned at me and asked cynically, "Cold?" The car slowed down and I sprang out, but it stopped immediately and I was again thrown back. There then followed the most dishonouring moments of my life which I cannot describe . . .'

But it was a Russian, a young soldier named Alexander Solzhenitsyn, whose poetry, translated here by Robert Conquest, best described what happened when the Red Army invaded East Prussia:

> *Collapsing chunks of slender Gothic*
> *Burn in an enormous mound.*
> *Across the narrow street the traffic*
> *Jams up solid, tightly bound:*
> *Some too fast and some too slow –*
> *Up steps, up thresholds, on they go,*
> *Russian drivers batter through.*
> *They twist and turn, devil-may-care,*
> *At any angle, anywhere!*
> *We're used to Asiatic jolting,*
> *Bumping, riding, crashing, bolting . . .*
>
> *A moaning by the walls half muffled:*
> *The mother's wounded, still alive.*
> *The little daughter's on the mattress,*
> *Dead. How many have been on it?*
> *A platoon, a company perhaps?*
> *A girl's been turned into a woman,*
> *A woman turned into a corpse . . .*

Slapping their shoulders they reach the house.
Now they're in. She stands there, numb.
They laugh. 'Get us some eggs then, Mum!'
And the housewife does her best,
Brings them apples, ripe and brittle,
They grabbed them, walked around a little,
A crunch between their teeth like frost.
And then they shot the housewife first,
Spattering with blood the carpet's pile.
The husband was bedridden, ill:
They cured him with a carbine burst.

'The Russians,' said the American statesman George Kennan, 'swept the native population clean in a manner that had no parallel since the days of the Asiatic hordes.'

Looking back, the Königsbergers saw nothing but fire, dust, ashes, and smoke curling around the spires of their Gothic churches.

Before 1939 | After 1945

Kaliningrad/Königsberg

From the port, it was a half hour's ride by rickety bus into the center of Kaliningrad. I asked the driver if he could tell me anything about Kalinin, a former Soviet president (famous for sending his wife to the gulag) who gave his name to the city.

'Kalinin? Something to do with Stalin,' he shrugged. 'I don't know.'

We approached the city through a corridor of low buildings and the crumbling facades of bombed-out houses, unrepaired after forty years. The bus lurched over potholes, broken asphalt, trolley tracks, and bits of old cobblestone road. The wide streets were empty of cars, as if they had been built for a larger, more populous nation. On the outskirts of the city, old trees lined some of the boulevards. As we drove, the trees disappeared, the terraced houses gave way to taller buildings, the wide boulevards opened out into large plazas, the odd bursts of brick architecture gave way to cement, the landscape grew starker, until finally the bus ground to a halt: we had arrived in the medieval city center.

'Cathedral that way,' the driver said. The doors swung shut, and the bus rattled away. The still air tasted of automobile exhaust and coal smoke. The sidewalks were vacant of people. Wherever one looked, there was nothing to see but high walls of concrete and steel. But it was not the clean, crisp concrete and steel of New York or Los Angeles. Here the tall buildings were cracked, broken, and sagging, as if prematurely aged. Their walls were pockmarked with dirt and building flaws, their windows were broken, their facades had grown black from pollution. Although already in a state of advanced deterioration, few appeared to be complete. Great hunks of concrete, rusted piping, wire, and sheets of plate glass covered with masking tape lay strewn about on the mud beside them. Piles of broken brick stood beside doors whose hinges were already rusted. Thick green fungus covered half-built walkways. Whole avenues were partially paved or blocked off for repair, heaps of dirt and sand covered the grass in the parks.

Occasionally, signs of another, older, order poked through the wreckage of the new. In one place, a concrete sidewalk came to an abrupt end, suddenly revealing a well-laid cobblestone road lying just beneath its surface; somewhere else, an old building leaned sideways in an empty lot, surrounded by nothing. It was possible, almost, to see how the streets of the old town – once twisted and narrow, covered with cobblestone, lined with the tall houses of the coastal merchants – had disappeared beneath Soviet avenues of cracked concrete; how variety – medieval stone foundations, baroque seminarium doors, classical columns, Prussian red brick walls, and delicate shop windows – had vanished behind spectacular monotony; how churches and pastry shops, farmers' markets, tobacconists, a university and schools and law courts gave way to numbered apartment blocks.

Yet the city seemed unconscious of its history. After an hour of searching, city map in hand, I found the only monument to the Soviet destruction of Königsberg: a tiny, underground museum, hidden away in a war bunker. Most of its displays contained battle dioramas, and a series of diagrams plotted the advance of the Red Army. There were artists' renditions of the burning of Königsberg, and mock German signs: '*Wir Kapitulieren Nie!*' (We will never capitulate!). The final room contained before-and-after photographs. Brick homes and churches before; identical concrete blocks after. Medieval churches before; empty lots after.

GERMANS

Outside, I tried to walk through the old heart of the city, but the street plan made no sense. The center of town seemed jagged, unfinished; it was as if someone had thrown down the mismatched boulevards and drab buildings on top of the older landmarks by accident, and then gave up the whole project for lost when he saw the hideous result.

'*Sprechen Sie Deutsch?*'

I spun around. An elderly man in a checked suit and frayed leather cap was staring at me, picking his tooth with a splinter of wood. We were standing on an island surrounded by polluted canals; behind us stood the roofless, floorless, windowless ruin of the cathedral, picked clean like the ribs of a great beast.

'*Sprechen Sie Deutsch?*'

I shook my head.

He didn't either, really, so we spoke Russian. He was from Pinsk, in Belarus. During the war he had worked as a slave laborer in a German prison factory near Berlin. The food was the best he had ever tasted. The women were the most beautiful he had ever seen. The houses were so clean, so neat! Afterward, he had not been allowed to stay in Berlin, but he had not wanted to go home either, so he made his way to Kaliningrad.

'This is more West,' he said. 'This is more like Germany.' His black teeth curled over his homemade toothpick.

I asked whether there were many Germans left. He shrugged.

'I don't know any. It would be better if there were more.'

He followed me around the ruins, leaping ahead to point out the graffiti-stained tomb of Immanuel Kant. One of those rare philosophers who achieved glory in his own lifetime, Kant was once Königsberg's most celebrated inhabitant. Despite offers from more famous universities, Kant refused to move out of Königsberg, leaving the city only once during his youth, to work as a tutor in a Prussian noble household. But people from all over Europe came to him, attracted by his fine conversation and his cook's good food as well as his erudition, reverently reporting his *bon mots* and words of wisdom back to their home universities, 'like Moses returning from Mount Sinai,' in the words of one admirer. Kant inspired fanatic devotion in

23

his pupils, including Johann Herder, the father of the notion of *Volk-geist*, who said of his master that 'he was not indifferent to anything worth knowing. No cabal, no sect, no advantage to himself, no ambition had the least influence on him compared with the development and illustration of the truth.' He also won the admiration of the Prussian officers and noblemen who constituted Königsberg's upper class. Once, dining at the house of a famous general, the philosopher accidentally spilled a glass of red wine on the expensive tablecloth. To show respect for his guest, the general kept talking, spilled his own glass, and then – as he was speaking of the Dardanelles – traced the shape of the straits in the red wine with his finger.

Kant was also a familiar figure in the city streets. He was a man of meticulous habit, and the inhabitants of Königsberg regulated their routines by his daily walks. When he died, people from all classes and all professions turned out for his funeral.

The man from Pinsk did not know much about Kant: 'I think he wrote books,' he said.

I turned away, and walked across a bridge that still had its prewar iron railing. The water seemed a long way below: perhaps the pollution had caused the Pregel River to run low, or perhaps it was just the end of the summer. In the eighteenth century, the bridges of Königsberg had inspired a great mathematical puzzle. There were seven of them, crossing both the Pregel and the canal, leading from the mainland and onto a small island. The question was: could someone follow a path that crossed each bridge once, and none more than once? Some of the greatest minds in Europe fretted over this weighty question, tossing and turning in their sleep at night – until Leonhard Euler, a Swiss thinker who took over the chair of mathematics in St Petersburg at twenty-eight, conclusively proved that 'if there are more than two areas to which an odd number of bridges lead, then such a journey is impossible.' Euler later became the court mathematician to Frederick the Great, but his experience in Russia stuck with him. Once, when the queen of Prussia reproached him for his silence, he replied, 'Madame, I come from a country where, if you speak, you are hanged.'

As I walked, trying to follow the course of Euler's bridges, the man from Pinsk kept following me. He seemed to be waiting for something. Beyond the cathedral, he leapt in front again.

'Look, look,' he said without irony. 'Communist Party headquarters.'

The building would have been difficult to miss: its exterior, the part that had been completed, was made of pink marble. Lopsided, its top half wider than its base, the building hunched over the center of the city like a witch on a broomstick. Its two mismatching towers were linked by what appeared to be bits of metal piping. Round windows punctuated its middle. Vast sheets of pointless granite encircled its base, but the pink building was unfinished. Scaffolding still covered its outside walls, and the wind whistled in its elevator shafts. Too expensive to tear down, too expensive to complete, its only remaining function was its original one: to blot out the memory of the Teutonic Knights' castle, which once stood in the same place.

I turned to go. The man grabbed my arm.

'Can you take me to Germany?'

'What?' I pulled my arm away. He clasped his hands together in a mockery of prayer.

'Can you take me to Germany? I want to go back to Germany with you.'

I said that I couldn't take him back and that I was not a German. He looked me up and down. He didn't believe it.

He grabbed my arm again.

'Any Deutschemarks?' he asked.

I gave him a dollar, and he scurried away.

Kaliningrad is one of the few places where Stalin succeeded completely in what he set out to do. He exterminated the East Prussians as thoroughly as the Teutonic Knights once exterminated the Prus, taking a few years instead of a century. He filled the city with outsiders. He destroyed the churches and the houses and the trees. He put concrete blocks in their place. He obliterated the past. 'If I were dropped in this town by parachute and asked where I was,' wrote Marion Gräfin Dönhoff, the publisher of *Die Zeit*, who spent her childhood in a palace near Königsberg and returned long after the war, 'I would answer: perhaps Irkutsk.'

*

In the afternoon, I walked into the offices of a local newspaper. It used to be called *Komsomolskaya Pravda*; now its editors were trying to find a new name. I asked if anyone knew how to find a German.

'Not a Soviet German,' I said, 'a Königsberger.'

The Soviet Germans are descended from the German peasants who farmed near the Volga, where Catherine the Great granted them empty land in the eighteenth century, or from the German merchants and engineers whom she and her predecessor, Peter the Great, imported to develop cities like St Petersburg and Odessa. Although thousands of them were now living in Kaliningrad, the immediate ancestors of the Soviet Germans were immigrants, still conscious that they lived in a foreign country. A Königsberger, although his ancestors came from Germany in the Middle Ages, was not an immigrant. Whatever it might have been once, Königsberg was not a German colony in the East before the war; it was Germany.

The editor, a woman with a man's haircut, thick bones, and a long flannel skirt, looked at me skeptically.

'Why?' she asked. 'It would not be an interesting theme for you.'

She took out a piece of paper and showed me the nationality breakdown of the Kaliningrad District.

'We are mostly Russians – I am a Russian – but we are also Lithuanians, Latvians, Estonians, Belarusians, Ukrainians, Armenians, Uzbeks, and Azerbaijanis. We have more than thirty nationalities in Kaliningrad; there are many interesting people to interview.' She was proud of Kaliningrad's diversity: her city was a tiny mirror of the Soviet Union. 'Why do you want to meet an old German?'

She had been born in Siberia, and spent her childhood at an army base on the Kurile Islands. Her parents had escaped the cold and poverty of Asiatic Russia by joining the army, moving west, and later, on retirement, electing to stay there. This was the path taken by many Russians of their generation. The Baltic coast – Lithuania, Latvia, and Estonia, as well as the Kaliningrad District – seemed more civilized, more European than Russia. As so many of the region's inhabitants had been murdered or deported, there was more space. There were even empty houses – sturdy, brick, Prussian houses – to be had for the asking.

The editor had lived in Kaliningrad for most of her life, but in school she had not learned that Kaliningrad had ever been a German city. History began with the Russian Revolution, and the next important event was the Second World War, the Great Patriotic War. After the war, her teachers told her, Stalin liberated Kaliningrad from Nazi occupation, but no one ever said anything about the city prior to this event. Now she knew more. She had seen photographs of the cathedral, and she was very proud of Kant; she thought Kaliningrad should be renamed Kantgrad. Already, she said, her generation considered itself 'different' from Russian Russians. They were Baltic Russians, a new nationality. For the moment they were rather passive, children of soldiers and sailors, but surely they would develop into a great trading nation; geography would have to win out in the end. 'Over there,' she said several times, with a wave of the hand, indicating Russia, which she believed to be a different country. Unconsciously, she had adopted the attitude of the Germans before her. Here, the Baltic coast, was civilized. There, the East – that was barbaric.

Yet her knowledge of the city's past was shallow. She spoke of Kant with the same veneration that Russians reserve for their canon of cultural heroes – Pushkin, Tolstoy, Dostoevsky – yet she had not read any of Kant's books: 'I don't think they are published in Russian.' The names of the city's other philosophers were new to her. Her interest in Germany was an interest in German tourism, German commerce, not an interest in the German past. Her plans for 'her' city were plans that would bring in German money. She hoped her newspaper would promote a free economic zone on the Baltic, an open border with Poland, trade with Germany. She spoke knowledgeably about the 'corridor': just as East Prussia had once had a Polish corridor between itself and Russia, so, too, was the Kaliningrad District now separated from Russia by a Lithuanian corridor. The problem of customs and transport would have to be solved – peacefully, she hoped.

As she talked of these things, the editor grew so excited that she picked up the telephone and, still talking, began to dial. She had a friend, she said, an economist. He could explain everything about the economic zone, everything about trade and transport. 'You should meet someone who can talk about the future, not the past but the future.'

But her friend was not at home. She put down the telephone. An airplane roared overhead, filling the room with sound.

'I think an old German would be an interesting theme,' I said.

'The only people who could find a German for you are the KGB,' she declared. 'They have the lists. And in our district, they are quite reformed. We know some of the young officers. But maybe you would like to meet a new German, one who has come here to visit, to invest? We know such people. There is a new society, a German society, that they have put together with the Soviet Germans.'

She picked up the telephone again.

'No, I met some of those already,' I said, 'on the boat.' She put the telephone down.

'Maybe you could call the KGB?' I said. 'There is nothing wrong with asking them if they know how to find someone.'

'If you wish. I will call the KGB, but I promise you nothing.' With a frown and a shrug of her shoulders, she sat back in her chair.

'Come back tomorrow,' she said.

There were no hotels in Kaliningrad that appealed, so in the evening, I took a taxi to Svetlogorsk – it was called Rauschen once, and Thomas Mann is said to have stayed there in the twenties – about an hour north of Kaliningrad.

'I am a Pole,' said the driver, speaking Russian.

His grandfather's father was a nobleman who fought in the 1863 Polish uprising against Russia; the czar's army exiled him to Kazakhstan, from whence he never returned. His grandfather worked in Kazakh mines; his father joined the Soviet Navy and sailed around the world. On one memorable trip he visited Galveston, Texas. The taxi driver lived in Pioneersk, not far from Svetlogorsk.

'Pioneersk?'

The driver saw nothing funny in renaming a city after the Communist Boy Scouts. 'I grew up there,' he said. 'I don't know what it was called before.' On his mother's side he was a Tartar and an Uzbek. But his native language was Russian, and he knew no other.

Approaching Svetlogorsk, he became nervous.

'Not supposed to go near here,' he mumbled.

He stopped at the bottom of a steep hill and gestured for me to get out. 'You'll find a hotel up there,' he said, and drove away quickly.

I walked up the hill slowly, passing big houses with towers and high Gothic windows – some wooden, some red brick, some stone. After a few minutes, I understood why the driver had wanted to get away so quickly. Each house bore a sign: 'First Division, Soviet Army' or 'Naval Officers' Club' or 'Military Sanatorium.' Svetlogorsk had become an army holiday camp, off-limits to civilians. Perhaps it had always had been that way. It was easy to imagine Prussian officers with large families coming here to pass the summer in the big, roomy houses and wide streets. But close up, the houses were covered with mold and the wood was decaying.

The only hotel not linked to a regiment stood as if abandoned in a field outside the center of town. The reception desk was deserted, and water dripped from the ceiling inside the hallway.

I rang the bell.

From somewhere in the background came the sound of a teaspoon dropped on the floor, and then silence.

I rang the bell again.

A door slammed. A woman with long gray hair and one unfocused eye came shuffling to the front desk. I asked for a room.

'Passport,' she said.

Her eyes widened when she saw the American eagle.

'Fifty rubles,' she said, naming the largest amount of money she could imagine. Fifty rubles, a month's salary, came to about $1.50. She grabbed the bills, looked at them carefully – in an earlier era, she would have bitten the coins with her teeth – and surreptitiously stuffed them into her pocket.

I made my way up the filthy staircase and down the dark hall. Opening the door, I beheld a remarkable sight.

It was not just that the hotel room was badly designed. It was as if someone had purposefully set out to create a room where everything was askew, where nothing worked at all.

Every item in the bathroom was poorly constructed, as if stray bits of old junk had been reassembled there instead of fixtures. The sink had no drainpipe, so water leaked straight onto the floor. The toilet flushed not with a handle, but with a bit of twisted wire. The shower head was set so low that any normal adult would have to kneel to wet his head. An inoperable ventilator, unconnected to any source of electricity, hung from the wall.

In the bedroom, the walls were covered in unmatching tiles. Half the room was muddy blue, and the other half hospital green. No one had bothered to make the tiles reach the ceiling, so several inches of unadorned cement lined the top of the walls. The beds lacked sheets and pillows. A small but vigorous cockroach was crawling across the floor.

Someone had ordered the construction of this hotel. Someone else had built it. Someone had placed the mismatching tiles on the wall, someone had installed the ill-fitting sink. Someone had chosen the colors of the paint, someone had failed to make the beds. Many decisions had been made, but no one had been responsible for the hotel room. No one was forced by the need for money or the need to keep a job or even by pride of ownership to make the hotel room pleasant. It was just a place, created to fill the plan of a distant bureaucrat who would never see it and would never care.

I thought of the Prussians, the original, pagan Prussians who worshiped trees. I looked out the window. Soft green hills, shrouded in mist, formed the backdrop to the great, gray ash heap that stood in the middle of the yard.

In the morning, I returned to the office of the newspaper. The mannish editor was formal and distant, still angry that I had not wanted to discuss economic zones and the bright future of Baltic Russia. But she had found what I wanted.

A young sergeant at the KGB, a friend of the newspaper, had on file the names of three Germans who still lived in Kaliningrad District.

'I'm not saying that this is all of them. But these are the people who registered "German" on their passports.'

One, a Mr Fritz R——, was in a mental hospital. The second was a woman who lived quite far away, several hours' drive, and she was quite possibly too ill to speak, being more than ninety years old. 'The third, Gerda Petrovna' – and the editor gave a Lithuanian surname – 'lives in the center of town. But she has no telephone.'

'Perhaps you would like to come with me?'

'I would not like to come with you,' said the editor firmly. 'I am not fond of knocking on the doors of people whom I do not know. And for me it is not interesting.' She turned away without saying good-bye.

The house was easy to find, although it was not in the center of Kaliningrad. It stood in a prewar suburb, one of the few that had been preserved, squeezed between other town houses with red-tiled roofs and small gardens. These former homes for the German working class now looked luxuriously individual.

Gerda Petrovna herself answered the door. She was a thin woman with a rigid spine and gray hair pulled back severely with pins. When I explained who I was, she smiled a surprised, mirthless smile.

'Come in,' she said. 'I have never met an American before.'

She led me through a dark hallway. The old family house had been divided into four apartments, and hers was the smallest. Standard Soviet furniture filled the only room: cheap bookshelves lined with unread copies of Tolstoy, a mass-produced carpet woven in mock-peasant style, a few plastic ashtrays. A curtain hung across the center, dividing the 'sitting room' from the 'bedroom.' An improvised kitchenette branched off the far corner.

'Masha,' said Gerda Petrovna, 'we have a guest.'

Another woman, as fat and soft as Gerda Petrovna was brittle, peered out of the kitchenette. Seeing me, her flabby cheeks began to quiver.

'A guest?'

'A guest from America,' said Gerda Petrovna firmly.

'From America! But I haven't cleaned the room, I have nothing to eat,' she began to wail while rustling toward me, wiping her hands on her apron in a panic. 'What would you like? Tea? There is no coffee . . . perhaps juice?'

'Tea is fine.'

Masha cleared some old dishes off the table, and ran back into the kitchenette to prepare tea. Pots began to bang against one another, and something fell to the ground with a crash. Gerda Petrovna ignored the sounds and turned to me.

'So what do you want to know?'

'I am told you are German,' I began.

'German? I am not German,' she said quickly. 'I am Lithuanian.'

'Oh, I'm sorry . . . I was looking for someone who lived in Königsberg before the war.'

'I did live in Königsberg before the war.'

'But you were not born here . . .'

'I was born here, but my mother was a Lithuanian.'

'So you spoke Lithuanian as a child?'

'I don't speak a word of Lithuanian. My mother moved to Königsberg as a young girl, and my father was from Hamburg.'

I eyed Gerda Petrovna, and she stared back at me, her face a perfect mask of blankness. Someone, or something, had taught her not to call herself German.

'So you speak German.'

'I used to speak German,' she corrected me, 'but I hardly remember it at all. For forty years I have spoken only Russian.'

Gerda Petrovna's mother was born in a port city north of Kaliningrad that is now called Klaipeda. Like Königsberg, Klaipeda was a Baltic city that spoke German. For many centuries it was called Memel, and it belonged to Prussia. In the carving up that followed the First World War, it fell to the Lithuanians, who joyfully renamed it Klaipeda. In 1938 Hitler demanded the city back, and declared Memel German again. After the war, Memel reverted to Lithuania, became Klaipeda, and so it remained.

Was Gerda Petrovna's mother a Lithuanian or a German? It depended on how one wanted to look at things. Born of Lithuanian parents in the last quarter of the nineteenth century, she lived in a region traditionally inhabited by Huguenots, German and Polish Catholics, German and Polish Jews, Lithuanians, Russians, and other peoples now forgotten. She spoke German, the lingua franca, in school and in the shops. She spoke German to her daughter. She spoke German to her husband. She was a citizen of Germany, and when the war came she had probably become a staunch supporter of the Reich.

I looked at the flower pattern on the carpet and understood that Gerda Petrovna was afraid. Soviet propaganda had found unpleasant words for people like her, former bourgeois Germans: fascists, enemies of the people. That would explain why her name had been Russified, why she had 'forgotten' her German. But surely, I thought, if she was still afraid to have opinions, she might at least have some memories.

Could she just describe something for me, I asked, could she describe, say, what Königsberg looked like before the war?

'Oh, it was an old city, it had old streets, narrow streets, old houses. I don't know, you ought to look in books. I really couldn't remember,' she said. 'I was only twenty when it ended.'

She had been studying at the pedagogical institute, she said, when the war broke out. During the war she had worked as a nurse in a clinic for the war wounded. There were ration cards and air raids, and that was all.

'I was only twenty,' she repeated.

I tried something more concrete.

'What happened on the day that the Red Army took the city?'

'Oh . . . we were in the basement of the clinic. And . . . they came, I suppose. I didn't see them.' I thought of the tanks, the soldiers, the infamous rapes, the people nailed to walls.

'I didn't see them,' she repeated.

'What happened to the Germans?' I thought: your friends, your colleagues, your relatives, your family.

'Oh, some of them died. My mother died – the others left.'

'Where did they go?'

'Germany, I suppose.'

'Why didn't you go with them?'

She shrugged. There seemed to be no answer.

'What did the city look like afterward?'

'It was wrecked, yes.'

'What did the center, the medieval town, look like?'

'I don't really remember.'

'Were you sad?'

'Was I sad?' She looked out the window. 'Probably I was.' I made one last effort.

'Isn't it strange,' I asked, 'to live here now, after all that?'

She turned back to face me. 'We are used to it,' she said finally, 'and that is all.'

The door burst open and in came Masha, carrying an enormous iron tea tray crammed with tea in glasses (the way Russians drink it), putty-colored cookies on a dish, a plate piled high with black bread, and another smeared with butter. She smiled a moist-eyed smile and laid the food before me.

Masha was from Russia, from Sverdlovsk. She came to the front line as a nurse. Afterward – well, it was not so easy to get back. Many soldiers were also forbidden to return, and many gulag prisoners forcibly repatriated to the region. The Soviet Union needed inhabitants for its new territories. Masha and Gerda Petrovna had met in the refugee camps in 1947. There was not much more to tell. 'We just stayed together ever since.'

They had lived in the small house, with its single divided room, for forty years. Through a crack in the curtain I saw that there was only one bed.

'We only want peace,' said Masha suddenly. 'We don't want war again.'

'Yes,' said Gerda Petrovna, agreeing quickly, 'and we don't want these national problems. I am a Lithuanian, Masha is a Russian, but we don't have problems, you see? Problems lead to war.'

'We want peace,' said Masha again. She said it using a Soviet slogan: *Miru Mir*, peace to the world, the kind of soothing phrase that used to appear quite often in the streets of Soviet cities, painted on billboards or on the sides of buildings.

'Peace to the world,' repeated Gerda Petrovna.

Was it possible to feel nothing about the place where one's childhood had gone up in flames? Gerda Petrovna had lived through the rise of the Nazis and the fall of Königsberg, she had seen an entire city deported and murdered, she had watched it fall under Stalin's grip, she had seen it populated by strangers. But she could not speak about it, or she would not.

Masha was saying something.

'Perhaps you are married?'

'Soon,' I admitted.

'Anushka!' said Masha, using a Russian nickname, 'How wonderful!'

Masha turned to Gerda Petrovna. 'How wonderful!' Relieved, the two ladies began chattering about weddings, and offered me more tea and cookies. Russian sentimentality, which allows total strangers to address one another with the greatest intimacy, came gushing forth.

They asked sly questions about husbands and babies, and giggled, holding their hands over their mouths. Is he American? Is he handsome? What does your mother think about it? When is the wedding, Anushka?

They changed the conversation to cooking, to the difficulty of shopping, to the availability of winter coats. They spoke energetically about how the weather had changed. They wondered whether this winter would be colder than last.

'Anushka,' said Gerda Petrovna, 'prices are going up all the time now. Things aren't like they used to be.'

'Anushka,' said Masha, 'potatoes cost three times what they used to, and it's almost not worth buying meat anymore.'

Perhaps this was the way they lived, always in the present. Perhaps that was easier. I rose to leave.

'Anushka,' said Masha, 'eat some more.'

Gerda Petrovna said, 'Come back again, Anushka. Call us, write us a letter!'

Cheerfully, they waved from the doorway.

In a square nearby I hired a driver. For twenty dollars, he quickly agreed to drive the eight hours to Vilnius. 'No problem, no traffic at night,' he said, and fell silent.

Past the great concrete blocks and the empty lots, we drove into the countryside. Evening had come, but even in the low light I could see that the fields were empty. Red wildflowers and weeds grew on what had once been densely cultivated land. Irrigation ditches had silted over from neglect. Storks nested on the rooftops of crumbling barns. In some places, men on horseback – Russian cowboys – drove cattle across the unattended fields. European farmland had been converted to Asiatic steppe. Every half mile or so, a radar dish thrust its round ear into the sky; clusters of antennas waved about in the still air. Soviet military bases were more plentiful than tractors.

The linden trees lining the road were the only living sign of the older inhabitants. The Germans who planted them had believed that their descendants would live to see the trees grow tall. Now the trees seemed to be taking a subtle sort of revenge on the Germans' conquerors. Along the road from Kaliningrad to Vilnius I counted seven wrecked army vehicles and a smashed car: the trees must have mesmerized the drivers.

I smelled smoke.

'What is it?' I asked the taxi driver.

'Hay,' he said. 'The collective farms burn the leftovers in the fall.'

I looked back toward the city. The fires in the fields lit up the orange sky behind us, as if Kaliningrad were burning once again.

Just outside of Vilnius, there was one more East Prussian to meet: I had been given the name of Petras Cidzikas on a previous visit. A few years earlier, Petras had lain down beside the Vilnius cathedral with his arms outstretched. He would not move or eat, he said, until certain Lithuanian political prisoners were freed. The fast had been successful. Another time he walked from Vilnius to Moscow, carrying a wooden cross on his back: 'People came out of their houses to watch me – it was as if they were remembering something they had forgotten long ago.' Petras was one of the first men in Vilnius to call loudly, strongly, and clearly for Lithuanian independence.

Lately, Petras had taken up the cause of Kaliningrad, which he called 'Little Lithuania.' This, he explained, was because the pagan Prus had been a Baltic people, related to the Lithuanians by blood and language. 'When they were exterminated,' he explained, 'it was as if a member of the family had died.'

His house was dark inside, and smelled like fire. A large wooden bowl filled with red apples and yellow plums stood on a long wooden table; books and dust lined the walls. Petras had black hair, a black mustache, and a black beard trimmed the way prophets trim their beards in silent films. Every so often he picked up a plum, carefully peeled off its thin skin with a small knife, held it up to the flickering candles, and, while still talking, bit decisively into its naked flesh.

Petras explained that he felt no compassion for the Germans who had occupied the Prussian coast for so many centuries: 'They deserved to have their city wrecked, it was built on someone else's land.' Anyway, the destruction had all been predicted.

Petras told the story:

When the last living Prussian priest came to the camp of the Teutonic Order, soldier-monks immediately bound him with rope and told him to state his demands. The priest stood up straight, despite his bound hands and body, and asked them, in the name of the Prussians who no longer existed, to stop cutting down the trees.

The Baltic peoples, he explained, believed that the gods lived in trees, and they worshiped trees as living things from which civilization came: fire, houses, shafts for weapons. The trees were sacred.

The Knights laughed. So the priest began reciting a curse: 'As long as you live here,' he said, 'you will never have peace on this coast.' The Teutons, although they were Christians, were superstitious, and they took fright at this curse. They threw the priest onto the fire, shouting that he would burn together with his false gods.

But the priest did not burn. He sat in the center of the fire and kept chanting, 'As long as you live here, you will never have peace on this coast.'

The Teutons pulled him from the fire, hung a stone from his neck, and threw him into the icy river.

But the priest did not sink. He bobbed on the surface of the water and kept chanting, 'As long as you live here, you will never have peace on this coast.'

The Teutons dragged him from the water, pulled their swords from their scabbards, and stabbed the priest in the heart again and again. All the time he chanted, 'As long as you live here, you will never have peace on this coast.'

Finally, he died. But the prophecy came true.

'For seven hundred years the Germans lived in Königsberg,' said Petras, 'and in a mere forty-five the Russians have swept it all away.' He bit into his peach with satisfaction.

Petras lived most of the time in Vilnius, but he felt a kinship with Kaliningrad that went far beyond ethnic ties. He had, after all, spent four years of his life inside a Soviet psychiatric hospital near Kaliningrad.

BETWEEN EAST AND WEST

The psychiatric hospital was not only for the mentally ill. It was also for dissidents like Petras, and it had no name. On the day he entered he was given a special designation: YCH OCH 216 CT2. The YCH stood for 'institution,' the OCH stood for 'special circumstances.' The number 216 was the number of the hospital, and CT2 meant 'cell number two.'

The 'doctors' forced Petras to take injections that put him to sleep or sometimes kept him awake. They bound him in a strait-jacket. They interrogated him, asking, 'Why are you so crazy? What is wrong with you?'

His guards entered his cell night and day. When he lay on the bed they would say, 'Why don't you sit?' When he read a book they would say, 'Why don't you sleep?' When he walked across the room they would say, 'Why are you not quiet?' When he looked out the window they would say, 'Do you want to escape?' In the night they would wake him, shaking him out of his grisly dreams, only to ask him, 'Why can you not sleep?'

Sometimes they gave him a cellmate, a thief or murderer, who would lean against the opposite wall and watch him.

Every day at least one of the other patients went mad. Petras himself was not sure how he survived:

'I began to think it was normal. I began to think, "This is how life is." And I stopped thinking about the outside world.'

But the hospital failed to take away his faith in the Catholic God. This he found unsurprising; after all, the absurd world of the hospital was only an exaggerated version of the absurd world of the Soviet Union, and the Soviet Union had never made him lose his faith.

Petras's religious convictions originated in his birthplace, a village called Šeštokai, which lay on the border between Lithuania and Poland. Šeštokai was the last stop on the old Russian railway line, and his family lived beside the eastbound station: trains left from Šeštokai and went straight to the gulags. In 1940, the year of the first Soviet invasion of Lithuania, and again in 1945, the year of the second invasion, Petras and his mother could lean out the window of their wooden house and watch the deportees gathered by the tracks, brown wool coats and cardboard suitcases stark against the snow. With bayonets at their backs, they scrambled onto the cattle cars that would take them to Siberia. One in ten Lithuanians was taken away: doctors, lawyers, owners of shops, rich peasants. The Soviet occupiers wanted to rob the nation of its leaders. A few came back, years later. Most did not.

'I felt an obligation to these people, and I searched for many years for ways to help them. I found the solution in the New Testament, where Jesus speaks about fasting and prayer. My mental energy helped to free them, and now that I have done what I can for the Siberian deportees, I wish to do the same for the inhabitants of Little Lithuania. I wish to free them, too.'

Petras believed that the former East Prussians were really Balts and not Germans at all. The Germans, he said, had never slaughtered as many people as they had married, nor had they accurately counted the numbers of peasants speaking Baltic languages. Right up until the war, the Germans had falsified the statistics, over-estimating the numerical strength of the descendants of the Teutonic Knights, under-estimating the number of Baltic peasants and workers.

But the Germans could not hide everything. During the nineteenth century, when Lithuania was part of czarist Russia, a Lithuanian nationalist revival had flourished in Königsberg; the first Lithuanian Bible was printed in Königsberg, along with Lithuanian newspapers and literature.

'Sometimes, when you go on foot there, when you walk in the woods near the old pagan temples, you feel something very strong. It is like the energy you feel in a church, or the energy you feel when a boy and a girl are in love and touch hands for the first time. People with a mystic sense can recognize it immediately, and when they pinpoint a grove or a field where it exists, historical sources usually confirm the place as the site of a temple.'

Petras looked up.

'Do you feel it?'

'Feel what?'

'Do you feel the house?'

I looked around the dark room. There was nothing there.

'The KGB have planted chemicals in it. People often fall suddenly

ill here; there is something wrong with the atmosphere. The air is tur-
bulent. Look' – he walked to the other side of the room and picked up
a plastic bag – 'this is a shirt that I am sure has been poisoned using
psychotropic means. I will take it to be examined by a chemist next
week.'

The KGB, he said, were very knowledgeable about psychology,
parapsychology, and black magic. In fact, the KGB were the world's
greatest experts on the use of herbs, potions, and chemicals to influence human thought. The KGB had even investigated the mystical
powers of Kaliningrad District, the special powers the pagans had
invested in certain places. 'The KGB are very, very interested in such
matters,' Petras repeated, 'which is why the Russians will struggle
hard before giving up Kaliningrad.'

I asked Petras if he believed that Little Lithuania would ever be
part of Greater Lithuania again.

He looked up at me, surprised.

'Of course,' he said.

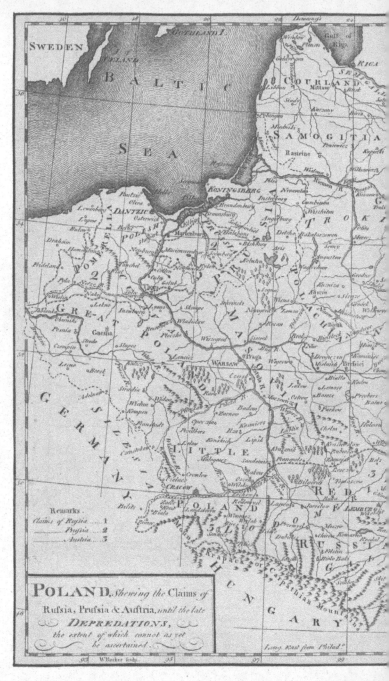

Matthew Carey, 'Poland, shewing the claims of Russia, Prussia, & Austria, until the late

the Creative Commons Attribution 2.0 Generic license www.creativecommons.org/

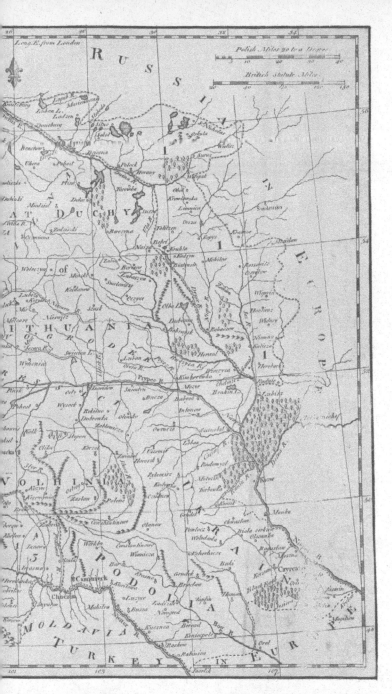

depredations, the extent of which cannot as yet be ascertained', 1800. (Licensed under licenses/by/2.0/. Photo: Norman B. Leventhal Map Center at the Boston Public Library)

PART TWO
Poles and Lithuanians

On he races in the rays of the low-hung sun, like a messenger from the dwellers in heaven. And long and far can the ringing of his horse's hooves be heard, for over the spacious plains is a widespread silence. No voices of merry nobles or of knights, only the wind whistling sadly as it bends the corn, only a sighing from the barrows, and from beneath the grass the groans of those who sleep on the faded wreaths of their ancient glory – a wild music, with words to it yet wilder still, that preserves the spirit of old Poland for those that are to come ...

– Antoni Malczewski, Polish poet

Forest and peasant knew no discord
Grew up together, aged in accord ...

– Antanas Baranauskas, Lithuanian poet

The affiliation of these republics to the Soviet Union will ensure their economic development and the flourishing of their national culture in every way; their entry into the Soviet Union will, moreover, greatly enhance their strength and ensure their security.

– Vyacheslav Molotov, Soviet foreign minister, offering a 'national contract' to the Baltic states in 1940

PART TWO
Robots and Lithuanians

When speaking of the history of Vilnius, it is best to start with the very oldest facts. For if the two main protagonists do not give the same account of their city's history, neither do they tell the same set of stories about their alliance – an alliance which became a common state, the Polish-Lithuanian Commonwealth – and in one form or another ruled much of the borderlands from the fourteenth century to the eighteenth.

The seeds of the empire lay in a sudden, late-thirteenth-century vacuum: the Slavic empire of Kievan Rus had dissolved, the Mongols were weak, the Turks had not yet arrived on the scene, and the Lithuanians, an unusually vigorous nation – the last pagan nation in Europe – burst out of their northern forests and pushed south and east toward the Black Sea, conquering Kiev and Smolensk and Polotsk, and a host of other cities in what later became Russia and Ukraine. The Lithuanians did not bother to force their religion or their language on the Slavic peoples whose lands they captured. Although they themselves remained pagans, and although Lithuanians at home continued to speak Lithuanian, a Baltic language, their leaders adopted the language of the Slavs they had conquered.

For a tiny nation, they had conquered a vast slice of land. But by the fourteenth century, they hit an obstacle. The Lithuanians were no match for the higher technology and greater cruelty of the Teutonic Knights, who, having conquered Prussia, were moving East as well. To counter the German threat, the Grand Duchy of pagan Lithuania sought a union with the Christian Poles.

47

For the leaders of both nations, the military and political advantages of union seemed well worth the price. They had no special love for one another, but both needed to fight the Teutonic Knights, and both needed protection against Mongol raids from the east. So in 1385 Jogaila, Grand Duke of Lithuania, promised to convert his people to Christianity, to bind his armies to Poland's armies. The Poles offered him the hand of their Princess Jadwiga, and status as a legitimate Christian, European king in exchange. A deal was struck. The Lithuanians converted in mass baptisms. Jogaila became Władysław Jagiełło, king of Poland. Jadwiga, forced to marry a foreign pagan three times her age, turned to a life of charity and died at twenty-four.

Together the two peoples soundly defeated the Teutonic Grand Master at Grunwald in 1410. After that, the stories differ.

If the march of the Teutonic Knights up the Baltic coast seemed critical to nineteenth-century Germans who wanted to understand their nation's role in the world, the saga of Polish heroism in Poland's eastern borderlands seemed even more central to Poles of the same era. Looking back from the garrets of nineteenth-century exile or the ruins of their estates, Polish patriots imbued the word *kresy*, the Polish word for 'borderlands' or 'marches,' with nostalgic meaning. Used only when speaking of the East, *kresy* implied a lack of demarcation, an endless horizon with nothing certain beyond: once upon a time, they told themselves, the fields and forests of the *kresy* were the outer rim of the known world.

The Germans of that era spoke of an East filled with barbaric peoples, but the Polish idea of *kresy* was one of emptiness – emptiness in contrast to the *pogranicze*, that is, the lands on the western border. The word *pogranicze* (literally, 'next to the border') implied the presence of guards and fences. For as long as anyone could remember, the *pogranicze* had been crowded with German-speaking peoples, the outline of the *pogranicze* had been defined, the lands on the other side of the *pogranicze* had been settled. But the *kresy*, to the Polish mind, had always been empty, like a blank page waiting to be inscribed; through valor and bravery, the Poles had put their mark on it.

'The last traces of human settlement ended at Tchehryn on the Dniepr River,' wrote the Polish romantic novelist Henryk Sienkiewicz. He had never been to the East, but he knew just what it had looked like:

> Beyond them lay the rolling emptiness of the Steppe that flowed like an uncharted, multi-colored ocean all the way to the Black Sea, the Caspian, and the Sea of Azov. Cossack life swarmed like turbulent wild bees in the distant *Niż* and along the streams and pastures hidden in the coils of the Dniepr beyond the cataracts, but nothing human lived in the Wild Lands themselves. It was a land as vast as all of Western Europe, subject in name to the dominion of the Crown of Poland but, in effect, belonging only to those who lived by claw, fleet foot, and arrows shot out of ambush in the night.

In the Polish memory, the year 1385, the date of the Polish-Lithuanian union, was important precisely because it represented the opening of the *kresy* to Polish influence. With the aid of the Lithuanians, the western and northern frontiers at last became peaceful, and Polish culture no longer met many obstacles to its gradual eastward spread. As the Poles remember it, this Polonization of the *kresy* happened peacefully. Polish tolerance and Polish goodwill allowed the local peoples to keep their religions and their languages if they wished; Jews thrived in the Polish lands, Catholics and Orthodox lived side by side, local customs were allowed to continue. Catholic churches soon appeared in small villages. The Lithuanian nobility married their daughters to Poles, and Polonized their names – by choice, as Poles remembered it. By 1569, Poland and Lithuania had adopted a union treaty – much in the same way that England and Scotland were unified one hundred thirty-eight years later.

Certainly, as the historian Norman Davies has written, the creation of the Commonwealth changed Poland forever. From a small country, Poland had became a large one; from a rather average central European country, Poland evolved into a unique, multinational state. With the addition of the Lithuanian borderlands, Poland acquired a new national destiny: the country became the easternmost defense of Christendom, a new bulwark against the pagans. Was it not a Polish king, Jan Sobieski, who defeated the Turks outside the walls of Vienna in 1683? Was it not the Poles who repulsed the Tartars, the Mongols, the Muscovites, again and again?

But while the borderlands made Poland large, their acquisition also contained the seeds of Poland's defeat. Partly because it was a nation of nations, the Commonwealth failed to become an autocracy like its Prussian, Austro-Hungarian, and Russian neighbors. Partly to serve wide-ranging local interests, the nobility (much like the Venetians, whose empire arose and fell at almost exactly the same time) elected their monarchs. Partly because it controlled so much territory, the Commonwealth could never agree on common goals, and the nobility gradually whittled away the king's powers to tax, to form an army, to build roads and castles. Beneath a strong government, the many nations of the Commonwealth might have joined together to beat off the Turks in 1620, the Swedes in 1654, the Russians in 1772. Instead, they weakened the empire incurably. Betrayal, treachery, and rebellions staged by Cossacks and peasants finally led to the near-breakdown of the state.

Piece by piece, the Commonwealth's three large neighbors nibbled away at its territory, and by 1795 they had agreed to divide the decaying Commonwealth into three pieces. Prussia got the Pomeranian coast and the prosperous Western cities and, briefly, Warsaw. The Habsburg empress, Maria Theresa, took the mountains and the lovely villages of Galicia, crying her apologies as she did so. ('The more she took, the more she wept,' said the Poles, 'and the more she wept, the more she took.') Russia snatched the great spaces of the East, renamed them 'western Russia,' and inflicted Siberian exile upon those who disagreed.

By the middle of the nineteenth century, those eastern regions had fallen into neglect. Robbed of their manors and their land, many of the Polish gentry had collapsed into genteel poverty. Families with ancient coats of arms and long pedigrees lived in miserable wooden hovels on the edge of forests, or at the fringes of estates belonging to Russian governors. Impassable, muddy roads led from one such 'noble' house to the next; their inhabitants wore crude homespun, and planted potatoes and beets in their gardens. Outsiders laughed at their pretensions to nobility. During the Napoleonic Wars, Murat, one of Napoleon's greatest marshals, visited for the first time what had been Poland's eastern lands. He was shocked by the dirt, the cold, and the filth in which the nobility lived. Napoleon had promised Murat the Polish crown, but Murat, after his visit, wasn't interested.

'What kind of climate, and what kind of terrible country is this?' he said to one of his comrades. 'Do these donkeys in Warsaw really imagine that the emperor will give me their kingdom? That would be a nice present. I wouldn't touch it at any price,' he said – and he never came back.

In their own imaginations the Polish noblemen remained just as grand as their medieval ancestors, and in the isolated villages and manors, it was still possible to live according to the values of the past, to inhabit an era that no longer existed. Czesław Milosz, a Polish-speaking poet born in early-twentieth-century Lithuania, grew up surrounded by talk of a more glorious past. 'I felt that I was only half present,' he writes in his memories: 'Too many shadows enveloped me: the clanking of sabers, the rustling of Renaissance gowns, the fragrance of old houses full of animal hides, hunting arms, coaches, rusted armor; and this robbed what was going on around me of some of its reality.'

Yet this era of defeat and nostalgia also gave birth to the greatest romantic writers and poets in the Polish language. While German historians pondered the legend of the Teutonic Knights and discovered a blueprint for Germany's destiny, Polish poets looked backward and saw a lost civilization, a romantic ideal, sometimes a place of wild, sublime beauty, sometimes a place of great calm. In 1883, Sienkiewicz described 'savage beauty ... billowing pastures where a mounted man could vanish like a diver in a lake ... a wilderness of forest, fallen timbers, sudden glittering lakes and rivers exploding into cataracts.' The poet Adam Mickiewicz, exiled in Paris in the 1830s, remembered

> those little wooded hills, those fields beside
> the azure Nieman, spreading green and wide
> the painted cornfields like a quilt
> the silver of the rye, the wheatfields's gilt.

He wished to return there, he wrote, 'to seek the sunshine and the shade alone, the homely plot and endless childhood days.' In Polish nineteenth-century mythology, nostalgia for childhood, nostalgia for a happier past, nostalgia for the glory of the vanished Commonwealth, and nostalgia for the open spaces of the *kresy* became one and the same.

Twice in the nineteenth century – once in 1830 and again in 1863 – the legend of the glorious past (together with the unusual cruelties of Russian rule) inspired rebellions within the Russian partition of Poland. Both times the Poles were trying to revive not only ethnic Poland but also all the nations of the former Commonwealth. Accordingly, they called on Lithuania – together with the Belarusians and Ukrainians who lived within the old Grand Duchy – to help them. In 1863 the Warsaw conspirators addressed their manifesto to 'the nation of Poland, Lithuania, and Ruthenia.' Some responded, but the rebellions were crushed. Poland remained divided for another half century until, unexpectedly, the three partitioning powers collapsed in the flames of World War I.

After the war, independent Poland was reborn, although Polish politicians differed as to what its shape should be. Some felt it should be a homogenous nation, for ethnic Poles only. Others – most notably Józef Piłsudski, Poland's great military commander – had other ideas. Himself a native of Vilnius and a descendant of Polonized Lithuanians, Piłsudski knew that Poland within the borders of 1772 – a Poland big enough and powerful enough to withstand Germany and Soviet Russia – was no longer possible. He knew that national aspirations among the borderland peoples had grown stronger. He proposed to bring the generous, tolerant spirit of the Commonwealth back, but not its political system. Instead of a reunified empire, he wanted

Poland, Lithuania, and Ukraine, three nations bound by common history and sympathy, to come together in a federation.

Stonily, the Lithuanians refused. Instead, they shouted independence slogans. They staked aggressive claims to wide tracts of land, well within what most Poles considered to be Poland. Most of all, they claimed the city of Wilno – which they called Vilnius – despite Polish expressions of hurt surprise.

The Lithuanians did not want to revive the Commonwealth, and the Commonwealth's noble traditions did not fill the Lithuanians with sentiment and romantic longing. On the contrary, the Lithuanian nationalists spoke of the Commonwealth not as a noble democracy but as a noble cheat. The Poles, they said, had cheated the Lithuanians out of their medieval kingdom, annexing lands that rightfully belonged to Lithuania. Polish aristocrats had cheated the Lithuanians out of their language; only the tenacity of Lithuanian peasants in isolated provinces had kept alive the Baltic tongue of the thirteenth-century pagans. In the nineteenth century, new nationalist poets drew on peasant traditions, writing of farms and forests, always making connections between Lithuanians and the flora and fauna around them, proving that the Lithuanians had an attachment to the land. 'The nightingale calls louder than the rest,' wrote Antanas Baranauskas, one of the nineteenth-century Lithuanian nationalist poets,

> In song full-throated, varied, full of zest
> Forever changing ever reaching to
> The heart, as Lithuanian folk songs do ...

Lithuanian culture was authentic; Polish culture was a foreign phenomenon that had drowned traditional habits and customs. Polish poetry was an alien import, Polish culture an alien imposition; the Polish language would have to be unlearned.

These nationalists agreed that the original Polish-Lithuanian pact had been born of necessity. Yet they did not consider it a union. The Lithuanians had not *joined* Poland in 1385, they complained: there had been two states, the Grand Duchy and the Polish Kingdom, with one Lithuanian king. The Lithuanians had been the stronger partner, not the weaker. Only Polish historians had contrived to make things look otherwise.

It was true, for example, that Władysław Jagiełło, the Lithuanian who became Polish king, had defeated the Teutonic Grand Master at Grunwald in 1410. But the real credit, the Lithuanians claimed, belonged to Jagiełło's cousin Vytautas, the Lithuanian Grand Duke, and his Lithuanian, Ruthenian, and Tartar legions. They had carried the day after Polish troops had fallen back.

It was also true that Lithuania had remained a duchy during the era of union, that Lithuania never became a kingdom in its own right. But that was due to an act of Polish perfidy, the nationalists said. In 1429, a gathering of European nobility at Łuck had determined that Vytautas should be crowned king. They planned a coronation ceremony for September 8, the birthday of the Virgin Mary, ordered a golden crown from Germany, and invited the ambassadors of various European courts. The King of Denmark came, along with the Grand Duke of Moscow and the Teutonic Grand Master and the Tartar Khan. For fifty days they ate and drank and celebrated. But the crown never arrived – the Poles had stolen it. Another coronation day was fixed, but Vytautas died before it arrived. He left no heirs. The Grand Duchy of Lithuania stayed a duchy, technically subservient to Poland, and over the centuries lost most of its autonomy.

Looking back from Russian-ruled Lithuania in the years following the collapse of the Commonwealth, Lithuanian nationalists did not remember a beautiful lost kingdom. Instead, they remembered the degenerate, Polonized aristocracy who quarreled and drank while the Commonwealth burned. They remembered the huge aristocratic estates, the private armies and private wars, the narrow lives of the Lithuanian peasants who served Polish masters. Instead of cheering the Polish revolutionaries in the nineteenth century, they drank toasts to men like the Radziwiłł brothers, considered traitors by the Poles, who fought on the side of the enemy during the Swedish invasions and hoped to revive free Lithuania.

Suffering under the czars (who forbade use of the name 'Lithuania,' suppressed the Lithuanian language, and insisted that Lithuanians use the Cyrillic alphabet), the Lithuanian nationalists did feel nostalgic, but their nostalgia was for an earlier time, for the era of Grand Duke Vytautas. He, a true Lithuanian, was their national hero, not the Polonized Władysław Jagiełło; the Grand Duchy's symbol – a man on horseback – was their national symbol, not the Polish eagle. The Lithuania they longed for was a pure Lithuania, a Lithuanian Lithuania, together with a Lithuanian Vilnius. Vilnius had been the original capital of pagan Lithuania and should be Lithuanian again.

Lithuania's claims to Vilnius were loud enough for President Wilson to hear. Germany, looking for a client state on the Baltic, also supported them. But the Poles furiously disagreed. Energetically, the Paris Peace Congress sought to determine the proper Polish-Lithuanian border. Legions of Frenchmen arrived with maps and survey charts; committees sat for hours in musty rooms perusing hundreds of documents, claims, and counterclaims. 'Wilno,' wrote Miłosz, trying to define the city: 'around two hundred thousand inhabitants plus tons of memoranda, notes, and stenographs in the League of Nations archives.' There was a move to create an independent Vilnius – a free city, not part of any nation, a separate canton. But in 1919, General Piłsudski cut the argument short. He instructed one of his generals to stage a 'mutiny' and to capture the city by force – which, very quickly, he did.

From Piłsudski's point of view, the invasion was no theft. The idea that Wilno ought to be Vilnius, a Lithuanian city, simply because it had been founded by Lithuanians, seemed to him absurd. The city had been called Wilno for centuries; half of its inhabitants spoke Polish, most of the others spoke Yiddish, and only a tiny minority spoke Lithuanian. Nevertheless, from 1920 right up until 1939, the Poles and the Lithuanians remained in a legal state of war. Throughout those years, Lithuanians fulminated against Polish plots; Poles complained of Lithuanians' perfidy. Occasionally a bullet flew across the border and someone was killed. But in light of what came afterward, the arguments seems quaint, like a war between toy soldiers.

For whatever their self-righteous arguments, whatever their claims of land, both the Poles and the Lithuanians expected their common history to continue. Just as the Königsbergers thought that their civilization would last forever, so did the Poles believe that the eastern Poles, the remnants of the Commonwealth, would always be there in

Wilno, and in the lands south and east of the city. Empires would come and go, but there would always be Polish churches and schools in the East; the inhabitants of tiny manor houses would always speak Polish to their servants, the cemeteries would always contain Polish graves, the places described by the Polish romantic poets would always be there to visit.

At the same time, the Lithuanians also believed that once attained, their little state would always be free; that, with independence, they had crossed a threshold and would never turn back. The Lithuanian language would become a national language, not a dialect; Lithuanian culture would become a national culture, not a peasant oddity. No one could ever again deny that Lithuania had its own right to exist. Metaphorically, the stolen crown of Vytautas had been returned, and between the wars the Lithuanians believed that there was no going back.

None of it mattered.

Between 1939 and 1945, war passed through both Lithuania and the Polish *kresy* – western Belarus and western Ukraine – three times. Whole villages disappeared in flames. Cities were destroyed in bombing raids. The nobility were exterminated, as the Russians, then the Germans, then the Russians again occupied their grand houses. Factories collapsed, fields burned, peasants, lost their homes and barns.

Cycles of hatred and revenge swept over the region as Poles and Lithuanians – along with Jews, Ukrainians, and Belarusians – blamed one another for the attacks. Encouraged by Soviet propaganda, some Jews collaborated with Soviet commissars; encouraged by Nazi propaganda, some Lithuanians welcomed the German Army and helped send Jews to Nazi concentration camps. Afterward, no one remembered that the Red Army had also murdered Jews, or that the Nazis had also murdered Lithuanians.

Lithuania and the *kresy* were caught up in a fever of suspicion and recrimination. Józef Mackiewicz, a Polish writer, later described the feeling of life in newly occupied Soviet territory in his book *Road to Nowhere*:

People had become very dangerous. Everyone could destroy everyone else. All one needed to do was to go the authorities and make a deposition. The accused man was finished. In the past, bearing false witness was punishable and ineffectual. One had to be careful not to harm oneself with hasty accusations. Now, the matter was simpler: a few accusations, and your enemy would disappear . . .

After the war, Polish Communists accused Mackiewicz of Nazi collaboration; even ordinary Poles often found his descriptions of life in occupied eastern Poland too macabre, and too frightening, to be real.

But often life was much worse than he described. From 1939 to 1941, Polish and Lithuanian communities alike were decimated by deportations – to Siberia, to the Arctic Circle, to camps in the Far East. 'We were packed so closely,' remembered one Lithuanian peasant afterward, 'if I ever had to know how to pack people again, I would do it. We were told to sit in the truck, and to spread our legs around the person in front of us. The truck then drove to the railway station, where sixty wagons waited for us: sixteen families fit in one cattle car. For a week, we were fed three times a day, and told not to leave the wagons. Finally, the trains could not continue, the ice was too thick. So we got out, and made our way by foot to the camp . . .'

After the war, the policy was continued: one in ten Lithuanians was murdered or sent abroad. At the same time, several million Poles from Lithuania, western Belarus, and western Ukraine were removed from their homes and sent West, to live within the new borders of Poland – which now included the former German territories of East Prussia and Silesia.

A famous Polish film, *Sami Swoi* (*Our Own Kind*), records this era. In the first scene, a family of eastern Polish peasants – barefoot, dressed in homespun jerseys, living in thatched huts – are feuding with their neighbors. Later the two families are dislodged and deported, placed on trains with their cows, their wooden pitchforks, and their goats. They travel day and night, across the flat land of western Poland, and finally arrive in German houses – sturdy, brick German houses (from whence the owners have left so recently that kettles are still boiling on the stove) – only to discover that, lo and behold, they are still living next door to one another, and they are still feuding. The film is meant to be funny, but it tells a true story: an entire civilization had been transported, materially and spiritually, from East to West.

When it was over, the mixed, multiethnic *kresy* had disappeared forever. Most of the Poles were gone from the region, most of the Jews were dead. The survivors were afraid and demoralized. Vilnius belonged to Lithuania, but it hardly mattered anymore. Poland still existed, but the last remnants of the Polish Commonwealth had disappeared. So, for the time being, did free Lithuania.

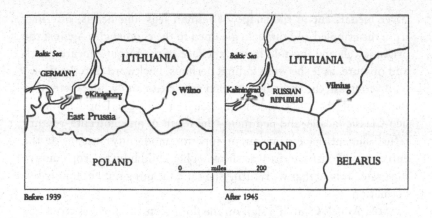

Before 1939

After 1945

Vilnius/Wilno

In Vilnius it was still summertime, although the calendar showed September. Girls in short skirts walked up and down Gedimino Prospektas, formerly HitlerStrasse, formerly Marshal Piłsudski Boulevard, stopping to look at the foreign fashion magazines for sale by the curbside. In a tree-lined square, three optimistic young men were squeezing the last notes out of an ancient upright piano, a ragged acoustic guitar, and a rusted trombone, while the fourth sang and passed the hat. All of the songs were Lithuanian except, inexplicably, a reggae ballad – 'The Harder They Come' – brought up to an oompah street-band tempo. Everywhere I went, Polish and Lithuanian voices competed for attention: Lithuania's new freedom meant that Vilnius's past no longer had to be discussed in whispers. The bandage had been removed from an unhealed wound.

At the Eastern Gate, a holy chapel tucked inside the old city walls, elderly Polish women walked up a medieval stairway on their knees and prayed for miracles; others squatted and begged for money from Polish tourists outside. The corridor leading to the icon of the Virgin Mary of the Eastern Gate was dark and cramped. Inside, hundreds of silver medals cut in the shape of human legs and hearts, offerings from the crippled and the sick, gleamed in the candlelight. Against the bright jewels and the gold frame, the face of the Virgin appeared dark and obscure, as if she were fading, perhaps, backward into the past.

By contrast, the cathedral seemed very clean and white. It stood at the edge of the city's oldest quarter, but its high Doric columns, neo-Classic facade, and pediment (the result of an eighteenth-century refurbishment) gave it an air of superior modernity. Just inside the entryway, a Polish tourist was showing her child how to drop coins in the grate: 'It is so that we return,' she said, meaning not her family but her nation.

At St Anne's Church a sign on the door stated that Mass would be said every week, in both Polish and Lithuanian. But a bilingual priest in a brown cassock told me that the Poles and the Lithuanians pushed and shoved one another during the break between the two services.

'It happens every Sunday,' he said, shaking his head. 'When the Poles stay too long praying, the Lithuanians feel they are showing off.'

Everywhere, street signs had been changed to Lithuanian; my Polish guidebook, of prewar vintage, was practically useless. I looked in vain for the hotels it mentioned – *Bristol, Europejski* – and for the restaurant *Naruszewicza*. But Polish words did remain in odd, forgotten places. Lampposts and the covers of sewers bore the names of the prewar Polish local authority. Brass mail slots on old doors were inscribed 'for letters and packages,' in Polish.

At dinner in an apartment in the old part of the city, china, crystal, and Oriental knickknacks – a brass Buddha, a Chinese paper fan – filled glass-fronted cabinets; the sitting-room window looked out onto a garden. The host was a cautious Lithuanian politician. The other guest was a German professor from Frankfurt, visiting Vilnius for a conference.

The German wore a stiff white shirt, a dark suit with a red vest, shiny shoes, and a tie. His beard was clipped short. The host wore the same outfit in the Soviet version: a wrinkled white shirt, a poorly cut suit, a mauve-colored vest, and shoes with rubber soles. But, being self-consciously Western, he had no beard.

Dinner was a heavy, complex meal served by the host's silent, high-heeled wife. A northern European weightiness hung over the conversation, which turned around the latest nationality crisis. Poles, part of the tiny remaining minority, had stood outside the Lithuanian Parliament that day, demanding Polish schools.

'We know,' said the host, speaking in carefully enunciated English, 'that our Russian friends stand behind these Polish agitators.'

The German professor nodded his assent.

'We know that these Polish agitators could not have organized such demonstrations alone. They must be helped by someone with a talent for these things.'

The German professor nodded again.

I asked whether it was possible for the Poles to want Polish schools and Polish universities and so on without calling in the KGB.

'No, no,' said the host. 'Impossible. And we know what it is that they really want, after all.'

The German professor nodded for the third time.

'And what,' I asked, 'do they really want?'

The host looked at me, surprised. 'Vilnius, of course. They want to invade us again.'

I raised my eyebrows.

'If they don't want it, why do they insist on calling Vilnius "Wilno"? Its proper name now is "Vilnius." Poles only call the city by its Polish name because they want it back, because they plan to invade.'

It was the first time I had run into the borderlands' confusion over names: Lithuanian Vilnius fought constantly against Polish Wilno, Ukrainian L'viv disputed Polish Lwów.

I tried to disagree: 'I don't think an invasion of Vilnius is imminent at all. Poles in Poland hardly know where to find the city.'

'You don't know these Poles like we do,' my host snapped back. 'You don't know what they are capable of doing. They did it in 1920, they can do it now. We must always be prepared for history to repeat itself.'

The German, suddenly troubled by the idea that history might repeat itself, furrowed his brow. We settled into our sherbet and talked about Russian politics – a nice, neutral subject – instead.

*

The next day was the opening day of Lithuanian schools. I told a taxi driver that I wanted to find the 'House of Young Pioneers.'

'There are no more Young Pioneers in Lithuania,' he said firmly, but he knew where it was.

The building, now called the 'House of Lithuanian Youth,' had been converted into a Polish school. In the courtyard amphitheater, little girls in black dresses with white lace collars and little boys in navy blue suits stood at attention, their parents looking on behind them.

'On September 1, 1939, little Polish boys and girls could not go to school at all,' the principal opened his speech. 'There is a long tradition of Polish schoolchildren in Vilnius, who always remained faithful to the ideals of Poland no matter who was the occupier. Remember Mickiewicz, Lelewel, Moniuszko, Piłsudski.'

A choir of girls in 'folk' dress – white aprons, flowered vests, garlands in their hair – sang the Polish national anthem, and a tall blond boy in glasses got up to recite the new school oath.

'Repeat after me:

I promise to be a good Pole.

I promise to study for the sake of the Polish fatherland . . .'

He rang the school bell, and three boys ran up to the podium to put on their white altar-boy smocks.

Mass went on. I wandered away to look at the Vilnius skyline. In the distance, an uneven patchwork of high tower blocks spread out beyond the river. But the Lithuanians had kept careful watch over Soviet-style urban development, so that the old buildings in the city center had been preserved. It was very different from ruined Warsaw, burned to the ground during the German retreat. Small nations must learn how to live with their conquerors, but large nations are condemned to fight back.

'Laugh, laugh, go ahead and laugh at our Polish schools and our songs,' said Stanisław that evening. Stanisław worked for one of the tiny Polish newspapers in the city. He had agreed to speak to me only reluctantly, and although he had preferred to meet for dinner, he refused to order any food. The restaurant catered to foreigners; it was not for him. I ordered potato pancakes with sour cream; this seemed to annoy him. When I told him that I had found the Polish school ceremonies amusing, he became even more annoyed.

'You are American, none of this matters to you. You can live anywhere, it doesn't make any difference. Americans can move every year, every week if they want to, the land doesn't matter to them. You are an uprooted people: if your ancestors had felt about their land the way we feel about ours, they would never have left it. But this is all we have, our land: our grandparents lived here, our great-grandparents lived here, we live here, and we have nowhere else to go. And we don't want to have anywhere else to go.'

Stanisław appeared to want to bite angrily into a steak, or to drink a glass of wine for emphasis, but there was nothing. He had to content himself with finishing off his glass of water.

'The Lithuanians? They lie, you know, they say one thing and they do another. They say we have the right to Polish schools, but look, that school you saw, that is the only one in the district. And parents who are less educated, they don't send their children to Polish schools anyway, they say it is better for their children to speak Russian, the language of the conqueror, or now Lithuanian, the language of the new power. Children are forgetting their language, children can't speak to their grandparents. When they forget their language, they lose their history, and then they know nothing.'

There was a loud crash behind us: the 'orchestra,' a not quite sober trio in matching dinner jackets, had begun to play 'The Girl from Ipanema.' Stanisław kept talking, but now he had to shout to make himself heard above them.

'It is better to be what you are. I know a man, born Polish, who went to Russian schools and lost the language of his childhood. He was an older man when I met him, but do you know what happened when we began to talk? He started sobbing, crying and sobbing, and he said: 'I am not a Pole anymore, but I am not a Russian either.' He had no nationality at all. Do you understand what a tragedy that is for a man? Can an American understand?'

My potato pancakes arrived. Stanisław kept talking.

'They say, the Lithuanians say, that we Wilno Poles chose the side of the Communists, that we defended the Soviet Union against free

Lithuania. If we did, how can you blame us? Lithuanian nationalism, you will see, it will be worse than anything the Russians ever did. The Russians never tried to deny our existence, they never tried to forbid us to exist. The Lithuanians don't want us to be here, they know that they are in the wrong, that this is our land, not theirs. They know that Vilnius is Wilno, that Wilno is our city, not theirs.'

The orchestra moved rapidly into 'New York, New York.' A group of American tourists at the back of the room began to sing along. Stanisław was becoming angrier and angrier, and his voice sounded dissonant against the lyrics.

Start spreading the news ...

'Just look around you. Who built Wilno? Who built the cathedral? Who laid out the streets?'

I'm leaving today ...

'Who were the great citizens of Wilno, the statesmen and the writers?'

I want to be a part of it ...

'Poles, not Lithuanians, but Poles. Back when the Poles were building palaces, the Lithuanians were peasants on farms, speaking a forgotten language that nobody else could understand!'

New York, New York!

'Polish was the language of culture, of diplomacy, of science in Vilnius.'

These vagabond shoes ...

'Without the Russians we are alone, we are alone in our fight against the Lithuanians.'

are longing to stray ...

'We have been forgotten by the Poles in Poland, because the Poles in Poland are not real Poles at all.

Right through the very heart of it ...

'They dream of going West, they dream of working in Germany, they watch American films, they don't value their homeland because they don't have to fight for it.'

New York, New York!

'We are the real Poles, we here in the *kresy*, we are the only ones left who believe in Polishness and who believe in tradition.'

He paused for breath.

'Them – *Koroniarze!*' he said, almost spitting. *Koroniarze* meant 'the people of the Polish crown lands,' as opposed to the people of the Grand Duchy. It was what *kresy* Poles used to call Poles from Warsaw, hundreds of years ago.

Stanisław kept talking. The hum of laughing Americans and German businessmen on expense accounts rose and fell around us.

'We will never give in, we will fight and fight to remain here.'

Stanisław promised to show me the sights of Polish Wilno – 'they are hidden beneath Lithuanian Vilnius, you'll never find them yourself' – but, disgusted with Americans, he didn't appear at the appointed time on the next day.

I went alone to the Polish cemetery. A vast slab of black marble engraved with the words 'Mother of Piłsudski, and the Heart of Her Son' lay on the grass outside the main gate.

'And just as well that he didn't live to see the day when his heart would be buried in a foreign country.'

A middle-aged Polish woman in a polka-dot silk top and blue, bell-bottomed silk trousers stood in front of the vast grave. Her midriff was bare. Her feet were squeezed into tiny, open-toed, rhinestone-bedecked sandals. Her fingernails sparkled with gold paint, her wrists jangled with gold bracelets, and gold earrings dripped from her ears. She wore shiny red lipstick and big, round, American sunglasses. Oddly, she was quite beautiful.

Her companion, a thirtyish country cousin in a dusty yellow shirt, was listening to her with dull attentiveness.

'They should have taken it to Kraków after the war, and buried it with the rest of his body. You see, Henryk, Piłsudski's body is buried in Kraków with the Polish kings, you must remember that he is almost like a king. But his heart is buried here, in Wilno, Polish Wilno, and his mother is buried here, too. Look, oh, look how poor the flowers are now.'

With an anguished little cry she reached down to rearrange the old daisies and blackened carnations that lay strewn about the grave.

She turned to me, apparently not distinguishing between her mute relative and a stranger. If anything, she seemed even more gratified to wail her laments in front of a foreigner, who might appreciate the depth of the tragedy far more than one of these ill-educated local Poles.

'It is a shame how they have forgotten,' she said angrily, pointing at her cousin.

Everything had been different when she was a child; back then, her family came to visit Piłsudski every month, and back then there were piles of roses, orchids, lilies, carnations, and humble daisies from the poor. Her family never lacked for money – they spent the summers by the seaside, she would have me know – so they brought a wreath, a big floral wreath with a sash on it. On holidays there were crowds of people, important people, mayors, generals, ministers, standing in front of the grave.

'We Poles cared about Piłsudski, we would never have let his grave go untended.'

She threw her hands up in the air, turned away from the grave in disgust, and turned up one of the cemetery pathways. She walked with tiny, mincing steps, balancing on her shoes like a trapeze artist on a tightrope. She kept talking all the time, assuming that I would follow and keep listening. Henryk, the local cousin, trailed a deferential five paces behind us.

Since the war, she had only been to Wilno a few times; she could count her visits on one hand. The trip had been difficult for ex-residents to make, and not many had wanted to try; after all, she pointed out, 'there isn't much left of old Wilno, is there?' Between the Soviets and the Lithuanians (and she didn't know who was worse) they had managed to destroy the city. This time she was here to look after her grandparents' graves, nothing else. Were they still standing? Probably some Lithuanian had knocked the tombstones down, because, she insisted, the Lithuanians were always going about knocking down Polish graves. The last time she saw them – 'oh, about five years ago' – they were still vertical.

'What would Grandmother and Grandfather think now, if only they could see Wilno, lovely Wilno now? What they would make of the street signs, all in Lithuanian?'

Her family, she would have me know, had done very well, thank you, despite everything. They had left Wilno in 1945, when the Russians told them that they would have to have Soviet passports.

'My mother said, "No, I will never sign my name to anything Russian," so we were one of the first families on the trains to Poland. We didn't know what would happen to us, whether things would work out or not, but we took the chance. Anything was better than the Soviet Union.'

Things turned out well in the end; she wasn't complaining. The family received a German house in Sopot, and she spent her childhood in a room with a window overlooking the sea. Her family had made money, running a small business even during the darkest years of communism. In her short lifetime she had been to Paris and to America. Once she went to Florida during the winter and there was a man there who wanted to take her to New York, but she said, 'No, – it is such a miracle to have sunshine in the winter, I will stay here, thank you.'

The path was rough. Henryk, despite his apparent youth, emitted short, sharp breaths as he pulled himself up the steep incline. She stopped speaking as she concentrated on picking her way among the sharp stones and clumps of weed. We passed weeping angels, toppled crosses, broken tombstones, old names: Chojewski, Milewski, Rutkiewicz, Paszkiewicz. We passed a Pole who had served in Napoleon's army, a famous Lithuanian artist, more relatives of Piłsudski, the family of Moniuszko, and the idealists of another century – young poets, young writers, young scholars. Just over the cemetery walls lay the plain graves of the soldiers who died for Polish Wilno in 1920. Someone had put little red and white Polish flags on top of each one.

Panting slightly, the woman finally stopped beside a small statue of Jesus. Ivy was creeping up his face, giving him an odd, leering expression.

'Here I always remember: stop at the Jesus statue and then turn down the hill. Granny and Grandpa are lying at the bottom,' she said, as if reciting a child's poem. Dutifully, we turned down the hill, treading through the carpet of weed, thorn, and broken stones.

At the bottom, she began to shout:

'*Oj Babcia, Dziadek!* Grandmother, Grandfather! You are still here!'

Two matching white stones stood in a small, square plot. Zofia, died 1945, aged fifty-nine. Rafal, died 1942, aged seventy-three.

She ran toward the graves. And, almost as if on cue, she began to weep loudly and ostentatiously, her sobs punctuating her sentences.

'Grandmother was so young, so young! She died because of the war, oh, look how weeds have grown, look how no one tends to the graves. Oh, what will I tell Mother, what will she say when she hears how there are weeds growing here, how there are broken bottles, how there is no trace of our family?' Henryk looked distantly embarrassed, and stood, respectfully, a few feet away.

Then, lament over, she stopped sobbing as abruptly as she had begun. Wiping the tears away, she stepped back from the grave, tripping slightly over the weeds.

She turned to Henryk: 'We have such fruits in Poland now, you can't imagine. Bananas, oranges, grapefruit, even kiwi. Have you ever tasted kiwi, Henryk?'

Henryk shook his head.

She shook her head, pitying her poor relations left behind in the old country. 'I don't know, really, why any of you bothered to stay here at all.'

One afternoon I told a professor at the Vilnius university about Stanisław and Henryk and all of the other Poles who still seemed to live in the Vilnius region.

'Nonsense,' said Professor Z——. 'There are no true Poles in the Vilnius region. Never were.'

The professor had a square jaw and a shock of gray, wavy hair. He bore a distinct resemblance to the mature Beethoven. The walls of his office were covered with maps, and the maps were covered with red circles, black arrows, and green lines. They looked like war maps, but they were language maps. They demonstrated the pernicious spread of Slavic languages north and east over the past several centuries. The Lithuanian language had struggled heroically to defeat these unsophisticated dialects, but to no avail.

Until the sixteenth century, he said, the people of eastern Lithuania and western Belarus spoke Lithuanian. There was a plague; it wiped them out. The new inhabitants spoke a Slavic tongue, proto-Belarusian. But they were not Poles.

'There were no Poles in Vilnius, and no Poles in the Vilnius region. There were no Poles in any part of what is now Lithuania and Belarus, except possibly a few émigrés. The Poles in Vilnius nowadays think themselves Poles because they are Catholic, and because their grandmothers went to Polish schools, but they are not Poles. They are the descendants of Lithuanians,' he said, tapping his map with a stick.

'In the villages, they will even try to fool you. They are very clever. You, a foreigner, to you they speak Polish. But among themselves, they don't even speak Belarusian, they speak *po prostu* – it means "simple speech." Poles can understand them, but this language has nothing to do with Polish. It is a dialect of Belarusian, not a dialect of Polish.'

Professor Z—— had traveled extensively in western Belarus, discovering Lithuanian influences everywhere. As he began listing them, he stood up and paced about the room, his gray hair floating behind him. The names of lakes and rivers, the names of towns – they were all Lithuanian. The surnames of the peasants – all Lithuanian. So-called Belarusian folklore, so-called Ukrainian folklore – all Lithuanian.

The phone rang, disturbing his discourse. He glared at it and picked up the receiver. '*Da*,' he said in Russian, '*da, da*,' and slammed the receiver down. He got up, and began to pace again.

'All of this was proven, you know – oh, it is a very long story and a very strange story indeed. I don't have time to tell it, but' – he sighed deeply – 'I feel that I should. You see, there is a book that proves what I am saying to you. But that book no longer exists.'

The book in question was the work of a lady scholar. Silent, ugly, and brilliant, she had spent the years between the wars researching the history of the Polish language in the Vilnius region. Patiently, she visited every village in the area, talking to peasants, writing down their phrases, listening to their pronunciation, recording their grammar. When she had finished two solid decades of research, she told her colleagues that she intended to write the definitive history of the Polish language in Lithuania and Belarus, focusing on the Vilnius region. For two long years she locked herself inside the baroque walls of the Vilnius university library, scribbling away. She revealed the results of her research to no one. Finally, in the summer of 1939, she completed her masterpiece. Her publishers rushed it to the printing houses – but they couldn't outpace the approaching German troops. In the bombing and chaos that followed, the manuscript disappeared.

'Such a tragedy for science,' sighed Professor Z——. 'Such a tragedy.' Many years later, some students accidentally discovered a few pages of the book in a warehouse. All of the research documents were missing, but some fragments on methodology and phonetics remained. Even from these scraps, the linguists of Vilnius knew that the book must have been a masterpiece. For she had hinted, in her Introduction, at a spectacular discovery: in nearly every village, she had found a few old people who spoke a unique, archaic form of the Lithuanian language.

It was revolutionary. For if Lithuanian was the ancient tongue of the region, then she had proved that the region always was, and always should be, part of Lithuania. Hysteria gripped the tiny world of nationalist language studies. Rumors flew. Some said the manuscript still existed, having been spirited to Poland by an enterprising language student. Others said it had been locked up in the archives of the Soviet secret police. Lithuanian scholars accused Poles of destroying the book. The missing pages, they said, proved that the Polish language had only been in widespread use in the Vilnius region since the early twentieth century. In retaliation, Polish scholars accused the Lithuanians of destroying the book. The Lithuanians, they said, were afraid the research of a Polish scholar might demonstrate exactly the opposite case.

Suspicion grew into scholarly warfare. Bands of competing academics went out to the same villages. Glaring at one another from above the horned rims of their glasses, they wielded notebooks and pens like weaponry. They interviewed ancient ladies in cardboard shoes, men in straw hats, barefoot children, and the better-heeled members of the new working class. They spoke to Communist Party members and farmers, drivers of trucks and diggers of potato fields, but none of them ever found evidence of what the lady scholar had hinted at in her Introduction. No one could prove conclusively, one way or another, that the land around Vilnius was definitely

Lithuanian or definitely Polish. The research could never be repeated: the old men and women whose speech the lady scholar had recorded were no longer alive.

Many years later, Professor Z—— sought out the lady scholar herself. She had survived the war, and taught at the department of linguistics at a university in western Poland. He had heard various rumors, strange stories. She was said to be a heavy, difficult person, not popular among her colleagues. She walked with a limp, and kept silent unless addressed. She would not see Professor Z——, so he wrote her a note. The next day, a messenger delivered the response to his hotel room. He opened the tiny envelope and took out the little card with the excitement of one about to uncover the secrets of his own past. But what he read led him to give up his search forever. There was no date, no salutation, no signature, just a single sentence written on the card:

'The book of which you speak did not exist, does not exist, and will not exist again. Please go away.'

The telephone rang again. Professor Z—— picked up the receiver and slammed it back down onto its cradle. The phone rang once more, like a whimpering animal, then fell silent. Professor Z—— slumped down in his chair beside it.

'Such a tragedy,' he sighed. 'A national tragedy. The missing link has been lost and may never be found.'

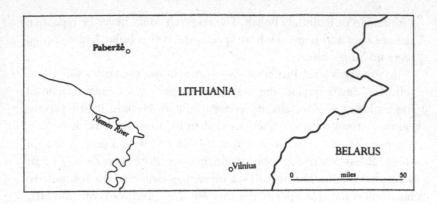

Paberžė

From Vilnius, I went north to Paberžė. From the windows of a car that moved with exquisite slowness and infinite caution over the gentle hills, I watched as fields alternated with forest. Every mile or so a lone white farmhouse or a dark blue lake stood out against the green. A Lithuanian acquaintance had told me to look carefully at the rural landscape, to ignore the towns: the spirit of Lithuania, he explained, had been preserved in the countryside. I hardly needed to try, as in this part of the country the towns were few.

In Paberžė there was hardly a town at all, only a church and a few houses. I carried greetings to Father Stanislovas from his friends in Vilnius, and he nodded his thanks.

Father Stanislovas wore the brown, belted cassock of the Capuchins – at last, he said, after all the years of hiding in civilian clothes – and a silver crucifix around his neck. He was a big man; his flowing hair had gone white. He spoke the perfect Polish of the prewar aristocracy, and he drank black tea out of a pottery mug.

'And how is it in America?' he asked. 'Do the Lithuanians there live as we do here? Do they keep their own language? Do they go to church? Or do they just become American like everyone else?'

I tried to explain how it was in America, how it was possible to keep one's own language, go to church, and still be American; many Americans, I said, did exactly that.

He sighed. 'I see, so it is just like the Soviet Union. Everyone is all mixed up, all the nations and the races. I suppose there are no real Americans, except the Red Indians?'

Father Stanislovas was the son of Polish gentry, born before the Russian Revolution on an estate not far from Paberžė. He had been christened Stanisław Dobrowolski, and was brought up speaking Polish. His father made money on the St Petersburg railroads, his mother thought herself a beacon of culture and enlightenment in an uncivilized land.

The illusion dissolved when their son arrived home from school one day and announced that he would no longer speak Polish. He wished to call himself a Lithuanian.

'Back then, everyone who lived in a *dwór*, a manor house, thought he was Polish,' said Father Stanislovas. 'But what kind of Poles were they? Ha! We were all Lithuanians, Polonized Lithuanians. We just thought ourselves more aristocratic if we spoke Polish. It meant nothing, nothing at all.'

Lithuania's aristocracy had spoken Polish since the fourteenth century. But after Lithuania won her independence in 1917, Lithuanian – a Baltic, not a Slavic tongue – became the national language. By the 1930s, the nationalists' great decade, Lithuania was shouting her uniqueness to whoever would listen. Other kinds of revolution were in the air, too. To desert the Poles and to cast one's lot with the Lithuanians – that was radical, that was a demonstration of support for the Lithuanian peasants and the working classes, as opposed to the degenerate Polish aristocracy.

In the spirit of the times, Father Stanislovas Lithuanianized his name, from Stanisław Dobrowolski to Stanislovas Dobrovolskis. New ideas were moving in him; he felt the call. He took the monk's vow of poverty in 1937, and his mother wept for her only son.

'I was so naive, I thought it would be the last important decision I would ever make,' he said, slapping his knee and standing up. He yawned and stretched: 'Time to pray.'

He handed his pottery mug to a blond girl who had been chopping vegetables behind us. She was the priest's housekeeper, and she did the cooking and cleaning at the Paberžė rectory, and translated the poetry of Rilke into Lithuanian when she had spare time. She also watched over the young people who came to stay. A few years ago, she told me, there wouldn't have been an empty bed in the place. Father Stanislovas had taken very good care of the long-haired dropouts and unhappy teenagers who found their way to Paberžė in the old days. But now that Father Stanislovas lived in the monastery at Dotnuva, a few miles from Paberžė, the soul of the place had gone.

'The scene,' the priest's housekeeper said later, using a word from Russian hippie slang, 'will probably move to Dotnuva.'

My eyes had adjusted to the darkness inside the rectory kitchen, and I could see dozens of copper pots clinging to the dark wood walls: copper kettles, copper plates, copper cups, copper frying pans, copper soup tureens.

'The People's copper,' said Father Stanislovas, stopping on his way out the door. After the war, he explained, the new regime had tried to requisition copper pots. Lithuania, the new commissars said, had to pay her debts to Russia. No one wanted to give anything to the Communists, but possession of a single copper mug handle could mean Siberia or worse.

Give them to me, Father Stanislovas told his parishioners: it is no tragedy when priests go to labor camps, because priests are meant to suffer. The tragedy is only for others.

By that time, he had already spent nine years in Vorkuta, a Siberian camp, where they fed him twenty grams of bread, sixty grams of fish, three spoons of buckwheat, and two spoons of soup every day. Those who didn't work received less. People died in the coal mines, collapsing on top of their shovels.

'After that, I wasn't afraid of some commissars and their nonsense about copper pots,' he said, walking out of the room.

In fact, the copper pots gave Father Stanislovas an idea. Under the Soviet occupation, old manor houses were being burned down, churches were being destroyed, and priests, teachers, intellectuals, aristocrats, and rich farmers were being murdered. The Soviet Union was trying to destroy Lithuania, and Father Stanislovas wanted to stop it. But he couldn't save many souls: banned from speaking publicly, the Paberžė parish church, miles from the nearest village, was his only pulpit. He couldn't save the truth: the Communists were already busy rewriting the past to make it fit the present. He couldn't save the Lithuanian language, even in its native land: Russian had become the language of administration. But he could save things.

'Go on, have a look in the back rooms,' said the priest's assistant. 'I will finish preparing lunch.'

I left the kitchen and discovered that Father Stanislovas had filled the first room of his rectory with iron crosses, the iron crosses that Lithuanian peasants once put up at every road crossing, at the entrance to every house, and on the tops of every gate and every tombstone. Some were Lithuanian crosses – one straight, traditional cross laid on top of another cross that wiggled like a sunbeam. Others were really crosses laid on top of circles, and still others had horizontal half moons mounted below them, or stars: an authentic Lithuanian crucifix combines a Christian crucifix and the pagan symbols for the sun, the moon, and the stars. Dozens of them, in all sizes, hung from the walls in a pleasing, repetitive pattern.

The next room contained bits and pieces of houses and furniture. Some belonged to an identifiable period – neoclassical, baroque, Jugendstil – and some were peasant carvings, but all dated from before the war and before the Communists, who no longer made such things as ceiling moldings, banisters, and chairs with carved backs. Door panels, window sashes, table legs, and the corners of a wardrobe hung from every wall, squeezed next to the heads of angels, the wings of gargoyles, the fat arms of cherubs, and odd twists of plaster that seemed to come from a ruined church.

In the third room hung big, elaborate keys, keys that could have been keys to castles; keys made of brass, bronze, steel, rusted iron, and tin, hung next to locks; heavy locks with wide catches and thick handles, small locks for luggage, rusted locks from stables. The keys and the locks hung along the wall in diagonal rows.

Folk paintings covered the walls of the fourth room. Some were old, like a cracked wooden painting of the Virgin and Child, or a faded Nativity scene with flat figures, skewed perspective, and misshapen animals. Some were new. When word got around that Father Stanislovas was interested in such things, old men remembered that they knew how to paint, and brought him gifts: Jesus, John the Baptist, St Matthew and St Luke, peasant girls bearing bread and salt, flowered fields, red farmhouses.

Father Stanislovas had a room for brass lanterns, a room for old books, and a room for old sacred objects – communion plates, chalices, altar bells – all of the bits and pieces necessary to celebrate Catholic rites. But best of all was the room beside the sacristy, where Father Stanislovas kept his vestments, the garments a priest puts on before saying Mass.

The vestments pre-dated mass production; each one had been made for a different ceremony, but each also seemed to have been made with a specific person in mind. There were black velvet vestments, with a cross sewn on in red, made for a priest with flair; there were flowered vestments for simpler souls. There were fancier embroidered vestments and there were vestments of pure gold thread, which hung like stiff aristocrats on their pegs. There were everyday vestments in white lace, and damaged ones, yellowed at the edges. There were vestments trimmed in silver foil, blue satin, and green baize silk; there were vestments for All Saints' Day and other feast days painted purple, magenta, crimson, and burnt orange; there seemed to be as many vestments as there were religious moods.

By keeping such things, Father Stanislovas was waging his own private war against conformity, against enforced equality, against the Soviet personality. Vestments, stoles, chasubles, ceiling moldings, and brass lamps were tools in his private battle against the officially sanctioned worship of the New. But there was something more, as well. Paberžė had the feel of a sacred place, but not necessarily a Christian one: rather than preserving these things purely for liturgical use,

Father Stanislovas had created rooms where God could be content when He visited Lithuania. Walking among the whispering fabrics and the rustling chains, I understood his respect for Christ, but I also felt the way I imagined a pagan would feel in his temple. The collections inspired a kind of idolatry, a worshipful respect for objects. It was impossible not to wonder whether Father Stanislovas preferred things to people.

There was no altar in the rectory, but a nineteenth-century engraving hung in one corner like a small shrine. It showed a wild-haired man haranguing a group of angry men with pitchforks and rifles. Horses with flared nostrils stamped on the edge of the crowd, chafing at the bit. In the background stood a small wooden church – the same church I could see out the window.

The man was Antanas Mackevičius, a priest and a leader in the anti-Russian rebellion of 1863. He had preached in Paberžė, in Father Stanislovas's church. Mackevičius – the engraver spelled it Mackiewicz, the Polish way – went to the gallows in the end, along with his co-conspirators, and Father Stanislovas had taken him for a model.

A daguerreotype of Mackevičius hung below the engraving. He had dark eyes, a cleft chin, ivory skin, and a ruffle of black hair. I thought he looked too handsome, more like a romantic poet than a priest.

'Beautiful, no?'

I spun around. The priest's assistant had entered the room.

'It is always that way with old photographs,' she sighed. 'People look more noble than they do now. Once I thought it was because the technique made the skin look purer and the hair finer. Now I think it is just because people were more beautiful in the past. Something inside them was better, and it showed on their faces.'

In the evening I rode from Paberžė to Dotnuva on the back of a truck. The wheat fields shone orange in the late afternoon sunlight, and the forests stood out black and green against them. Here, off the main road, the farmhouses were fewer; I saw no people. The cloisters at Dotnuva had belonged to the Franciscans until the nineteenth century, when the Russians turned the monastery into a barracks and th̶ ̶ ̶ jail. After the war, the Communists turned the jail into a school for the mentally retarded and then into a warehouse. When the Soviet Union collapsed, the monastery reverted to the Franciscans. The Franciscans gave it to Father Stanislovas, a Capuchin, because he was willing to restore it.

Everyone at the monastery said that only someone brave like Father Stanislovas would have dared take on the restoration of a building like Dotnuva, with its collapsed ceilings, rotted walls, and sunken floors – especially since there were only four other Lithuanian Capuchins left to help. One was over ninety, and the other three had entered the order only a year or two previously.

'But what we lack in numbers, we can make up for in faith,' Brother Francis told me. 'Faith in God and faith in the nation.' Brother Francis was one of the young monks, and he was deadly serious when he said that the plight of the motherland herself had induced him to take his vows.

'For Lithuania. I did it for Lithuania.'

We were walking around and around the churchyard. From time to time, the noise of an electric saw on wood, or a hammer on metal, floated over the wall. Other than that, only the voices of the builders pricked the still country air. Brother Francis took very small steps, and spoke very rapidly in Russian:

'It all started with a simple question. Every day, I woke up and asked myself: Why did Christianity come to our people so late? For a long time, I worried that it was because we were somehow lower in the eyes of God. I worried that Lithuanians were not so blessed as other nations. I worried that our nation had somehow sinned in the years of its infancy, and that the sin had prevented us from conversion until the fourteenth century.'

Brother Francis stopped abruptly in front of a broad oak tree, stared at it for a second, and then turned his gaze on me.

'But one summer, after much meditation, I divined the real reason. I understood that the spirit of God has always lain deep within the Lithuanian soul. You see, our pagan religion was concerned not with the worship of idols, but with the worship of trees. We spoke to the trees, we believed that God lived in the trees – and I believe that we knew Christ through the trees. We understood Him through what He had created.'

Brother Francis glanced at the tree again, and continued walking.

'I believe that our late conversion was a blessing. Because of it, Lithuanians have a clearer understanding of Christ than other nations. We are a simpler people, we are closer to His truths, just as Christ is closer to the simple people than He is to intellectuals. The day that I understood this was the day I decided to take my vows. I wanted to devote myself to God's people, to the simple people – to the Lithuanians.'

He was still moving at a furious pace. I could see that he was working himself up to talk about what *really* bothered him:

'Take the Poles, for example.'

I nodded.

'They brought Christianity to Lithuania, did they not? God revealed the divine truths to them many centuries before He revealed them to us, is it not so? But now they are a proud nation, and their pride makes them incomplete. They suffer from this pride, for this pride prevents them from learning the things we could teach them. They cannot accept that we are further advanced than they in spiritual matters. They cannot accept that our intuition, our feeling for the poor and downtrodden, is far more important than their learning and tradition.'

Nevertheless, I felt that Brother Francis still wished the Poles had not received His Word first. I also felt that Brother Francis still wished it had not been the Poles, of all people, who had brought His Word to Lithuania. Could it not have been someone else, perhaps the distant French?

He stopped at the gate.

'Now you must excuse me. It is time for evening prayers, and after that we retire to our cells. I wish you luck; your task is important. If you are going to tell the world about Lithuania, then you will be telling them about the path to God. Lithuania is the path to God.'

I slept in a novice's cell that night. The walls needed plastering, and the floor was unfinished. A battered wooden desk, a narrow bed, and a battered lamp were the only furnishings. Next to the lamp sat a copy of *The Samuel Beckett Reader*, in English, and an English-Lithuanian dictionary. On the homemade shelves, *Twentieth-Century Playwrights* stood beside what appeared to be liturgical pamphlets. A tall porcelain stove heated the room, and a horseshoe hung upside down over the door for good luck.

When I turned out the light, I noticed that the bars on the window made the pattern of a cross; I wondered if the novice who usually slept there had ever noticed.

Breakfast was cinnamon toast, cooked by a cheerful, slovenly girl wearing a floor-length skirt and a leather band tied around her fore-head, Indian style. She stood over a vat of soup, stirring it slowly; pieces of soiled cutlery lay strewn about the kitchen. It was still early, but morning prayers were over and the monks were already at work. Through the window I could see Brother Thomas clambering over the roof to get to a loose tile, his cassock flying in front of him like the billowing brown jib of an exotic ship. Father Stanislovas was on the ground shouting up at him, stalking about the building site like an irate landlord overseeing his peasants.

What the priest's assistant had called 'the scene' was already gathered around the kitchen table, where about half a dozen straggly-haired young people sat sipping tea without milk or sugar. They were there because they had dropped out of school, or because they had drug problems, or because it had been too hard to fit into Communist Lithuania. Now they had nowhere else to go.

One especially fragile young man wanted to practice his English with me. He spoke cautiously, curving his lips around every word to get the pronunciation right. He was a sculptor, but his father had disapproved of artists. He was restoring the statues that stood in the nave of the monastery church. They were almost beyond repair – Mary's nose had been knocked off, and St Joseph's arms were gone. It took real talent, he said proudly, to do the job properly.

He told me that the local Polish landlord had built the monas-tery church in the eighteenth century, using an odd technique: brick mixed with large, uncut stones. His descendants had kept it up until the war.

He couldn't imagine where the money came from these days: 'perhaps from the Vatican.'

After that, we ran out of things to discuss, so I asked him if he would consider becoming a monk. He shot me a frightened glance.

'How did you guess that I am thinking of this?'

He had been wrestling with his vocation for months. Sometimes he would be just on the verge of approaching Father Stanislovas with the idea of taking vows – and then something would hold him back. He wanted the life of work and prayer, but the glamour of travel pulled at him like the temptation of sin. He knew that to live outside Lithu-ania would be to live outside the Church. 'But I want,' he stammered guiltily, 'to see Paris.'

He bowed when we said good-bye. He counted himself lucky, he said, to have met an emissary from the outside world that day.

Perloja

The history of Perloja begins in 1387, the year that Grand Duke Vytautas granted the village a charter, as well as the lucrative privilege of repairing the road that led south from Vilnius. The Perlojans, who knew the river fords, also became the duke's messengers; Vytautas himself declared that no inhabitant of Perloja could ever be made into a serf.

Such were the origins of Perloja's great and unusual loyalty. It was not a one-sided feeling: the leaders of Lithuania always felt an equal devotion to the humble Perlojan villagers. Once, in the middle of the sixteenth century, a mustachioed Polish landlord in the local *dwór* declared his disdain for their ancient status as free men, and claimed landlord's rights: he told the Perlojans to bring in his hay. The Perlojans sent a message to the king so quickly that soldiers from Vilnius arrived before the haying had begun. The landlord had to let the Perlojans return to their own farms.

'And so it continued,' said Daiva, a Lithuanian friend. 'Go and ask them what happened next.'

From Vilnius, I set out by car for Perloja. We left early in the morning – the driver, a Lithuanian Pole who spoke no Polish, complained in Russian that he suffered from lack of sleep – and drove due southwest. When we arrived, the village lay hidden beneath the damp curtain of an autumn fog. Perloja's few hundred inhabitants seemed to be in hiding. Their small wooden houses, each one placed a respectful distance from the next, appeared shut up and silent. The statue of Vytautas stood alone in the market square, the two shops were empty, the gates of the dingy little church were locked shut.

The priest was away, but in a small house in the outskirts of the village I found the historian. Through the window he saw me coming. He opened his door with a greeting and then apologized when he learned what I wanted: he had nothing to present me in writing. People called him the historian, he said, but he was an old man now, and he was having trouble getting it all written down. His eyes were failing – the legacy of snow blindness and a childhood spent in Siberia – and his hands shook when he tried to write. Still, his cheeks shone pink with health beneath his white hair, and he remembered everything.

'It's a very ancient place, Perloja, there are not many about who know the whole history. A very ancient place,' he said.

He apologized for not having any biscuits on hand. His wife had died a few months before, and he couldn't keep things in the house the way they were supposed to be. But he was happy to talk. He spoke of Vytautas, he spoke of the Middle Ages; he spoke of the seventeenth and eighteenth centuries, when Perloja went into decline. Impatiently, he waved his hand over the nineteenth century and czarist Russia – that was a 'bad patch' – and skipped right to the part of Perloja's history that he liked the best.

'It was 1918,' he said, 'and it was anarchy.'

The Russians were in retreat. The Germans were pressing down from East Prussia, but they knew they had lost the war. The Poles were fighting for whatever they could get, with their cobbled-together army and mismatching uniforms. The Lithuanians were still weak, and thieves roamed the countryside around Perloja in disorganized bands. It seemed, from all reports, as if Perloja would fall within the borders of Poland. Distressed by this state of affairs, the Perloja Parish

Committee sent a deputy to Vilnius to complain. But the Frenchman from the League of Nations refused to see the grubby emissaries of a Lithuanian village; he had the whole border to draw, after all.

Since the world would not listen to their grievances, the Perlojans took matters into their own hands. They called a town meeting in the square, beneath the statue of Vytautas. Various speakers described Perloja's august history, its service to the ancient cause of Lithuania's freedom, its patriotism. Others denounced the perfidy of the League of Nations, and the injustice of the Poles and the Russians, all of whom were fighting to include Perloja in their territory.

Finally, the man who would later be called the president, stood up. He looked around him. He looked down at his fellow villagers and saw descendants of the Grand Duke's messengers. He looked at the statue of Vytautas and saw the patron of Perloja. He looked into the distance at the small plots and cornfields, and he saw land that had been plowed by a free people for six centuries, and he knew what he had to do. He held his shoulders up, threw his head back, and declaimed:

'Today, the twenty-third of November, in the year 1918, I declare the first day in the history of the independent Republic of Perloja!'

The villagers cheered.

'It was our finest moment,' said the historian happily, 'our very finest moment.'

Soon afterward, Perloja held elections. The village chose a prime minister, a finance minister, and an interior minister, as well as a judge, who later won great admiration for his strength of character when he sentenced a wife-beater to be beaten by his wife. Plans were laid for a new town hall, paper money with a portrait of Vytautas on one side, chief clerks, and a flag. The priest took it upon himself to organize the army.

'Now, the priest, he liked to have a drink,' the historian admitted, 'and he didn't stay in any one parish for too long, not even Perloja. But he was a noble man, and we overlooked the problem. A noble man – he donated his wealth to the republic and his time to its army.'

The army could call up three hundred men when it had to, from Perloja and the surrounding countryside. These soldiers had guns, stolen from the czar's army, as well as uniforms, sewn by their wives. They even had one spy. He was lame, but he could imitate the voices of birds and animals; he could change his clothes to look like an old woman. When the army wanted to know something, they sent him. Then, of course, Perloja had its president, the man who had dared to make the independence speech.

The historian leaned back in his chair. Memory was taking over from science. The president had been part of the historian's very own childhood.

'The president – he had twenty hectares and a reputation as a good farmer. He was brave – yes, very brave – and he always fought right in the field, alongside his men. My father was not a warrior, but if the president said there was an enemy to be fought, my father would go to fight him. The president moved away from Perloja after the war – worked on the railway – said he couldn't bear to watch it change – but he came back here to die. He lived to be ninety-seven. Died last year. A fine man. He taught me everything I know . . .'

The historian stopped in midsentence, and looked up to make sure that I really cared: Perloja was his whole life's work, Perloja was not to be mocked, or taken lightly.

'What happened to the republic?' I asked.

'That's the sad thing,' the historian said, shaking his head.

Troubles with the Poles began in 1920. It seemed that the new border, drawn up at Versailles, left some of the Perlojans on one side and some on the other. Nobody seemed to want to recognize the Perlojan Republic, so there were arguments and even skirmishes. No one died in these fights, although the Polish police did occupy the village several times. Every time they marched down Main Street, the houses would be empty: the Perlojans ran to the caves so that the town should not be burned.

In 1923 there was a great battle, the greatest of them all. The Perlojans attacked the new Polish border guards and assaulted a surprised French demarcation commission, telling them never to come near Perloja again. Even when the Lithuanians themselves sent a unit, the Perlojans continued to fight, and it was only when they captured one of the Lithuanian soldiers that they realized they were fighting their own people. From him, they learned how they had been betrayed by the League of Nations.

'Tragic times,' the historian said, shaking his head.

The captured Lithuanian explained to the Perlojans that the European diplomats had already drawn the border onto their maps. The world was not going to recognize the Republic of Perloja. Even Lithuania could not recognize the Republic of Perloja. Sadly, the Perlojans laid down their arms in the square.

In 1924 the republican leaders agreed to abide by the laws of Poland, but they put up a plaque to the republic inside the church.

In 1944 the men of Perloja joined the anti-Soviet resistance. Sixty died in the woods, and sixty more, including the president, the prime minister, and the judge, went to Siberia with their families; more than three hundred people were deported altogether.

In 1957 the new regime tried to take down the statue of Grand Duke Vytautas, but failed, despite the successive use of tanks, a blowtorch, and explosives. The republican leaders, fearing that the Poles might try to damage the statue, had reinforced its pedestal and body with concrete, and lined its insides with steel railroad ties. The blowtorches of the commissars had no effect on the steel, and the explosives only damaged, ever so slightly, the tip of Vytautas's sword. For forty years it remained the only statue of the Grand Duke still standing in Soviet-occupied Lithuania.

'I am organizing the local militia again,' said the historian. 'We have meetings on Thursdays – twelve of us attend regularly. Come to our drill sometime if you have the chance.'

Ona Baubliene lived on the other side of Perloja, and at first I thought that she, like the priest, might be away. No one answered when I knocked on the door of her tiny wooden house. I peered inside but saw only an iron stove, a single bed, and a black cat.

When I finally found Ona, she was standing in her muddy field, hands on her hips, surveying the pile of dirty potatoes she had just scraped out of the earth. Her green plaid shirt and thick brown skirt hung off her body in folds, her white headscarf gave a severe cast to her flattish face. Her boots were black and heavy, as they had to be in such wet country. She had all of her teeth.

'He is alive, I know he is alive, if that's what you want to know,' she said.

Ona Baubliene was the wife of Perloja's greatest partisan hero, but she wouldn't come and have a cup of tea. The ground would be frozen soon, there were still potatoes to dig, and a neighbor was coming with a horse this afternoon to help. The fog had cleared, the sun was out – it was a pity not to work.

'If you want to talk to me,' she said, 'you have to stand right here.' And that was the beginning of the story, because Ona Baubliene's potato patch lay right in the center of what had once been disputed land.

'That side of the Merkys was Lithuania before the war,' she began, pointing toward the rushing stream that ran alongside her field. 'This side was Poland.' Nowadays, the Perlojans crossed the Merkys on a suspension bridge made of rope. Once, Ona explained, there was a sturdy wooden bridge instead of a suspension bridge, and Polish soldiers stood on her side of it.

Back then, the Perlojans didn't like the Poles: 'You can't like anyone who speaks a different language and stands in your backyard holding a rifle, can you?'

The Poles forced Ona's elder brother and his friend Jonas to serve in the Polish Army, so they plotted revenge. During their leave, they asked Ona to smuggle secret army documents to relatives across the border. In those days girls did what their elder brothers told them to do – and Ona was in love with Jonas. She sewed the papers into her skirt.

'You take up the hem of the inner skirt like this, you see, folding it over twice, and then you just put a few stitches along the edge right *here*,' said Ona, demonstrating.

Ona was driving her geese across the bridge when the Poles stopped her, frisked her, and found the papers, shouting, 'Sabotage! Spies!' Ona's brother and his friend Jonas spent the years before the war in a jail near Kraków. While they were gone, Ona grew tired of waiting and married Baublys.

Fate had tied her to a hero. Baublys was tall and blond like many

of the Perlojans. He was too young to have fought for the Perlojan
Republic, but he loved the village as much as anyone else. He had a
famous tenor voice and played the accordion; he was a hunter and an
excellent shot. Years later, a local Communist Party member told Ona
that her bandit husband had shot at him in the forest. She looked him
in the eye and said, 'I don't believe it. If he had aimed at you he would
have hit you.'

Baublys's career as a man of great escapes began in 1940, just after
the Soviet occupation of Lithuania. At first the Perlojans had been
pleased by the changes. The new borders put Perloja as well as Vilnius
back on the Lithuanian side, and the Polish guards disappeared. But
then, very quickly, the rumors began. The Russians, who seemed to
own nothing at all – why else did they covet everyone else's land? –
were rounding up all peasants who owned more than thirty acres.
There were stories of cattle trains and transport trucks, tales of Siberia
and people who disappeared without a trace.

One day when Ona and her sisters were out in the fields, they
heard a great drumming noise, as if an army were approaching: a man
was running over the bridge, shouting, 'They are coming, They are
coming!' All of the women lay down among the tomato plants in the
vegetable garden. Baublys and the other men ran to the barn – but the
Russians saw them. A little bit later, they led one of the neighbors and
his two sons out of the yard and took them away to Siberia. Baublys
was not among them. He emerged a few hours later, covered with
bran and oats, grinning from ear to ear.

When the Germans came in 1941, no one knew anything about
Nazis, but once again everyone thought the change was for the good.
Perloja was still in Lithuania, and Baublys, flushed with patriotism,
became chief of the local Lithuanian police. That was all very well –
until things began to go sour. The Germans were also suspicious of
the Lithuanians, and began locking up those whose loyalty they
suspected; there were terrible stories, as well, of what they were doing
to Jews. Eventually, the Germans ordered all Lithuanian police,
including the Perlojan police, to the Eastern Front. A handful of Perlojan policemen forged passports and hid themselves in barns and
outhouses, but a Pole from Rüdiškės betrayed them. Only Baublys

ducked out of the cellar where he was hiding, and rode home that night on a bicycle.

By the time of the second Soviet invasion, in 1944, the Perlojans – wiser now – no longer believed that any change was for the better. Baublys's brother, cursing the new occupiers, retreated with the Germans and went to live in Australia. But Baublys, invoking the ideals of the Republic of Perloja, refused to leave his village in her hour of need. Instead, he ran away to join the partisans in the forest. Soon afterward, three railroad junctions, two post offices, and a commissar were said to have fallen victim to his grenades.

Now Baublys was no longer just a man with a talent for escaping prison; he had also become a genuine hero. In their kitchens and gardens, in hushed voices and whispers, all of Perloja spoke of nothing but Baublys, always calling him 'Merkys,' his partisan alias, taken from the name of the stream that ran through Ona's potato patch. Neighbors brought food to Ona in gratitude for the deeds of her husband. Men tipped their hats to her in the street. For two years Ona felt as if she were married to one of the tree gods of her ancestors. By day her husband lived, invisible, in the forest; by night, in the lulls between acts of sabotage, he paid surprise visits. Until 1947, there still seemed to be hope. In that year, the commissars sent Ona to Siberia, where she remained for fifteen years. She never saw her husband again. Much later – 'oh, it was sometime in the 1960s' – a woman told Ona that the Perloja partisans had died in 1949, when the commissars surrounded their bunkers. There were twelve of them left. They burned their papers and shot themselves. But one man was said to have escaped, and everyone believed that it had to be Baublys.

Throughout the gray fifties, the sullen sixties, the stultifying seventies, right up until 1989, the police interrogated Ona. Every spring, almost always at planting time, they came to her door, asking for news of Baublys.

'And if I had seen him,' she told them every spring, 'do you think I would be telling you?' There was nothing for her to be afraid of; she had already been to Siberia.

Ona leaned against her fence, a broken-down affair made up of wooden staves, old plastic, and wire. 'I am sure he is still alive, somewhere out there in the forest,' she said. 'He was never a man to shoot himself, and he is certainly not a man to be caught. Soon he will come for me.' She was sure that he wanted to see his grandchildren. She was sure he wanted to hear of his fame, she was sure he would want to see the photograph of himself, dressed as Merkys the partisan, in a new history of Lithuania that had been published in Vilnius.

The air was beginning to cool. The clouds were moving faster across the sky – the wind was behind them – and the sunlight was fading.

'I am waiting,' Ona told me. 'Soon, very soon, I am sure he will decide that it is safe to come out.'

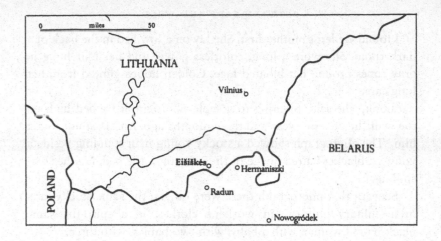

Eišiškės

From Perloja I took a bus heading south into the disputed territory so beloved of Professor Z——; this was the region where Lithuanians melted into Poles who melted into Belarusians. Already the hills and lakes of northern Lithuania were giving way to more open country, flatter fields.

South of Vilnius, all of the villages looked alike. Each had a Catholic church, an Orthodox church, a town hall with a columned porch. Each had a market square lined with neat, square houses whose colors – the lemon yellows and pastel greens of prewar taste – gave away their age, the way a preference for older fashions always gives away the age of a woman who continues to wear them. Almost every village also had at least one large, two-storied stone building, usually filled with farm machinery: that was the synagogue. While the villages in this part of the *kresy* were Polish-speaking before the war, they were usually at least half Jewish as well. After the war a few Poles had remained, and so had some Jews.

In Eišiškės, a village that looked just like the others, there were two Jews left: Gellert and his mother.

I found Gellert's mother first. She lay on a low bed in the back of a dark room. She wore a long, colorless gown, and her hair hung in gray ropes around her bloated face. Golden hoops glinted from her long ears.

'Look,' she said, pointing to a sepia photograph framed high on the wall, 'he died one year and three months ago. And I cannot forget him.' The photograph showed a stocky young man standing beside a younger, blacker-haired image of the woman in the bed. Neither was smiling.

Beneath that photograph there were others: the same stocky man in a military uniform, in worker's clothes, in a suit; the same black-haired woman with a baby, with two babies, with three.

'I went to the cemetery yesterday and told him that we were going to leave. I waited to hear what he would say. But this time he did not reply.' She began to moan softly.

'Only silence, only silence. The last time I went, he said, "Don't forget, you will lie beside me, don't forget you will be with me soon." He was waiting for me, he said. But this time – only silence.'

Once she was gone, there would be no one left, no one to visit him, no one to tend his grave.

'What is it like in Israel? I think it is hot, very hot, very hot. And I think I will die in all that heat.'

She had spent her childhood in Gomel, deep in Belarus, and she spoke Russian with a strong Belarusian accent, trading her g's for h's. Her family had always been poor, but her grandfather, a rabbi, owned a whole library of thick, leather-bound Hebrew books. They were gone now – everything was lost in the war. Her grandfather was killed, her mother was killed, her father was killed, her sister, her aunts, her uncles, and her cousins were killed.

'I don't remember Hebrew now,' she said. 'I don't know how to speak to him except in Yiddish, and I am afraid that the dead speak only Hebrew.'

She turned her face to the wall.

Gellert appeared. 'Ignore her,' he said, and shut the door. I told Gellert that I had stayed in the Hotel Gellert in Budapest, and his round face lit up.

'I think it is a very famous name, yes? I think a lot of famous people are called Gellert.'

Gellert was oblivious to his mother's stream of complaints; he was trying to think about the future. He showed me a telegram from his daughter in Israel. She had enrolled in an English-language course, and her husband was already working on a construction site. He had heard that an Israeli Jew could earn more in a month than a Soviet Jew could earn in a year.

'Here, he would have been a teacher,' Gellert shrugged. 'Look how I live on a teacher's salary. No one should have to live in such a place. Tell me: would a teacher in America live in such a place?'

I saw his point. The flat was small and dark. There were only two rooms – five people had once lived in them – and one could hear the grandmother moaning and muttering through the paper-thin walls. The toilet had not flushed for months. Instead of a refrigerator, a box hung out the window. Instead of a stove, a single burner leaned against the wall in the hallway.

Gellert was interested in Jews, but he didn't know much about them and had not had much time to learn. He was going to Israel for the children, he said, and he was going to Israel because there was no way to get to America. Immigration rules were tough for people without relatives. Someone had convinced him that Israel would be just like America anyway.

'It is the fifty-first state, yes? I am told that it is the fifty-first state,' he said, his eyes wide with an immigrant's hope.

He wanted to know if things in America were like things in Eišiškės. 'Do you have bicycles?' he asked. 'Or does everybody drive a car? Do your villages look like our villages?'

I said they didn't, not really. Gellert shook his head in admiration. He could not imagine what a different kind of village would look like.

'Do you have, say, books that look like this?' He held up a book, *History of the Political Economy of the Soviet Army*. I said we had books like that, but the contents would be different. He nodded his head sagely, but he didn't really see what I meant.

Gellert offered to drive me to Radun – if I didn't mind riding in a Soviet car. 'I am sure it is not nearly as good as an American car, but what can I do?' He shrugged hopelessly. 'I cannot buy an American car in Eišiškės.' The car was indeed very old and moved very slowly, with sharp, jerky motions. It had no muffler. Over the noise of the sputtering engine, I told Gellert that I didn't mind, but he kept shouting back apologies anyway. He knew how cars were supposed to be, he had seen them in films.

We drove along curving, tree-lined roads, the only remaining evidence of once-great estates; most of the land around Eišiškės had been owned by one or two great men, Gellert explained proudly, and these great men built the roads as well – although he admitted they hadn't been repaired much since. The car coughed and groaned when it hit the potholes, and leaned precariously on its side as it rounded each corner. We seemed to be safe, though; there was hardly any other traffic.

Over the noise of the engine, Gellert shouted, 'You want to know what I think? I think Lithuania is now going to be for the Lithuanians, Russia is going to be for the Russians, Ukraine is going to be for the Ukrainians. Places will belong, you know, to their people. So now . . .' The car retched and moaned.

'What?'

Gellert said something, but the car gurgled and spit.

'What?'

'Israel will be for the Jews, yes? Is it like that?'

'Yes!'

To get to Radun, we had to cross the Lithuanian-Belarusian border, which had been in existence for all of a week. Gellert shook his head; he found it strange to think of Belarus as a foreign country. He slowed the car to a nervous wheeze as we approached the border.

On the Lithuanian side, flowers planted in the shape of a cross lay on the ground by the border post. They marked the place where a Soviet soldier had shot a Lithuanian border guard; in the early days of free Lithuania, defense of the borders was defense of the idea of independence itself. Those early border guards were not merely watching traffic but also guarding their country's new sovereignty.

Yet the border was a new one. For centuries and centuries – right up until 1939 – Eišiškės and Radun were simply *kresy* villages, belonging to no one in particular. In both villages, Polish clerks and Jewish shopkeepers dominated town life. In both villages, peasants speaking both Slavic and Baltic dialects brought produce for the market; Polish or Russian landlords ran the surrounding estates, kept up the manor houses, and endowed the churches. The dirt roads were frozen in winter, muddy in summer.

After the war, the Holocaust, and the deportation of the Poles, the borders were redrawn. Eišiškės and Radun fell into the separate Soviet republics of Lithuania and Belarus. At first this didn't matter much, but little by little, people found that it did. Lithuanian had become the official language of Eišiškės, and the peasants were forgetting Belarusian, while in Radun, hardly anyone spoke Lithuanian anymore. Lithuanian roads were better cared for than those in Belarus, so Eišiškės had more contacts with the wider world; Radun sank further into provincialism.

Now the two villages would belong to two separate countries. It was as Gellert said: Lithuania would be for the Lithuanians, Belarus for the Belarusians. Israel would be for the Jews.

Just as we passed the flowers, one of the Lithuanian guards, crisp and uniformed, stepped into the road and put his hand out for us to stop.

Gellert's face grew blank.

Wordlessly, the guard looked over the car. He opened the trunk and looked inside. He kicked the tire. He peered into the backseat, leaned menacingly over the steering wheel, and had a good, long look at me.

Then he put his face next to Gellert's and asked, in a low, threatening voice, whether we could drop him off on the road to Lida.

Gellert nodded yes, and the guard got in the backseat and closed his eyes.

On the Belarusian side, an empty bench leaned against an empty customs post. We rolled smoothly over a piece of fallen rope.

'Now I can tell people that I have been abroad,' said Gellert happily.

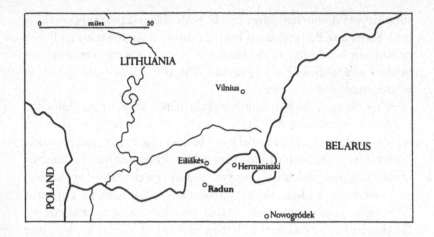

Radun

Meyer Chaimovich had been born in Radun, brought up in Radun, and he fully intended to die in Radun. He didn't believe in nationalism, he believed in internationalism. None of this Israel nonsense for him; he thought his friend Gellert a fool for going there.

Meyer Chaimovich was very short and misshapen. His head seemed to rest, neckless, on his shoulders, and his arms were too long for his body. His thighs were much thicker than his calves. His left arm was cut off at the elbow: a war wound. Meyer Chaimovich had been a partisan.

'People were happy when the Soviet soldiers arrived here,' he said. 'They said the Soviet Union would be better than Poland. And they were right. It is better.'

Meyer Chaimovich had been a Bolshevik before the war. The Poles put him in jail three times for Communist agitation.

'There is nothing wrong with communism,' he said. 'The problem here is that no one works. People think manna will fall from heaven, but manna only falls from heaven in the Bible. If people would work, then communism would be a success.'

A large television dominated the only room in the cottage; Russian rock groups gyrated to silent music on its wide screen. Meyer Chaimovich couldn't bear to listen to the sound, but he couldn't bear to turn it off either. The television was a token, proof that the Soviet Union had brought the modern world to Radun.

'In Polish times there were no televisions, only radios,' he said.

When Meyer Chaimovich had been wounded in the war, it was Russians who helped him, not Jews. He had spent three days in a Russian house, and Russian women had bathed his head with towels. Yet in Polish times, rich Jewish ladies turned their faces away from him in the street because his father was a blacksmith, his grandfather was a blacksmith, and if it hadn't been for the war, Meyer Chaimovich would have been a blacksmith, too.

From his life experiences, Meyer Chaimovich drew the following conclusions: Some Russians were good, some Russians were bad. Some Jews were good, some Jews were bad. In Israel, some people were good and some were bad. In America, some people were good and some were bad. In the new Belarus, some people would be good and some would be bad. Therefore, all of this moving around was pointless. 'The place where you were born, that is the place where you should die,' said Meyer Chaimovich.

In the afternoon, we walked to the Jewish cemetery. It lay beside the Voronova road, just outside of town. All of the tombstones had been removed, and at first it looked just like an empty field. But the ground was uneven – there were lumps where the coffins still lay, thinly covered with soil.

Meyer Chaimovich kicked one of the lumps, and began explaining how it was that he had escaped being buried there, too.

One day, he said, not long after the occupation began, the German military command simply announced that all of the Jews in Radun had to report to the synagogue. The people came to the rabbi, and the rabbi told them it was God's will. If God wanted the Jews to go to the synagogue, then everyone must go. So they went, knowing what was going to happen and not knowing at the same time.

At the synagogue, the Germans organized the Jews into a line and told them to walk to the cemetery. They turned to the rabbi, and the rabbi said they should walk behind him. Germans followed on horse-back, and Lithuanians followed with guns; being local, the Lithuanians were hated even more than the Germans. They often shot Poles as well as Jews, and had unpleasant ways of asserting their new super-iority over their old neighbors. But on this particular day, none of the Lithuanians were local.

'They were not from our village,' Meyer Chaimovich remembered. 'We did not recognize them.'

When the Jews arrived at the cemetery, the German soldiers showed them a space beside the cemetery and told them to start dig-ging. Again the Jews turned to the rabbi, and again the rabbi told them it was God's will. Again the Jews knew what was happening and did not know at the same time. They began to dig. But Meyer Chaim-ovich knew.

'I said to myself, It is time to leave. I said to myself, I won't dig my own grave, I won't dig my own grave. I saw one of the Lithuanians beat someone over the head, and I knew they were nervous. Some-thing was certain to happen. So I ran.'

He had told the story so many times that he had no more sorrow left, only the memory of the adrenaline and of the running and of the excitement of the escape. He grinned, and pointed toward a distant tree.

'There was a barn there, at that time – it was burned down later – and I ran and hid behind the barn, where they could not shoot at me. Then, when I heard them coming, I ran for the woods. The Germans followed me on their horses, but that field is full of stones, and the horses couldn't run on the stones. Once I got to the woods, I kept run-ning and running, and they never caught me.'

Meyer Chaimovich stayed with the Soviet partisans in the woods from May 1942 until June 1944, when the Soviet partisans liberated Radun. After that, he came back to Radun and learned that his father, his mother, his first wife, and his daughter were buried in the ditch next to the Radun cemetery, where the Lithuanian police had shot them.

The Jews of Eišiškės, he said, had been shot in the same way. The Jews in most of the villages near Radun had been shot in the same way. In this part of the world, there had been no locked ghetto, no trains, no camps. Here, so far from civilization, the sentiments of the local population did not need to be taken into account; death did not need to be hidden. The local police could be counted on to cooperate, or at least not to fight back. So there was no need, as in Western Europe, to take the Jews somewhere else to die.

Meyer Chaimovich smiled again at the memory of his lucky escape, so long ago, and walked toward the overgrown ditch.

Beside it stood a tall monument with a red star on top. The paint was peeling off the star, and it looked as if someone had been chipping away at the plaster as well. Chunks of it lay in piles on the ground, next to broken beer bottles, so it was just barely possible to read the inscription:

HERE LIE BURIED 1,137 PEACEFUL SOVIET CITIZENS SHOT IN 1942 BY GERMAN FASCISTS

I asked why it didn't say that they were Jews.

'They were peaceful Soviet citizens,' he said. 'That was what they were.'

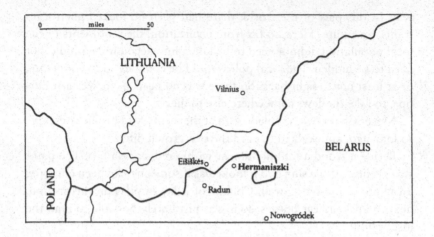

Hermaniszki

Hermaniszki lay to the east of Radun, across a forest and a swamp; I went there in search of a priest from Lublin called Father Andrzej.

I found him in the churchyard, sweeping the walkways. Father Andrzej kept himself busy in order to drive evil thoughts away.

'Idle hands find the devil's work to do,' he said.

Every day, Father Andrzej taught two Polish classes to Belarusian Poles who had forgotten the language (or perhaps never knew it), and rehearsed two catechisms. On Sunday there were three village Masses to be said – in Hermaniszki, Woronowa, and Bieniakonie – plus adult Sunday school. After forty-five years of godlessness, there was a lot of work for a Catholic priest in Belarus. Visitors marched in and out of the rectory, newly renovated with money from Poland, their eyes widening and their mouths falling open at the sight of the Sony television, the carpets, the indoor toilets, and the tiny dishes filled with chocolate candy wrapped in colored foil.

Just a few days before, Father Andrzej had discovered the Hermaniszki church records hidden in one of the sacristy walls, where the last priest seemed to have stuffed them at the end of the war. The oldest dated from 1801, and the priest pointed triumphantly to the Polish names: MATEUSZ, GREGORZ, ANTONI.

'*Zawsza Polska*, always Poland,' he said proudly. The records proved to him that Hermaniszki, now part of Belarus, had always been Polish.

The archives also contained a copy of a letter sent to the Archdiocese of Wilno in 1930, calling for the archbishop to issue a resolution against the Bolsheviks, 'A People Who Fight Against God and Faith.'

'Prescient,' said Father Andrzej.

He had first heard the call to missionary work as a child, and he prepared himself to proselytize in South Korea. God intervened via the missionary hierarchy and sent him to western Belarus instead. It was a blessing, for in Belarus every convert to Catholicism was also a convert to Polishness. The Soviet state had forbidden God and Poland to its citizens, and both had been nearly lost. But a new era was dawning.

'We brought the Word, and we brought Western civilization here in the fourteenth century,' he told me. 'It is our task to do it again.'

We took tea in the rectory with Father Andrzej's organist, who kept looking at me and laughing. He had never expected to meet an American, and certainly not now, not at the end of his long life. If he had known, he would have brushed up on his English.

Afterward, Father Andrzej gave two of his Polish-speaking parishioners, Hania and Maria, permission to speak to me instead of attending morning Mass. 'It will be better for you to talk to them than to me,' he said. 'They can tell you what happened to Poles here,' he said. 'They can tell you much better than I.'

We all sat on wooden benches in the sacristy. Hania frowned. I didn't understand. She shook her finger at me; I still didn't understand. Finally she leaned over my ear. 'You mustn't cross your legs in front of a priest,' she whispered. 'It is immoral.' I uncrossed my legs, but they didn't lift their eyes to look at me until Father Andrzej had left the room.

Hania and Maria were elderly ladies, identically dressed – except that Hania wore a white woolen scarf with pinkish spots, and Maria wore an orange scarf of frayed cotton. Both were clad in faded flower print dresses, dirty white aprons, and heavy leather boots that had been cobbled and recobbled again. Their round red noses, jutting chins, and big hands made them look like figures out of Breughel, and they spoke Polish with strong eastern accents.

'The other priest, Pilecki, was here until 1939—' Hania began.

Maria interrupted her. 'No, no, my dear, Romanowski was here until 1939. Pilecki was before him.'

'Of course, there was Jubiliewicz before that—'

'And Osobski came just before the war—'

'But I am sure that Pilecki was here until 1939—'

'Perhaps you are right, my dear, perhaps you are right, but wasn't Hermanovich preaching just a bit during the German times?'

'It doesn't matter, though, does it, because after that there was no one,' said Hania. 'No priest at all.'

They fell silent. Since when, I asked, had there been no priest?

'From the war,' said Maria. 'We have had no priest since the war, when the Poles went out and the Russians came in. They call them Belarusians, you see, but we aren't stupid. We know they are Russians. That is why they don't like us. Russians don't like Poles.'

Without a priest, the villagers of Hermaniszki held their own services. 'Just we here in the town by ourselves, for quite a few years,' said Hania. 'All by ourselves. We didn't have a priest, but we tried to do things the right way.'

They had all tried hard to remember the prayers, and said Mass as best they were able. Sometimes someone read a sermon. 'It wasn't as good as the real thing, of course, but we made do.'

But eventually the authorities heard about the services. The idea of one little congregation defying both the laws on atheism and the laws establishing Russian and Belarusian as the official languages was too much for the Soviet regime. Four policemen arrived in Hermaniszki, looking for the keys to the church: they were going to lock it up forever.

'Our friend Masha, may she rest in peace, she had the key,' Hania said. 'But when the policemen came to her, she looked the head officer right in the eye and said, "No, sir, I don't have any key at all."'

So the policemen went to the village mayor and asked him for the key.

'He knew Masha had it,' said Maria, 'but he looked those Russians right in the eye and he said, 'No, I don't have any idea where that key is.''

The policemen began to beat the mayor in his house. Then they dragged him out into the street and kept beating him so hard that the whole village heard him screaming. Finally they broke both of the mayor's arms and trampled his garden. Then they nailed boards to the church door and hung a new sign: NO ENTRY.

A few weeks went by. The villagers prayed in the churchyard, or in private houses when it rained. Then, one day – actually, it was All Saints' Day – Maria ran into Hania on the street.

'Hania whispered, "Maria, they have come to wreck the church! They have come to wreck it!"'

Four soldiers had arrived with a green army truck, and they were measuring the width of the walls to see how much force it would take to topple them. People ran out of their houses to watch, shocked. The church had been part of the town since before their grandparents' time. Everyone had been baptized there, everyone had been married there. Not everyone was pious, mind you, but everyone felt it was no business of the Soviet government to destroy it. So as the soldiers tied a battering ram to the truck, preparing to destroy its sixteenth-century walls, the villagers came, one by one, and sat down in front of the church.

'We were all there,' sighed Hania. 'Even the sinners, even the Cybula girl who had the baby before marriage, and even Jacek, who drank, and even old lady Pawlak, who lived over the hill and never spoke to anyone. And, of course, me and Maria and Masha, and the mayor and Maciek and Antoni and Rutkiewicz and everyone else. We all sat in front of the truck and we told those soldiers we would not move, and we would not let them have our church.'

Eventually the soldiers went away.

After that, Masha and Maria and Hania, along with the mayor, and Marek and Maciek, and one or two other pious men and women from Hermaniszki, all went to the local council building in Woronowa to protest. Not everyone could come, only those without state pensions or state jobs to lose. But it didn't matter, because the Woronowa council refused to see them.

A month later, a slightly smaller delegation went to the county council in Grodno to protest. People were beginning to be afraid, and they thought the Grodno council might lock them up in jail. But it didn't matter, because the Grodno council paid them no heed either.

Finally Maria and Hania packed up themselves some *kielbasa* and a few loaves of bread and went off to Minsk: 'Days we waited. Days! We slept in the train station. Finally they let us in to see the vice deputy president of Belarus for religious affairs. He took one look at us and said, "My dear ladies, what are you causing so much trouble for? Why do you bother me?"' Hania shook her head.

'Actually, my dear, he said that it wasn't his department—'

'No, I am certain he said it was just a bother—'

'Anyway,' said Maria, 'He wouldn't help, at first. But then we asked him if he had been baptized a Catholic, and he lowered his head and said yes. And then we asked him if he spoke Polish, and he said yes. Then we asked him if he wasn't ashamed to be destroying things that belonged to other Catholics, and he didn't answer. Finally he looked up and said, "You can use the church." And so we did. We went running home and told everyone they could go in again.'

'Oh, you should have seen it,' said Hania. 'The windows all broken, the altar smashed. The icons were gone, the paintings were gone, and the books were all gone, too.'

'We all brought flowers from our gardens to make God feel better about it,' said Maria, 'and we decided to repair it.' They cleaned the floors, painted the walls, fixed the windows. A local man painted new pictures over the altar, replacing the stolen paintings. 'He was a real artist, a real artist,' Hania insisted. They had begun to tend the cemetery as well, setting right the tombstones and filling in the robbed graves.

'And then, just about a year ago, God sent us a Polish priest.'

Maria began to cry.

'There, there,' said Hania, patting her shoulder.

'For the rest of my life, I will thank God every day for giving us back our church.'

'Shhhhh,' said Hania.

'We love our priest, we do, we give him presents, we are so happy that he is here—'

'Now, now,' said Hania.

'They stole it all from us, they did. This is Poland, madam, not Belarus, and our president is Piłsudski. This is not godless Russia, we are not godless Russians, madam, we are Catholics, we have always tried to do the right thing.'

Feeling awkward, I walked into the church, leaving the two ladies to recover. The nave was clean and sparse; the floors had just been scrubbed. A slightly antiseptic smell hung in the air, mingled with the odor of damp. Father Andrzej was just finishing Mass. He blessed the congregation, and then the organist began to play. A few of the notes were off-key, but I recognized 'Boże coś Polskę,' a nineteenth-century hymn:

> God, you have protected Poland
> Through so many centuries
> Given her strength and glory . . .

I looked up. Over the main altar, the God of Maria and Hania and Masha and Maciek, as imagined by the 'real' artist, was reaching down toward earth from a cloud. His arms were too long for his body, his face was too flat. But his eyes were beautiful, almond-shaped – almost Byzantine – and painted blue. Bright red flowers with bright green leaves floated in the air around him, just like the flowers that grew in the gardens of Hermaniszki.

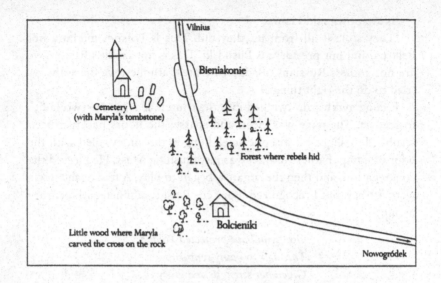

Bieniakonie

In the evening the rain poured down and the taxi I had hired to take me to Bieniakonie kept stopping, stuck in the mud. The driver swore in Russian while he waited for the wheels to spin free. By the time we arrived, it was almost dark; in the center of the village, the heavy gray sky seemed to be pressing down with disproportionate strength on the tiny wooden houses, like a slab of metal crushing twigs. I paid the driver more than we had agreed and ran toward Pan Michał's pale green door.

Inside, the house seemed bigger than it looked from without. 'Pan Michał isn't here yet,' said Pani Teresa. 'Lord knows where he has gone off to, in all of this weather.'

Pani Teresa was a short woman with bright red circles on her cheeks, a tiny turned-up nose, and white hair rolled up in a bun. She wore three layers beneath her apron: flannel petticoat, woolen underskirt, and cotton overskirt. She spoke an outdated form of Polish: in his absence she referred to her husband as Pan Michał, Master Michał. In his presence she called him Pan Mąż, Master Husband. She kept her house very neat, but her kitchen was full of dirty pots and last year's jam jars.

'Don't like washing them,' she said. 'Haven't got the time.' She paced around the kitchen and brushed a wet cloth over a few glasses: 'You'd like some tea, of course, and dinner. Go on, go on and sit down. You needn't worry about helping me.'

I wandered back into the sitting room. It was very warm and smelled of coal. Lace curtains hung from the windows, a cast iron stove stood near the kitchen door, and a ragged assortment of Polish and Soviet books had been stacked haphazardly along some home-made shelves. The Virgin Mary of Częstochowa, Poland's most miraculous icon, hung on the wall opposite. I had seen her blackened face often in Poland – her portrait hung in every church, Lech Wałęsa always wore her picture on his lapel. Finding her here, in a place that felt very far from Poland, made me feel oddly at home.

Quite suddenly the door swung violently open. There was a loud crash; the bookshelf had fallen face down onto the Turkish carpet. A white-haired man strode into the room.

'Pan Mąż,' cried Pani Teresa, rushing from the kitchen. 'Master Husband!'

'Pani Żona!' cried the man. 'Lady Wife!' He ran forward to embrace her, pushing away the tattered books and papers that had fallen onto the floor in front of him.

'Master Husband,' said Pani Teresa, stopping her husband dead in his tracks, 'we have a visitor. She is a poetess from America.'

I started to protest at the description, but Pan Michał put his index finger to his lips. When I stopped talking, he opened his bright blue eyes wide, formed his mouth into an 'o,' and began to declaim, in perfectly rhyming Polish verse:

> I said it once, and now I repeat:
> I am not a poet, I am not a writer,
> I have only a bit of a poetic soul,
> And I write, because my soul tells me I must.
> I think there are others, who when they 'hear' something
> Take pen and paper, and then write, too;
> It's not enough in life, just to eat bread,
> You must leave something for your children's children.

We are witnesses, of how much changes,
And so we must write down our own descriptions
Of our local legends, which are already almost lost;
They have almost disappeared, no one writes them,
Oh, we must not let it happen, the disappearance, the erasure
Of our folklore, and so I announce:
Let each man, according to his abilities, become a local expert,
Let you – there is no other – you who know the stories,
Let no legend about anyone, about anything, be forgotten.

He raised his arm with a flourish and took a diva's bow.
I applauded.

'Pleased to meet you, happy to greet you,' he said. He spread his arms in a great flourish, and a few more pamphlets and bits of paper flew up in the air like butterflies.

'I am not really a poet,' I said, 'just a journalist.'

'It is always a delight,' said Pan Michał, 'meeting one who likes to write.' As he spoke, he hopped about the room like a bird, picking up books and putting them down again, buttoning and unbuttoning the top button of his white shirt.

'Honestly,' said Pani Teresa, coming in from the kitchen. 'Can't you see the girl is tired? Let her rest. Don't bother her with these exhibitions! Such a man I am married to!' She turned to me: 'Have some tea, dear. It will make you feel better.'

'Better, better,' muttered Pan Michał. 'What word rhymes with better?' To the great irritation of his wife, Pan Michał preferred to speak in verse. It was a question of aesthetics: he believed that rhymed couplets were the highest form of speech and that only the most plebeian sort of conversation failed to scan. For small talk, he used impromptu rhymes. For larger topics, he kept a mental repertoire of long poems, specially tailored to certain occasions. Most of them concerned local legends, some of which had a greater ring of truth than others.

One of his favorites, he told me, was the story of how Bieniakonie got its name. 'In the very oldest days, before anyone got used to modern ways, there was a horseman named Bień,' he explained. Bień liked to ride; the root of the word for 'horse' in Polish was *koń*. Hence the name: Bieniakonie, the place where Bień likes to ride.

It was a bit too simple to be true. I glanced at Pan Michał. His eyes opened wide and his eyebrows rose upward, as if to deny he could ever invent such a story.

'Lots of local names have legends attached to them,' he said.

I asked about the nationality of the local people.

'Eh,' he said, waving his hands in disgust, 'these people here aren't Polish or Russian or Belarusian or Lithuanian or anything, they are Bieniakonian. They speak Bieniakonian, their own dialect; it doesn't have a proper grammar at all.' He thought for a moment.

'Some used to be Polish – I remember from back then – but now their interests changed and they have switched their tongue and pen.'

Of course, that did not apply to Pan Michał himself. He knew exactly what he was. 'Let me tell you,' he said, 'there are still some of us Poles here, and we don't like to be forgotten. We don't like to be told that there aren't any of us left out in the East':

> *Our wound is still painful; despite the years that flee*
> *It hurts us, we kresy Poles, that we are not free.*
> *And on this wound, many are still pouring salt,*
> *Even from the fatherland.*
> *Do they know how our pain increases, in their Warsaw souls,*
> *When they tell us that we are not Poles?*

He paused, and thought for a minute. 'I can't decide whether it should be "their Warsaw souls" or "the depths of their souls," but never mind.'

Yet Pan Michał had never been to 'Poland,' or rather he had never been to the lands west of the postwar borders. He did have many acquaintances in Warsaw and Kraków, and he had even been published there – he showed me a scrappy leaflet titled *Songs from the East*, published by the Society of Eastern Poles in Warsaw. A few of his poems were featured in it, and there was a short biography. Pan Michał read it aloud: 'Michał Wołosiewicz, a folk poet still living in the *kresy*.' Someday he would visit Warsaw, but what was the hurry?

He was already recognized in Poland, he had already attained a measure of fame.

Anyway, Poland was a state of mind, not a place. Pan Michał didn't need to see its capital, he didn't need to visit its cathedrals, he didn't even need to spend much time with Poles. 'Poland is here, too,' he explained. 'Poland is still here.'

I asked about the origins of his poems. Most of them were products of his boyhood, he said, 'back when Bieniakonie lay on Polish land, back when things were really grand.' And all of them, he explained, had been inspired by a single, fortuitous encounter, one meeting that had changed his life. He grew suddenly serious as he explained. He sat up straight in his flowered armchair, put his hands on his knees, and recounted the story.

In those days (he said), Pan Michał sometimes worked for a local farmer to earn extra money. In the neighborhood lived an old blind lady, and from time to time the farmer's wife would ask Pan Michał to bring the old blind lady leftover sacks of flour and bits of sausage to eat. During one of his visits, the old blind lady – after thanking him profusely, as she always did – told him that she had lived through one hundred and two springs, summers, and autumns. But she didn't know if she could live through one hundred and two winters.

Pan Michał imitated her, in a high, stagey, old woman's voice: 'I think one hundred and one winters are quite enough!'

In her childhood, the old blind lady had been a servant on the old Puttkammer estate, Bolcieniki, not far from Bieniakonie. She remembered how things had been: the garden parties, the guests visiting from Wilno, the suppers on the terrace, the four-horse carriages, the wine cellars, the racks of ham drying in the storage house. She also remembered the old countess, whose sour, unhappy presence had set the tone on the estate during the final years of the nineteenth century.

At the mention of the countess, Pan Michał had listened more attentively.

'What was the countess like?' he wanted to know.

'Oh,' said the old blind lady, 'she was unhappy, everyone knew she was unhappy. She was hardly ever seen with her husband, not even in church. People said she was in love with someone else, you know how people talk.'

Tall and gaunt, the old countess seemed to live in the past, the old lady said. During the day, she wandered the estate, picking flowers and twisting them into garlands as a young girl would. She kept her bedroom decorated with the white and gold furniture that had been fashionable in her youth, wearing muslin gowns long after the style had changed. When her own fingers grew too arthritic, she insisted that her maid play the popular tunes of the early nineteenth century, always on the same ancient harpsichord she kept in the salon. By the time she passed away in 1863, she was considered a great eccentric.

Pan Michał switched on the old lady's voice again:

'After she died, people said her ghost rose from the grave. People said she was going to meet her true love in the little wood after nightfall.'

The old lady told him about the small cluster of trees that stood beside Bolcieniki, the old manor house – it lay just a few miles away from Bieniakonie – and that very day he went for a walk there.

It was like a magic journey. On his way, he touched every old tree he saw and wondered if, one hundred and two years ago, it would have looked the same. He picked a small white flower along the path and wondered who might have sniffed such a flower before. He lifted bunches of leaves into the air, tossed them up, watched them fall, and wondered who might have watched similar leaves fall in a similar way.

Then he came upon the stone. He looked at it, and Pan Michał knew that the stone had belonged to the countess – to Maryla, that is, only to Maryla, the heroine of the greatest love affair in Polish literature. On that stone, Maryla had met Adam on midsummer night's eve, and on that stone Maryla had sat and waited for him to return.

Pan Michał stood up straight and tall: 'And from that moment on, I was a poet.' He began to recite:

> *A strange legend circulates among the people*
> *That on midsummer's night comes that moment*
> *That the pious dare to call a miracle*
> *When once again, Adam is together with Maryla.*

And the River Solcza like a watchful mother
Glitters in the brilliance of the silver moon,
And the white fog lightly kisses the lovers
So that no one can see them from afar.

And only in the morning,
When others are waking from dreams,
Do their whispers of love vanish;
For they have returned to their graves ...

And leaving behind these wooded hills and these green meadows
They return, as they must,
She to the Bieniakonie cemetery, beneath the familiar maples

And he to the Wawel Castle crypt, buried in historic gloom.
And again run the days, and the sun rises, the sun sets,
Adam and Maryla patiently wait
For midsummer's night – when they will be young again –
To come to the Solcza River, to meet one another.

As he finished his poem, Pan Michał bowed again. Then slowly he sat down on the corner chair with the red cushion, and sunk his chin into his hands. He sat there for a minute, gazing out the dark window at the pouring rain.

'Adam and Maryla patiently wait for midsummer's night,' he repeated, 'when they will be young once again.'

Pani Teresa came back into the room.

'Now' – she turned to me – 'here is tea with honey and something extra.'

Whatever it was, it put me to sleep immediately.

Who was Adam Mickiewicz?

The conventional version of his life (the one found in Polish history books) says that he was the greatest of all Polish poets and a freedom fighter, born near the ancient Polish town of Nowogródek on Christmas Eve 1798, just three years after Poland had been partitioned out of existence. Bad luck had cast Nowogródek beneath the rule of the Russian czar at that particular moment in history, but

Mickiewicz's family (so Warsaw scholars claim) were staunch Polish patriots who taught their son to feel the strong beat of national pride. When he began to write, his earliest verse naturally evoked his yearning for Poland's freedom:

> *Hail, hail, thou dawn of man's new liberty!*
> *Salvation's sunrise will disperse the night!*

The Russian police did not see the poetic value of the *Ode to Youth*, but thought it might well be subversive. They sent him to prison at the age of twenty-four; Mickiewicz was on his way to becoming, in his own lifetime, Poland's national poet.

Adjusting his pen and his ambitions, Mickiewicz then lived for a time in Moscow, Odessa, and St Petersburg, frequenting the literary salons of the day and disguising his verse to pass the censor's eye. During this time he created a poetic character called Konrad Wallenrod, a medieval Lithuanian who disguised his true nature and passed himself off as a German. At the height of his career, when he had become Grand Master of all the Teutonic Knights, Wallenrod finally revealed his true identity and betrayed the Germans to save Lithuania from destruction:

> *I have done this – how great and proud am I*
> *So deep to wound the hydra-headed beast,*
> *So many veins to sever at one blow!*

When they manned the barricades in 1830, Polish insurrectionists called out the name of Wallenrod; when he defended his decision to declare martial law in 1981, General Wojciech Jaruzelski invoked the idea of Wallenrod; Mickiewicz had created a national myth.

Later he left Russia, where spies made the life of a Polish patriot too difficult. He traveled – to Switzerland, Bohemia, Italy, France – and lived among other Polish exiles, experiencing, as they did, the quick rise of hope upon news of a rebellion at home, and the quick rush of sorrow at news of its failure. During this era he wrote *Pan Tadeusz*, a poem packed with all the caricature figures of Polish *kresy* life: the poor squires and the rich lords; the beautiful young girls; the Russian spies; the silent priests; and the handsome, brave young men who populated the mythic Poland of the poet's youth. Generations of Poles used *Pan Tadeusz* as the blueprint for their dreams; Mickiewicz had written a national epic.

Toward the end of his life, Mickiewicz fell under the spell of a mystic and became convinced that he alone could save Poland from her conquerors. He traveled to Constantinople, where he hoped to organize an army of invasion. There he died of cholera in 1855. Already enshrined in the Polish canon as Poland's greatest poet, Mickiewicz died a martyr to the national cause.

Or did he?

Belarusian scholars have looked into this story, told so blandly and predictably by the Poles, and have drawn other lessons. One team in Minsk has uncovered what is, perhaps, the smoking gun: Mikołaj Mickiewicz, Adam's father, was a Polonized Belarusian. Thus Adam Mickiewicz – or, rather, Adam Mickievič – was a Belarusian, not a Pole.

Geography supplies the rest of the Belarusian scholars' argument. Navagradak, they quite correctly point out, was no Polish city, but rather an ancient outpost of Kievan Rus, the state from which all Belarusians descend. Although ruled by Poles for many centuries, and although briefly Polish in the twentieth century between the two world wars, Navagradak lies in a Belarusian-speaking region, in what is now rightly called Belarus. The Mickievič family spoke Belarusian at home, using Polish only for the sake of propriety. To get into a university, to hold official posts, the family had to speak Polish, despite any desire to the contrary.

Mickievič (say the Minsk scholars) fought valiantly against these strictures. As a young man, Mickievič wrote his most important verse in Belarusian. Most of this has unfortunately been lost, perhaps even destroyed (they hint) by Polish nationalists, who even question its very existence.

Certainly many of his major published works are based on legends that exist in Belarusian dialects. Thus he derived the themes of *Forefathers' Eve*, his great epic drama, from local stories of the twice-yearly pagan sacrifice to the ancestors. Thus *Grażyna*, his tale of a woman who sacrifices her life for her people, is set in 'the castle high on

Navagradak's slopes,' not far from where Mickievič lived. Thus legends of fairies who haunted the beautiful blue Lake Świteź, near Navagradak, inspired him to write a poem about a man who fell in love with one such sprite.

That Adam Mickievič considered himself a Pole, and that he has been so unjustly claimed by Poles as a great hero – these are mere historical mistakes, results of the imperialist colonialism to which Belarusians have been subject for the past eight hundred years. Only now, as the Belarusian nation valiantly begins to shrug off its chains, can the Belarusians claim their national hero – Adam Mickievič – as their own. Were he alive today (the Minsk scholars assert), he would undoubtedly take up their national struggle with the same fervor he so mistakenly applied to the Polish cause in the nineteenth century.

Or would he?

Before drawing final conclusions, another group of Mickiewicz scholars, these based in Vilnius, must also be heard. They claim to have proved, beyond any reasonable doubt, that Adomas Mickevičius, were he asked his nationality today, would look his interlocutor in the eye and say: 'I am a Lithuanian.'

Certainly (the Vilnius scholars say) Naugardukas, the birthplace of Mickevičius, is a Lithuanian city, ancient capital of one of the eleven palatinates into which the Grand Duchy was once divided, and an old haunt of Mindaugus, one of Lithuania's greatest rulers. Sadly, the Slav onslaught had pushed ethnic Lithuanians to the north by the time of Mickevičius's birth, thus depriving the poet's family of their native language. Slav aggression left the family with only scant knowledge of their true heritage.

But this evidence was enough to push young Adomas in the right direction, for the Lithuanian case rests on far more than mere geography and genealogy. It also requires an intelligent interpretation of Mickevičius's poetry. Take, for example, the opening lines of *Pan Tadeusz*, known by heart to every schoolboy in Poland and Lithuania:

> *Lithuania, my fatherland! Thou art like health,*
> *For how to value thee, he alone can tell,*
> *Who has lost thee. I behold thy beauty now*

In full adornment, and I sing of it
Because I long for thee.

Polish aggressors have long asserted that 'Lithuania' in this context refers to a province of Poland. Some even dare to assert that this 'Lithuania' had the same relationship to Poland as Wales does to Britain. Similarly, the Belarusian nationalists insist that 'Lithuania' refers to lands ruled by the Grand Duchy, including all of Belarus, and not to ethnic Lithuania. But *Pan Tadeusz*, the Vilnius scholars rightly point out, is no epic of Poland, nor has it anything to do with that species of nation which the Minsk scholars describe as 'Belarus.' Indeed, its full title, exactly as it appeared on bookshelves in the year 1834, was very specific:

Pan Tadeusz
or
The Last Foray in Lithuania

Obviously, Mickevičius intended his poem to describe the return of the Lithuanian prince to his own country, after many years in the wilderness abroad. The allegory is clear: the poet was calling the Lithuanian gentry to 'return' to their own native language and culture after years spent in the 'wilderness' of Polish cultural domination.

Careful study reveals that Mickevičius's secret loyalties go far beyond this one poem. Look, for example, at *Konrad Wallenrod*, the great revolutionary epic that was so widely misinterpreted by Polish insurrectionists. The poem is undeniably the tale of an ethnic Lithuanian. Konrad, when he drinks too much, often begins to babble in a mysterious language his Teutonic comrades fail to understand; his ties to his past are maintained by the presence of a Lithuanian bard.

Again, the allegory is there for all to see: if you cannot fight the enemy, join his army, just as the Lithuanians joined the Poles. Learn his language, just as the Lithuanian princes learned Polish. Have your revenge later.

At this point in every discussion of Mickiewicz, the Warsaw scholars, the Minsk scholars, and the Vilnius scholars would come to blows if they met one another, which they never do. But occasionally there is another group, or even a single scholar (visiting, perhaps, from Tel Aviv or New York), who comes out with the fourth, highly disputed explanation of the poet's national origin. When this happens, all of the other scholars come running back with notebooks, old papers, quotations, and interpretative theories to prove, definitively, that Mickiewicz was not a Jew.

True (they all admit), a rumor to this effect was current in the poet's lifetime. His St Petersburg acquaintances spoke of it with the special Russian combination of horror and respect for Jewish ancestors, and one of Mickiewicz's rejected Moscow lovers claimed as much on the day he died. Most of the debate focuses not on the poet but on his mother. Her maiden name, Majewska, happens to be one that many converted Jews took when they entered the Roman Catholic Church. Just at the end of the eighteenth century, there had been a large wave of such conversions, many inspired by the messianic teachings of Jacob Frank. At this time, all of these converts received the status of minor nobility, and a new coat of arms. Barbara Majewska may have been among them.

Were it just a question of a mother's name, the theory of Mickiewicz's Jewish origins might easily be dismissed. But later in his life, the poet showed an unusual sympathy for converted Jews, maintaining close relations with several Frankist families in Warsaw – and, most telling of all, marrying one: Mickiewicz's wife, by whom he bore five children, was also a descendant of Frankist converts.

Forgotten after his death, this theory, according to the Polish-Lithuanian poet Czesław Miłosz, was revived in 1953 by an Israeli scholar. Much of his case rests on a Hebrew pamphlet, published in 1879, that quoted Mickiewicz as saying, 'My father's origins are Mazurian, my mother was a convert.' While this pamphlet is remembered by other authors, no copies of it survive. Some speculate that they were destroyed, on purpose, by those who wished to protect the Polish nationality of Poland's national poet.

Of course all of these theories were thrown to one side in the Soviet era, when Mickiewicz was suddenly and quite unexpectedly discovered to be a great internationalist. After the Soviet invasion of eastern Poland in 1939, an editor of the newly founded *Red Banner* newspaper declared that Mickiewicz's patriotism derived not from Polish sentiment, but from the joint Polish-Russian struggle against czarism. Reports were prepared on Mickiewicz's Muscovite friends; anticlerical symbolism was discovered in his work. *Ode to Youth* was reinterpreted as a Communist revolutionary tract, and a student visiting the new Mickiewicz museum in Nowogródek wrote that the poet 'could not foresee that Poland would become an oppressor, the prison of the working people. If Mickiewicz had known, I think it would have broken his heart.'

In the summer of 1940, the city of Lwów held a wartime jubilee in the poet's honor. All of the town's literary scholars, together with the man who translated Mickiewicz into Yiddish and the man who put his verse into Russian, gathered to lay a wreath under the poet's statue. They read Marxist interpretations of Mickiewicz's poetry aloud, and finally an actress got up to read excerpts from *Pan Tadeusz*. But somehow the event didn't have quite the impact the Soviet invaders had expected. Years afterward, one of the participants recalled it:

'At one point the voice of the great actress broke, and tears streamed down her face. The audience was not ashamed of its emotion, but felt that Mickiewicz was suffering with the nation, and radiated like a bright ray of hope through his verse . . .'

Of course, there are also a few facts about Adam Mickiewicz that are not open to interpretation.

We know, from records of the time, that he grew up in Nowogródek. We know that he saw Napoleon's army and its Polish units pass through Nowogródek on the way to Moscow. We know that he registered at Wilno University in 1815, where he soon joined the faculty of philology. And we know that he and a small group of friends formed a literary circle called the Society of Polymaths in 1818, which vowed to propagate 'Reason, Liberty, and the Progress of Mankind.'

We also know that in 1819, Adam – who was then just beginning to enjoy a small reputation as a talented young poet – encountered a local aristocrat, Maryla Wereszczakówna, while staying at her parents' home in Tuhanowice.

At their first meeting, he thought little of her, as she was not especially pretty. She was given to fainting fits and bouts of neurasthenia, thought to be signs of a poetic nature at the time. She spoke French and German, but her reading habits tended toward sentimental novels, and her manner was sometimes affected. She was quite cool toward Adam. As the daughter of a grand family, she was out of his reach – and she was betrothed. Her husband-to-be, Count Puttkammer, owned an estate called Bolcieniki, one of the wealthiest in the district. Adam went away from Tuhanowice amused by her wit and entertained by her small musical talent – she played the piano and possessed a competent singing voice – and thought nothing more.

But over that winter, he began to read more deeply the work of the romantic poets, whose names were just beginning to filter into the consciousness of Wilno. Couplets, phrases, whole verses of the new poetry echoed in his mind as he gazed out his window at the falling snow. He turned it all over in his mind and found that he had abandoned his Enlightenment principles. He became obsessed with Lord Byron, the one man who combined within himself the two roles that Mickiewicz longed to play: that of a great poet and that of a hero.

In the summer of 1820, Adam returned to Tuhanowice and encountered Maryla again. This time, possessed by notions of predestination, and convinced that irrational love could triumph over cool reason, he saw something he had missed before. He describes, in *Pan Tadeusz*, the sensations of that first meeting:

> *Then, looking up, he suddenly caught sight*
> *Of a young girl upon the fence in white,*
> *That to her breast her slender form enclosed,*
> *Her shoulders and her swanlike neck exposed.*
> *The girls in Lithuania wear this guise*
> *At early morn – but not before men's eyes ...*

Suddenly her sentimentality, her penchant for white dresses and long novels, her fondness for trees and flowers – all the things that had seemed slightly silly the year before – held new attractions. He fell in love, hopelessly. But her parents could hardly allow Maryla to leave Count Puttkammer to marry a penniless poet. Long walks in the woods, poetry recitations, discussions of God, art, and music – none of it counted for much against the count's vast estates, his forests, his fields, his serfs. She was happy to flirt with him, even after her marriage. Tradition says that at midnight, on midsummer night's eve, they once met by a special stone in the little wood near her husband's house. But nothing, not midnight meetings, not the poems dedicated to her beauty and her charm, nothing could tear Maryla away from the life her parents had ordained for her. Deeply depressed, Adam returned to Wilno. He refused to eat for a time, and later argued with his friends, accusing them of mocking his purest sentiments when they tried to dissuade him from his hopeless, and perhaps slightly ridiculous, love for Maryla.

Then, on the night of October 23, 1823, the affair came to an end. The czar's soldiers arrested Adam and banished him to Russia. He never returned to Wilno, to Tuhanowice, to Bolcieniki, or to Nowogródek, and he never saw Maryla again.

But he enshrined his memories of Maryla in his work, in poems dedicated 'To M . . .,' in his depictions of young girls, in verse and in prose. With the feverish, romantic imagination of an exile, he linked the memory of Maryla with the home he had lost. Over time, his failure to win Maryla and his failure to win Poland's freedom seemed to him one and the same. Much later, staying with friends in Switzerland, he remembered her:

> *Ungrateful One! When today, in these mountains soaring heavenwards*
> *My steps are slowed by the ancient ice*
> *And I rub my eyes, misty in the driving rain,*
> *Then I look for the northern star in the blackened sky*
> *That by its light I may seek Lithuania, your home, and you . . .*

But of Maryla's feelings about Adam, of Maryla's later life, of Maryla's marriage, of the woman who inspired the greatest romantic poems in the Polish language, of those things we know almost nothing at all.

In the morning, the sun shone bright and hard. The houses in the village seemed more substantial, as if they were part of the earth itself.

Their pale green and blue exteriors matched the colors of the grass and sky.

Pani Teresa showed me her square vegetable patch ('a row of spinach, a row of tomatoes, a row of cabbage, a row of onions, a row of leeks, a few potatoes, and we'll get through the winter') and the small wooden chicken house behind it. She milked her cow, fed her birds, and tossed a few extra grains into the shrubbery for the crows ('keeps them out of my tomatoes').

After breakfast, Pan Michał bounded into the sitting room. 'Are you ready?' he asked. He could hardly contain himself at the thought of a companion. His wife had stopped coming with him years ago, and he was tired of visiting the local monuments alone. 'Are you ready?' he asked again. 'Are you ready?' It was a long journey, he explained – we had, oh, at least an hour's walk ahead of us. I said I was ready. 'Good,' he said gravely. 'Let us be off.'

We went first to the cemetery of the Bieniakonie church. Few of the other tombstones were in place, and the graveyard looked oddly empty, as if it had been robbed. But Maryla's tombstone was still there, standing beside those of her daughters. Count Puttkammer was buried elsewhere; he was a Protestant. Reverently, Pan Michał traced the inscription with his finger:

> Marya of the Wereszczaków, Countess Puttkammer
> Born 1799 December 24
> Died 1863 December 28
> Let her rest peacefully forever, O Lord

'They shared a birthday, Adam and Maryla,' said Pan Michał. 'Christmas Eve.' He stood up straight:

> This modest tomb, amid the green cemetery
> has hosted many visitors over the years
> For one of the world's great geniuses
> has cast a shaft of light upon it.

When he finished speaking, Pan Michał leaned down and fixed the dirt around the flowers – which were fresh, I suspected, thanks to him. 'Never fear,' he said, standing up, 'I will show you everything that I hold dear.' He began fumbling for something in his pocket. Furtively, he pulled out a document, looked around the cemetery, and handed it to me.

'Don't tell anyone,' he whispered.

It was the death certificate dated 1921, of Karolina, Maryla's youngest daughter. Pan Michał would not say exactly how he had come to own it. Someone simply knew that he was interested, and procured it for him; record offices and libraries had been pillaged so many times over the past forty years that no one had discovered its absence.

'The first of many mysteries that you will see: for the tomb itself is dated 1923.' He shook his head: it was true. The tomb and the death certificate showed different dates. Pan Michał contemplated this mystery for a moment and then shrugged. 'We must be moving on,' he said, 'there is still so much to do.'

To get to Bolcieniki, the house where Maryla spent her married life, we had to pass back through the village and into a dark forest. Pan Michał had spent a good part of the war in that forest, but he wasn't much interested in talking about that. Those were hard times, he said, hard times. Many people lay dead in that forest, but he wouldn't specify. He preferred to think of the woods as they had looked in a different era:

'This is the road Adam took when he came here from Wilno. He walked along it, with his very own feet, because he was too poor to hire a carriage, even for a treat.'

Perhaps Adam had even touched the very same grains of dirt. The road had never been paved, and we had to navigate some deep puddles left over from the previous night's thunderstorm. The woods looked unkempt; perhaps there was no one to take care of them, no one to carry away the dead branches. As we approached the estate, the trees gave way to fields which were equally ragged. The old Puttkammer estate had been transformed into a collective farm and then neglected.

'More is gone every year,' Pan Michał sighed. 'More monuments disappear, more houses collapse, more churches cave in. But soon you will see the manor house – ah, Bolcieniki still survives!'

But the Bolcieniki manor house was a disappointment, too. The collective farm had removed the towers and flattened the roof. The main part of the building had become a workers' club; the wings had become offices. No one had tried to preserve the park. The barns – big, eighteenth-century stone barns, with thatched roofs and chimneys – stood empty. A few sullen workers rode horse-drawn hayricks about the place, but there was no evidence of real economic activity.

The collective farm was named for Yuri Gagarin, the first Soviet cosmonaut in space. Pan Michał had written a poem about him:

> Although Maryla has long been asleep beneath the earth
> Her name is still linked with Adam's tomb
> And with this palace of red brick.
> But there was no sign to mark her memory
> From the time that the administrators took it over.
> What a shame that in the kolkhoz named 'Yuri Gagarin'
> So little is known of Adam and Maryla.

'Shakespeare invented Romeo and Juliet,' Pan Michał said with a sigh. 'And Romeo and Juliet are famous. But the story of Adam and Maryla is true, yet no one here, where they lived, knows about her.' He walked around the side of the house and peered through an empty window frame, still talking.

'No one here even knows about Mickiewicz. I told a local woman about him, I said he was a friend of Pushkin. And she knew all about Pushkin – the Russians taught everyone about Pushkin – but nothing about Mickiewicz. So she said that if he were a friend of Pushkin, she would have heard of him. But she had not – so she did not believe me.'

'Since then, I have translated my poems, not into Belarusian but into Bieniakonian, to explain to people who they were, and especially who she was.'

We walked around the back side of the house; the smashed glass panes of the conservatory glittered in the sunlight. From the back porch, a path, neat and clear of underbrush, led down a steep hill to the wood where Adam met Maryla on midsummer night's eve. Pan Michał knew the way, of course – he had been here more times than he could count. 'Maybe a score, maybe more. Who knows?' He hummed to himself as he walked through the forest, occasionally stopping to point out unusual trees. He knew all of their names. Count Puttkammer himself had imported some of them from foreign places. Pan Michał picked off the bark of one and explained how it could be used as cork. He picked a leaf from another and told me that it made very good tea.

Then we turned around a large oak tree and came upon the stone.

It was not an unusual stone at all, just a big and rather flat granite rock that lay in a little clearing surrounded by small bushes and mossy rocks. Weeds grew around its sides, and dry brown pine needles lay strewn on its surface. Nothing about it was much worth noticing, except that in the very center of its flat face someone had carved the sign of the cross.

Or rather, someone had sat, day after day – perhaps using a smaller stone or even a penknife – and etched, over and over, the sign of the cross. Months or even years had been spent patiently carving two deep lines into the granite.

This was their arranged meeting place, and this was where, years afterward, Maryla had gone to mourn her lost lover. Pan Michał took his cap off, reverently, and motioned for me to sit down.

'Sit, sit, sit in the place where Maryla sat over all those years. Sit and feel what she felt, the wicked hand that life had dealt.'

I sat. The woods suddenly seemed empty. I could hear nothing except the wind brushing the tops of the pine trees and the occasional snatch of birdsong. After a minute, Pan Michał began to recite again:

> Already, another century is coming to an end.
> But in our fatherland,
> And everywhere that Polish is spoken,
> The name of Maryla
> Like a refrain
> Will always be heard.

He stopped for a moment, and I thought he might begin to weep a little, as he had almost done the night before. Instead, Pan Michał began to speak again, rather angrily, almost as if he had been conducting an argument in his head.

'I must take her side, you see,' he said. He had stopped rhyming.

'She has been mistreated by history. Women are jealous, and they have been cruel to her. They say she was callous because she did not marry Adam, or they say she was greedy because she married for money. But in those days, you see, it was really the parents' choice. She could not help it if she was not allowed to marry Adam. And later in her life' – his arm swept over the stone – 'she was very sad. She had trouble with her husband, trouble with her children. In her lifetime, Poland never became free again, and that, too, made her unhappy. But we have forgotten all this. History has neglected her later life.'

Reverently, he kissed the tips of his fingers, and touched the stone. 'History has neglected her,' he said sadly, 'but as long as I am alive she is not forgotten.'

I looked at him and saw the face of a young man in love.

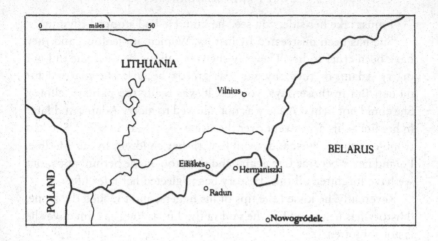

LITHUANIA

Vilnius

BELARUS

POLAND

Eišiškės

Hermaniszki

Radun

Nowogródek

Nowogródek

Along the road leading south from Bieniakonie to Nowogródek, Mickiewicz's birthplace, the landscape opened up. Farms grew bigger, fields wider, and we left the forest behind. If I narrowed my eyes, I could see a single line: the place where the flat brown earth met the flat blue sky.

Nowogródek itself was a sad little town, worn down by czarism, communism, and poverty. It was bigger, but not nearly as tidy as Bieniakonie. Its churches sagged, its market square was filled with weeds, its town hall was still marked by a hammer and sickle that nobody had bothered to remove. People walked slowly, drove slowly, and sipped their tea slowly, as if they knew that nothing important would ever happen to them. Only the castle spoke of better times, with its mossy, crenelated towers and narrow windows, designed for archers.

Near the tower stood a mound of earth, a monument to Nowogródek's only famous citizen. Just before the war, when Nowogródek still lay in Poland, Mickiewicz's admirers had gathered handfuls of earth from all the cities their hero had ever visited – Moscow, Constantinople, Odessa, Paris, and Rome – and brought them to

Nowogródek. By that time his body, like Piłsudski's, was already buried in Wawel Castle in Kraków, beside the kings of Poland, but some felt that Mickiewicz's exile's soul could only be put to rest properly in his hometown. Quite recently someone had planted a Belarusian flag on top.

In the Catholic parish church, a plaque commemorated the great Battle of Chocim in 1620, when the Poles fought a bitter battle against the Turkish infidel. The Polish Army carried the day, but nine great warriors, some from Nowogródek, had died to save Christianity. On the plaque, nine headless men stood in a circle, their heads rolling about on the ground beside them: 'May they rest in peace,' the sculptor had inscribed beneath.

Beside that plaque was another one, only recently put back into place. It praised the valor of those Polish citizens of Nowogródek who had fought the Bolsheviks during the Polish-Bolshevik War of 1920. More recently, one of the chapels in the church had been refurbished and dedicated to the memory of the local nuns murdered by German soldiers in 1941. A border town is a border town, and nearly always at war.

Mickiewicz's house was not difficult to find. New paint set it off from its shabby neighbors; the fresh green walls and white trim radiated benevolence. Inside, the floors positively glowed with wax, and the windows sparkled with polish. Five tour guides, all local girls dressed in neat blue suits, stood stiffly in the hallway. A Polish philanthropist was paying their salaries, and from the way they tiptoed around the rooms and spoke in hushed voices, one could see that here, deep in Belarus, 'Poland' stood for culture, civilization, and new paint. They gazed curiously at me when I walked in, and held a whispered discussion over who was to guide me; I was the first visitor of the week, and they wanted to make a good impression.

The winner, by virtue of her rudimentary English (that qualified her to guide a foreigner), was a peroxide blonde with blue eyes. She dipped and swayed on her white, high-heeled shoes and carried a long rod with a brass tip.

In the first room, she pointed the rod at a table.

'This table, it is not original,' she said.

In the second room, she pointed it at an elaborate, mock Jugendstil wall clock.

'This clock, it is not original,' she said.

In the third room (it was empty) she made a little speech:

'This was office of Mickiewicz father. This is picture of Mickiewicz father. Mickiewicz father was lawyer. He wrote verses also.'

In the fourth room, she pointed her rod at a group of low, battered chairs. One lacked a leg, and the paint had been scratched off the others.

'This is children's room. This are chairs from that time,' she said proudly.

'Original?' I asked.

'Original,' she said firmly.

On the wall hung an etching of a schoolhouse.

'This school, it is where Mickiewicz studied. It does not exist.'

We walked into the hallway, and she pointed her rod at a spot where the wooden floor had warped.

'This hump, it is a mistake by the builders.'

I stared at the peroxide blonde, looking for a hint of humor in her carefully made-up face. There was none. She had not been trained to tell jokes. Still, she was curious. Her gaze kept running up from my shoes to my hair and back down again. As we turned to go up the stairs, curiosity got the better of her professional training.

'Where are you from?' she asked.

'America,' I said.

'Oh,' she put her hand to her mouth. 'This is the first time I speak English with an English-speaking person. I thought you were a Pole – I am sorry, sorry for mistakes!'

Formally, she reached out her hand.

'Hello. My name is Svetlana. Pleased to meet you.'

'My name is Anne.' We shook hands gravely.

'You have heard of Mickiewicz before?' She didn't seem to believe it possible.

'Yes.'

'Where did you learn of him?'

'I don't remember. He is famous.'

She smiled happily. 'Yes, I have told people that he is famous, but no one here believes me. Only Poles know him.'

'Where did you learn about Mickiewicz?'

'Not from school, he was forbidden in school. From books. And my grandmother tells me a little – she is Polish. She was Polish nobility. My father was Polish, too.'

'Are you Polish?'

'No,' she said. 'I am Soviet. I mean – I am Russian.'

She turned to the painting on the wall.

'This is house where Mickiewicz was born. It does not exist.'

I nodded. But the tour had ceased to be of interest, even to the guide.

She turned to me again. 'Have you come,' she asked, 'for the reading?'

'What reading?'

A real actress from Warsaw had come to read Mickiewicz's poems in the Mickiewicz museum. It was a great event; the outside world very rarely came to Nowogródek.

'I am afraid I hadn't planned to stay the night.'

'But such a shame, such a shame to come all the way here, all the way to the hometown of Mickiewicz, and to miss such a reading!' She tapped her rod on the ground.

'Why don't you stay the night? You can stay with me.'

'I wouldn't want to impose—'

She stood up very straight. 'You are not impose. It . . . would be an honor to have you stay. You can stay in the house of my grandmother.'

I hesitated.

Svetlana grabbed my arm, glanced around quickly to see that no one was about, and lowered her voice to a pleading whisper.

'You must stay. You must stay. You must understand, I read Mickiewicz now every day. I try to know this language, this Polish. I try to know it better so that I can understand him. But there are no books here, only one – it is a Russian biography of him, I have taken it from our library. I need – I want – to talk to someone who knows of him. You must stay. You are the first person I meet who knows of Mickiewicz from outside, the first person I can talk to about him.'

Svetlana's grip on my arm tightened.

'You must understand. My parents, my family, live outside of Nowogródek. On a collective farm. In the country. All of my life I want to leave. And I did leave, I went to work in Vilnius. But the wife of my brother, she dies. One day she is dancing at the wedding of her friend, and the next day she is dead. It happens sometimes among women here, no one knows why. She leaves two small children. My brother, he cannot care for them. I must come back. I must do everything for these children. Even tonight, I must go back to their house after the reading to feed them, to put them to sleep.

'At first I was very unhappy,' she continued. 'I am thinking, Nowogródek is – not interesting. Very much not interesting. But slowly, slowly, I am changed. Slowly I learn about Mickiewicz, I learn that he, too, comes from Nowogródek. He is from here, and I am from here. And he is a great poet. So Nowogródek must be interesting. I start to learn about it, and now I want to learn more. I go, last year I go, on a pilgrimage to Poland. To the shrine at Częstochowa. It was something special, it was different. The people there were different from people here, different even from the Poles here. The Poles here, they hate the others, they hate the Belarusians, they hate us Russians. But the Poles in Poland are not like them. They are more open, they are friendly, they are not closed and hard like our people here. They know about West, they know about God. So now I go to the Catholic church. I am the only Russian there. I used to be proud to be Soviet, but there is no more Soviet Union. Now I want – to be with them. I want to be one of them. I want to be a Pole. I want to be Polish.'

She let go of my arm.

'I want to be a Pole,' she said again, softly.

I agreed to stay the night.

The reading was to begin at six, but by five o'clock the local poetry lovers had gathered in the salon of the Mickiewicz house. They walked delicately on the new wood floors, trying not to scratch them, while the tour guides put on a great show of activity, moving chairs about from one room to the next and talking to one another in loud, self conscious voices. The older ladies watched them with great admiration, and I leaned over, trying to eavesdrop:

'That one is Krystyna's granddaughter, don't you know? She isn't married yet, such a shame. Now that other one, the little brunette, she is related to Paszkowski. She married his cousin last year . . ,'

When the actress walked in, they parted to let her pass.

'So distinguished, so beautiful!' they murmured.

The actress was a woman of a certain age. She wore a long black skirt, a black silk blouse, and a black shawl across her shoulders. Her eyes were lined with deep black mascara, and her long black hair, streaked slightly with gray, cascaded down her back. She made a great show of lifting her skirt and adjusting her shawl as she stepped up onto the podium in the small reading room and took stock of her audience. There were, perhaps, twenty people in the room.

'It is a great joy,' she said, 'to see that in Mickiewicz's town, deep in Belarus, there are still some people who honor his name.'

She bowed her head, as if in prayer. It was a gesture meant to indicate great sorrow, as if she were meditating on the sad absence of Polishness from these hallowed fields and villages after so many decades.

After her moment of silence, she lifted her head and began to recite the first chapter of *Pan Tadeusz*:

> *Lithuania, my fatherland! Thou art like health,*
> *For how to value thee, he alone can tell,*
> *Who has lost thee. I behold thy beauty now*
> *In full adornment, and I sing of it*
> *Because I long for thee.*

As each new character was introduced, she took on a new voice: high and lilting for Zosia, firm for Tadeusz, deep and ponderous for the count. She spoke very slowly, and with each new event she demonstrated her emotions with a great waving of arms and a gnashing of teeth. It was high drama, just what the local poetry lovers had come to see.

But *Pan Tadeusz* is quite a long poem, and the audience, attentive at first, began to lose its original enthusiasm. Just as the actress reached the famous mushroom gathering scene, one of the old ladies began snoring softly. As Tadeusz began flirting with his Aunt Telimena, some of the tour guides were politely yawning. Hardly any of them spoke Polish well enough to understand the nineteenth-century language.

'I see some sleepy faces,' the actress said, wagging her finger, at the end of Book Four. 'Perhaps I will read some ballads':

> To anyone heading for Nowogródek ...
> Remember to stop your horse ...
> Lake Świteź there spreads out
> In the perfect shape of a circle
> The forest is packed tightly around
> But the lake is smooth, like a pane of glass ...

The actress stepped up the pace. She made her shawl into a veil of death, and then a flag; her face took on the lovesick longing of Adam for Maryla, and then the fiery patriotism of the man whose country is under occupation. By the end of the performance she was sweating profusely, although the evening was cool. Her mascara ran down her face in black lines.

The audience, now fully awake, cooed and sighed at the end of every verse. But it was not the poetry that held their attention, nor the melodrama. The attraction lay rather in the place-names – Nowogródek, Lake Świteź, the Niemen River – and in the descriptions of churches and white manor houses. These were their local landmarks, their local sights, their local customs being described. To have poems about them emerge from the mouth of an actress made them special; it meant that their forgotten town was part of the wider world.

When she had finished, the actress took a deep, sweeping bow. One of the tour guides ran up to give her a bouquet, and she took another bow.

'The pleasure is all mine,' she said.

The audience clapped politely.

She bowed again.

'Thank you all,' she spoke very slowly, as if to children. 'Thank you all. Thank you for honoring Mickiewicz's name, thank you for keeping Polishness alive. Thank you for defending Polish territory from the Belarusian incursion.'

I felt a hand on my shoulder.

'Was she not wonderful?' Svetlana breathed. 'Such beauty I have not seen before. I did not know that anyone could speak with such a voice.'

Civilization had come to Nowogródek that night.

As we left the Mickiewicz museum, Svetlana's shining eyes faded into a dull glaze and worry lines appeared around her mouth. She began to apologize. Her grandmother, she explained, did not really live in a house. She lived in one of the concrete apartment blocks in the center of town.

'Perhaps it is not what you are accustomed to. Perhaps it is not good enough, perhaps you expect something better,' she worried.

I told her that it didn't matter, but it did. The drive from Bieniakonie had been long and tiring. When we entered the building, I knew I had made a mistake.

The stairwell smelled of sour milk and sewage. The light was broken, and the elevator was broken. The door swung open at a touch – the lock was broken, too. Inside was worse.

Svetlana's grandmother was over ninety years old. Her huge body was grotesquely bloated. Her legs were thick and round like tree stumps; the quivering layers of her stomach hung down below her knees. A filthy rag, yellowed with age, was wrapped around her misshapen head. Dirt and trash covered the floor of her single room: old melon rinds, stale bread, melted candle wax, empty pill bottles, dirty spoons and cups, coffee grinds, and tea bags. Yellowed newspapers stood stacked on the table and the chair, which were the only furniture aside from two beds.

The room smelled of poverty and old age, but a far worse stench came from the bathroom. The walls were damp with mildew, and there was no hot water.

The old woman complained, in Polish, that no one had been to see her for three days.

'You know I have to take care of Mikhail's children,' Svetlana answered in Russian.

'So what? You work too much anyway,' she said, still speaking Polish. 'No man will marry a woman with red hands like yours.' Svetlana blushed, mumbled more apologies, and promised to return in the morning 'to do a proper cleaning.' She rushed around the room for a bit, trying to clean up, putting sheets on the extra bed, and avoiding my gaze.

'I am so sorry, so very sorry,' she kept repeating. 'It is so dirty here, so very dirty. It is just that no one has time to clean . . .'

'Don't worry, don't worry,' I kept saying in reply. But when the door slammed behind her, I wished I had tried harder to leave.

Claustrophobia descended. I reached over to open a window.

'It can't be done,' said the grandmother. 'Hasn't been opened for fifteen years.'

I was trapped.

'Hasn't opened for fifteen years.'

The old woman wanted to talk. She had been born into a family of Polish gentry – a 'noble family,' she called it. They had lived in a big house in the country, an estate with land and peasants. But during the First World War, her father was forced to sell his cows, and the family had moved into Nowogródek. Their house had fourteen rooms and a garden, and it stood right in the center of town. During the Second World War even that house burned to the ground; her mother and father were murdered, and the Bolsheviks stole the silver, which had been locked up in a trunk. After that, she had lived on the collective farm with her son, and then for a time in Minsk with her daughter.

'This is all I have now,' she said.

Her two brothers had gone to Poland, but her husband had refused to leave Belarus. He was having an affair with a local woman, and the local woman wouldn't leave. Or that, anyway, was one version of the story. Some said that it was not stubbornness but drunkenness that prevented him from leaving. At any rate, when the trains filled with Poles and Polish possessions pulled out of Nowogródek, he was asleep in a gutter and could not be raised.

'Now he is dead,' she said, 'but we are still living here. The terrible harm he has done to me still lives on.'

She fell silent. I tried to lie on the sagging bed, but it was too lumpy.

The slightest movement caused it to creak and moan. I tried to read a book, but the old woman's heavy breathing – it was a noise like air coming out of a tire – disturbed me. After a while, I simply stared at the ceiling, looking for patterns in the cracks, and tried not to let the stench make me ill.

Then she spoke again.

'Things were better in Polish times,' she said. 'Except that there were too many Jews.'

I sat up.

'There were too many Jews. Even Piłsudski, our great general, had a Jewish wife. They were everywhere. And they didn't do any work. They didn't ever do an honest day's work. They only knew how to trade and haggle. I don't like Belarusians, and I don't like Russians – these people are not civilized, they don't know how to do anything – but thank God I am not controlled anymore by the Jews.'

I stared at her. The yellow light from the single bulb made her face look as if it were made of rubber or plastic. 'What happened to them?' I asked. 'Where did they go?'

She rocked her grotesque body back and forth on the chair and looked at me sideways.

'Hitler got rid of them for us,' she said softly. 'Hitler killed them all off. He did terrible things, Hitler, he killed those nuns in the parish church, but he did us a service when he got rid of all the Jews.'

'All of them?'

'Not all. There was a Jewish woman in this building, Oh, she was a clever woman. She bought her flat for two thousand rubles two years ago when the Bolsheviks let people buy their flats, and now she has just sold it for twenty thousand rubles and gone to Israel. Oh, they know how to do business, those Jews, they know how to cheat honest people.'

It was too much.

'Do you think I would cheat you?' I said.

The old woman looked up, startled.

'I said, do you think I would cheat you?'

There was a silence. She looked at me sharply, carefully.

'You're not ... one of them, are you?' she asked me after a few moments.

On hearing no reply, the old woman's features shriveled in confusion, and I felt suddenly sorry for her. She was ignorant, poor, and dirty; her life had been one long series of misfortunes. The world into which she had been born was well and truly dead, and she had witnessed its passing. Nowogródek was no longer a Polish town, secure in its possession of Poland's greatest poet. Now it was a Belarusian village, full of poor people who knew nothing of what had been there before, and the old woman was a ridiculous antique, a burden to her children and grandchildren. Why argue with her?

After a minute, she heaved herself out of the chair, turned toward the tiny plastic statue of the Virgin that stood in one corner, and, with great awkwardness and discomfort, got down on her knees to pray.

'Lord,' she prayed, 'forgive me for what I have said to this girl.'

She went on, mumbling the Lord's Prayer, Our Father, Hail Mary, praying for Poland, praying for herself, praying for me. I turned my face to the wall.

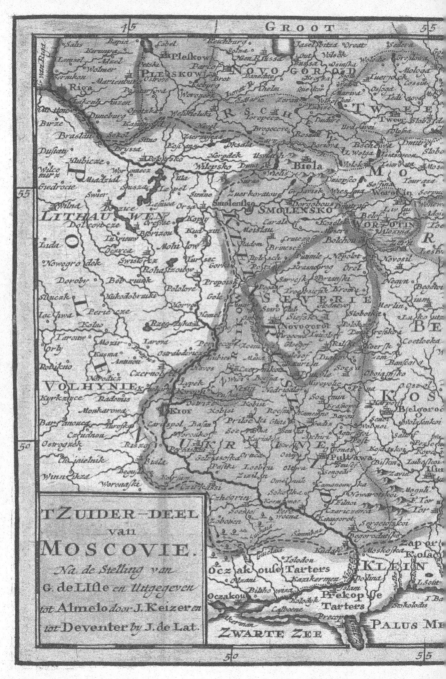

Jacob Keizer, 'T Zuider-Deel van

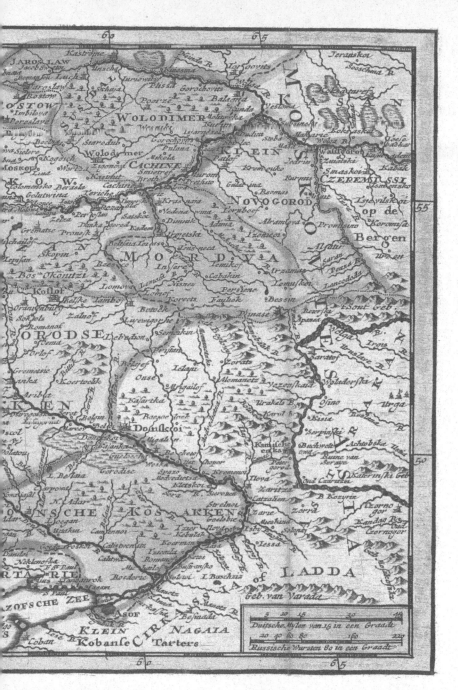

Moscovie', c. 1734–47.

PART THREE
Russians, Belarusians, and Ukrainians

Patriotic Russian historians notwithstanding, when the Lord created mankind He did not place the Russians where they happen to be today.
            – Richard Pipes, Russia under the Old Regime

He cherished this map as the darling of his heart. It represented to him a great and living ideal to the service of which his life was devoted. He could talk for hours about it, elaborating this point and that point, recalling historical events and folklore, and place-names and heroes of the past. Here he was born. Here his wife was born. Here a battle was fought. And so on ... He reveled in frontiers, and, taking a pen, he proceeded to draw a great many more ...
            – A. MacCallum Scott, describing a
                    Belarusian nationalist, 1925

Where is the Cossack host, and where
Are the red jerkins scattered?
Where the freedom-destiny?
The Hetmans and their banners?
Where is it scattered? Burned to ashes?
Or has the blue sea drowned
And covered over your high hills ...
            – Taras Shevchenko, Ukrainian poet, 1839

PART THREE

Russians, Belarusians, and Ukrainians

When discussing Russians or when thinking of Ukrainians, when examining Belarusians or when pondering the Eastern Slavs all together, it is best to begin at the beginning, and the beginning is Kievan Rus. According to the eleventh-century *Chronicle of Bygone Years*, the oldest existing East Slav history, Kievan Rus came into existence in the year 862. This was, the chroniclers tell us, a time of great discord among the perpetually warring pagan tribes who lived along the Dniepr River in what is now Ukraine, Belarus, and western Russia. We don't know why; perhaps there was a particularly severe set of quarrels, perhaps an especially bloody invasion. In any case, the unrest finally forced the leaders of the region to seek a solution:

> They said to themselves, 'Let us seek a prince who may rule over us, and judge us according to the law.' They accordingly went overseas . . . and said to the people of Rus: 'Our whole land is great and rich, and there is no order in it. Come to rule and reign over us.' They thus selected three brothers, with their kinsfolk, who took with them all the Russes and migrated . . .

The people whom the chroniclers called Russes were Scandinavians, elsewhere known as Normans or Vikings, and the land the chroniclers called Rus was probably Sweden. The Rus dynasty, later known as the Riurikids, apparently agreed to 'rule and reign' over the Slav lands for financial reasons. They had just discovered a new waterway – from the Baltic, through the White Sea, down the Dniepr River, and into the Black Sea – and immediately spotted the commercial possibilities. With control over the waterway, the Russes would also control the lucrative trade between Scandinavia and Constantinople, providing slaves, furs, and wax to Byzantium in exchange for gold and jewels.

That seems to have been the limit of their ambitions. Rather than impose an alien, Scandinavian culture onto the East Slavs (as the Teutonic Knights might have), and rather than use subtler methods of cultural persuasion (as the Poles did), the Riurikids over time absorbed the language and habits of those they ruled. Within a few generations they had taken Slavic names (Helga became Olga, Waldemar became Vladimir) and married into local families. Kiev grew, thanks to its position halfway along the trade routes between the Baltic and the Black Sea, but relations with the more distant cities of Rus remained loose and ill defined. Rus was hardly even an empire at all in the modern sense: the historian Richard Pipes has compared Rus to the great British trading companies of the seventeenth and eighteenth centuries – the Hudson Bay Company, say, or the East India Company.

Thus established, Kievan Rus developed very quickly. Trade between Byzantium and Scandinavia made it rich; contacts with Western Europe grew. In 988, the character of Rus developed further when Prince Volodymyr, the Riurikid leader, decided to convert. As the early chroniclers would have it, he rejected Islam because it prohibited alcohol, and chose Byzantine Christianity over the Roman version because the Byzantine Mass was so splendid. Whether or not that is true, the citizens of Kiev were baptized en masse in the Dniepr, and onion-domed churches, encrusted with gold mosaics in the Byzantine style, grew up in the city and surrounding countryside.

By 1037, Rus was at its zenith. In that year, Prince Iaroslav the Wise began building St Sophia, the cathedral that would become the Orthodox equivalent to St Peter's in Rome. Modeled on the Hagia Sophia in Constantinople, St Sophia had thirteen cupolas and pillars made of marble; Greek and Byzantine artists filled the apses above the altar with stiff saints draped in togas, Virgin Marys with almond-shaped eyes, angels speaking in Greek letters. At about the same time, Prince Iaroslav also received Bishop Saveraux, who had come to ask him, on behalf of King Henry I of France, for his daughter Anna's hand in marriage. 'This land,' wrote Bishop Saveraux upon returning from Rus, 'is more unified, happier, stronger, and more civilized than France itself.' Disputes between Catholic and Orthodox were still in the future, and the bishop's suit was successful. Anna became the first, and the last, Kievan princess to become queen of France. Daughters of Prince Iaroslav also married kings of Hungary and Norway; one of his sisters married a Polish king and another married a Byzantine prince. For this reason the prince is sometimes remembered as the 'father-in-law of Europe.'

But just as it quickly rose, so did Kievan Rus rapidly decline. As time went on, Italian merchants established more direct routes between Constantinople and Western Europe, bypassing Kiev; the Rus princes began to feud among themselves, and separate principalities began making their own laws and setting their own tariffs. At the beginning of the thirteenth century, a Mongol king who called himself Genghis Khan – the Khan of Khans – mobilized his people for an assault on Europe and Central Asia. By 1240, Genghis Khan's grandson had reached Kiev. With its capital burned to the ground, its commanders dead, its churches plundered, and its people fleeing across the countryside, the Riurikid dynasty disappeared; Kievan Rus had lasted for a mere four hundred years.

Almost immediately, the controversies began. For despite its short life, Rus spawned an unusually large number of historical disputes: why the Riurikids were called 'Russes,' for example, is a point of great contention. Some say the word comes from *Ruotsi*, the Finnish word for Swedes. Others say it comes from the Rus and Rusna rivers in central Ukraine. Still others speak of Roslagen, the Swedish coast north of Stockholm, or of *rhos*, the Persian word for 'light.' In the twentieth century, those in the *Ruotsi* camp – these included Hitler – argued that Kievan Rus came into being only thanks to the Germanic genius of the Scandinavians, who took a motley group of tribes and made them into a trading empire. Those in the Rus and Rusna camp – and these included Soviet as well as Russian and Ukrainian nationalist historians – argued that although the Russes may have cooperated a bit with the Scandinavians, the Eastern Slavs had been far more important than the Scandinavians in the creation of Kievan Rus. To suggest otherwise, wrote one Soviet scholar, 'denies the ability of the Slavic nations to form an independent state.'

Rus and Rusna, Ruotsi and Ros: it is all very well for outsiders to laugh. For Kievan Rus – however brief its history, however much it borrowed from others – was the outstanding achievement of the medieval Eastern Slavs. All three nations that evolved from Kievan Rus – Russia, Ukraine, Belarus – can legitimately claim to be its spiritual, or geographical, or cultural heirs. Yet so little is known of Kievan Rus, so much has been lost; it is so hard, when considering the distant past, to know what is true and what is false. Records are scarce, guesses have to be made on the basis of fragments and icons and golden-domed churches; so many mistakes can be made; so few people can know what actually happened.

They are more precise than any official document, more interesting than analysis, more eloquent than prose: the best way to read the history of Russia is to look at maps. Not the new maps, but the old, yellowed maps with the place-names still showing, or the maps of many shades that portray, inch by inch, the progress of Russian rule. And all of these historical maps start with the tiny statelet of Muscovy, one of the many successors to Kievan Rus. In the year 1300, the Grand Duchy of Muscovy measured about twenty thousand square kilometers, an area that would have fit easily within one of the smaller modern European states – Portugal, say, or Belgium. In that same year, Muscovy was not even independent. While the southern states around Kiev fell beneath the milder rule of Lithuania and later Poland, Muscovy – from the time of the Mongol conquest until the end of the fifteenth century – was ruled so harshly by Mongols and Tartars of the Golden Horde that traces of their tyranny remain in the Russian language. The Russian words for knout and for chains, for example, have a Mongol origin.

Nevertheless, from its tiny base (and from its state of abject submission), the maps show Muscovy expanding outward from the end of the fourteenth century, almost indiscriminately, in the wake of the Mongol retreat. Inspired perhaps by the need for farmland, or perhaps by a love of power inherited from the Golden Horde, Muscovy first sacked and destroyed the trading state of Novgorod, with its links to the German-speaking Baltic, digging out even the foundations of buildings so that they should not rise again. Later the Muscovites dealt a similar blow to the Khanate of Kazan, and then to Livonia on the Baltic. From century to century, in fact, the maps show Muscovy growing in concentric circles, taking first a bit of Asia, then a slice of Europe, here and there some land in the Caucasus. As its sheer size gave it confidence, Muscovy moved with more vigor. One by one, the simpler, weaker peoples on its borders, east and west, north and south, disappeared into the Muscovite state. Whereas West European empires grew after the West European nations had already been established, the Russian empire grew along with Russia – so much so that it became impossible, as Richard Pipes has written, for Russians themselves to distinguish between their own country and lands belonging to people they conquered. So much so that Russians after the collapse of the Soviet Union found themselves living in an 'unnatural' situation. The borders of their country, post-Soviet Russia, did not correspond to any previous 'Russia' in history.

In the seventeenth century, the Russians – for that was the name they now used for themselves – began their assault on the region they called *okrainy*, the borderlands, the eastern edges of the Polish-Lithuanian Commonwealth – lands that had once belonged to Kievan Rus but had escaped Mongol rule. The Russian czars began slicing territory from eastern Ukraine in the seventeenth century. By the end of the eighteenth century, they had begun to focus their efforts on the heart of the Commonwealth itself: first the lands to the west of Smolensk, then Minsk, then the rest of Ukraine, then Brest and Wilno, and finally Warsaw itself. It was a special kind of invasion: far more than any of its other conquests, the conquest of the *okrainy* was destined to change Russia itself, just as the conquest of the *kresy* had changed Poland.

Part of the change was geographic: because Russia now shared frontiers with Prussia and Austro-Hungary, Russia was, for the first time, a serious player in European politics. But the transformation was also intellectual. For the first time, Russia had occupied a large region that was technologically more advanced than itself. Poor by the standards of Western Europe, the lands of the Commonwealth were highly developed compared to those of Russia. In acquiring them, Russia acquired innumerable artistic treasures, baroque churches, and Italianate estates, as well as a clutch of universities, libraries, and scholars. The Russians also acquired educated people, which mattered particularly in the cases of Estonia and Latvia, nations whose confident elites would eventually give the Russian empire one third of her officials. The Polish aristocracy, while less influential in St Petersburg than the German-speaking Balts, would also dominate the *okrainy* bureaucracy until the end of the empire. Polish remained the language of higher education in much of western Russia until the mid-nineteenth century.

Perhaps most importantly, Russia had also acquired a relatively highly educated, mainly Catholic populace. Although Russia also ruled Muslims, Protestants, and nomadic pagans, Catholicism was close enough to Orthodoxy to present a challenge. Catholics did not convert to Orthodoxy as other peoples might; Catholics did not acknowledge Orthodoxy as superior. Not only that, many Catholics insisted that their religion was more advanced, more intellectual; many mocked the elaborate rituals of Orthodoxy, the secrecy of Orthodox priests, the ignorance of Orthodox peasants.

These challenges to their ideas and status presented themselves to Russia precisely at a time when the Russians, having suddenly expanded to a great and unwieldy size, first began to examine their own nature. Confronted with more advanced, more confident nations in the West – not only Poles and Lithuanians but also Germans and Frenchmen – they began to ask, 'Who are we?' 'What sort of nation are we?' 'What right have we to compare ourselves with Western nations?' They came up with a historical answer: We are the inheritors of Kievan Rus. Our czars are descendants of the princes of Kievan Rus; we have a historical right to conquer the peoples to the south and west of Muscovy, because their land is the ancient patrimony of Kievan Rus. Even if the Slavs of those regions are different from us, even if they are better educated, we have the right to rule them because we are the inheritors of their historical ancestors.

Officially the conquered *okrainy* were called the 'recovered territories.' Officially Russia was retrieving traditionally Orthodox land from pernicious Polish-Catholic influence, saving historically Orthodox people from the domination of the Polish-Lithuanian Commonwealth. Officially there had been no conquest, merely a 'putting right' of a traditional wrong. When Catherine the Great struck a medal in 1793 to commemorate the second partition of Poland – the one that gave her a large swath of Ukraine – it read, 'I have recovered what was torn away.'

Official doctrine happened to coincide very well with the intellectual trends of the nineteenth century. By the 1830s, the emerging Russian intelligentsia had thrown up a group of philosophers known loosely as the Slavophiles, thinkers who claimed, among other things, that the Russian language was the father of the other Slavic languages; that Russian culture surpassed all other Slavic cultures; that Russia, which had contributed so little to world art and culture in the past, was destined to play the leading role in the future; that Moscow, the descendant of Byzantium, was to become the new Rome. Slavic nations that challenged Russia's claim to historical superiority, the ideological basis of Russian expansion, deserved to be crushed. Ivan Aksakov, one of the best-known nineteenth-century Russian philosophers, spoke of the Poles as 'this miserable, haughty, arrogant, and thoughtless tribe, which in addition has been burned through and through with Catholic Jesuit morality.' Men like Aksakov thought, and spoke, even less of the Ukrainians – who also claimed to be descended from Kievan Rus – dismissing Ukraine and renaming it Malorossiya, or Little Russia.

But even writers and artists who would not have called themselves Slavophiles, even those who fought against the despotic nature of the Russian state, even they joined the chorus of scorn for borderland cultures. Dostoevsky, who went to prison for conspiring against czarist rule, despised Polish pretensions to nationhood and put dozens of unattractive Poles in his novels, including the silly aristocrats who cheat at cards and toast to Poland 'within the borders of 1772' in *The Brothers Karamazov*, as well as the charlatan count whom Aglaya marries at the end of *The Idiot*. Even Pushkin – like Dostoevsky, a liberal critic of the czars – wrote of 'all Slav rivers flowing into a Russian sea' and was angered by Western sympathy for the Polish and

Lithuanian rebellion of 1830. After it ended, he wrote a poem titled 'Reply to the Defamers of Russia':

> *What is it that you fuss about, orator of the people?*
> *Why do you threaten Russia with anathema?*
> *What has so upset you? An uprising in Lithuania?*
> *Well, leave us alone: it is a quarrel between Slavs,*
> *An old, old, fight, a domestic row.*
> *Fate decided it long ago. You won't change anything . . .*

Eventually the hatred fostered by government propaganda and encouraged by the poets translated itself into suppression of any Pole or Ukrainian who showed literary talent and anyone who spoke with a distinctive voice – as well as anyone who spoke of independence or sovereignty. In two separate edicts, czarist Russia banned the use of the Ukrainian language.

Yet although the Russians destroyed as much of the other Slavic cultures as they could, the insecurity created by Russia's domination of the nations around her borders remained. Occasionally it appears in Russian literature. Toward the end of *Anna Karenina*, Karenin, Pestsov, and Koznyshev argue about the Russification of the borderlands. While Karenin, a high state official, supports the process, the others are bothered by it:

> 'I did not mean,' he [Pestsov] began over the soup, addressing Karenin, 'that we should set about absorbing other nations on principle, but that it would come about naturally if our population were larger.'
>
> 'It seems to me,' said Karenin languidly, and with no haste, 'that amounts to the same thing. In my opinion, only a nation with a superior culture can hope to influence another. A culture that—'
>
> 'But that is precisely the question,' interrupted Pestsov in his deep voice – he was always in a hurry to speak and always seemed to be staking his whole soul on what he was saying. 'How is one to recognize a superior culture?'

The conversation ends inconclusively; but the question of 'superior culture' – did Russia have one or not? – goes unanswered.

Every so often there was a dissenting voice. In 1836, Piotr

Chadayev, one of Russia's great intellectuals, looked at the maps and the history of Russian expansion and came to a conclusion different from Pushkin's fury, different from Dostoevsky's scorn:

'Contrary to all the laws of the human community, Russia moves only in the direction of her own enslavement and the enslavement of all neighboring peoples. For this reason it would be in the interest not only of other peoples but also in that of her own that she be compelled to take a new path.'

By order of the czar, the Russian state declared Chadayev insane.

The Poles believe that the Germans used trickery – forging the Kruszwica Act, fooling even the Pope – to win control of East Prussia. The Lithuanians also believe that the Poles used trickery to win control over Lithuania, preventing their Grand Duke from becoming a king by stealing his crown. Perhaps, then, it is not surprising that the Ukrainians too believe that the Russians had won control over Ukraine through a trick.

The story begins in 1648, the year that the Ukrainian Cossacks rebelled against Polish rule. Their leader was Bohdan Khmelnytsky. In his fictional *Trilogy*, Henryk Sienkiewicz describes him as he appeared in Polish folk memory:

'There was a strange and rare quality in the man's stormy face, a poorly hidden sense of power pulsing like a flame, along with all the tell-tale signs of an iron will and an inner strength beyond anything that an ordinary man might find in himself . . .'

Born a Polish nobleman, Khmelnytsky had the strength and charisma to lead the Cossacks against their Polish rulers, but not the political gifts to unite them into an independent force afterward. The glorious year 1648 was followed by many months of chaos, remembered in Ukrainian history as 'The Ruin.' The Cossack leaders quarreled among themselves; a Tartar invasion was feared; Ukraine, it was decided, needed a strong protector. Khmelnytsky met the czar's envoy in Pereiaslav in 1653, and determined to ally the Cossacks with the Russians. By January of the following year, a treaty was drawn up; a ceremony was planned. Khmelnytsky swore an oath of fealty to the czar, and expected the czar's envoy to swear an oath of fealty to the Cossacks.

At the last moment, the czar's envoy refused. The czar, he said, swore oaths to no one.

Khmelnytsky stalked out of the church, then stalked back in. He swore the oath.

Within a decade, most of Ukraine was firmly under Russian rule. There would be no second chance for Ukraine to establish its independence for three centuries.

Ukraina: the very word means 'borderland' in most Slavic languages. In Russian, the word is close to *okrainy*. In Polish, *u* means 'beside,' while *kraina* is an old, slightly archaic way to say 'land' or 'region,' as in *kraina baśni*, 'fairyland.'

Until the twentieth century, Ukrainians were, like Belarusians, often called Ruthenians, Ruśini, Ruskyi, or Rusyns – words derived, of course, from 'Rus,' but distinct from Russia or Rossiya. Red Ruthenia is an old name for western Ukraine, the region around L'viv; White Ruthenia, or Belo-Rus, is the name that stuck to Belarus. The old eastern tail of Czechoslovakia, which now lies in Ukraine, still calls itself Sub-Carpathian Ruthenia (to distinguish itself from the rest of Ukraine), but otherwise the name, as applied to Ukrainians, survives only in old books and old expressions. Polonized Ukrainian noblemen, for example, used to refer to themselves in Latin as Ruthenians of the Polish nation, *gente Rutheni natione Poloni*.

Ruthenians but not Russians: from the very earliest days of Russian overlordship, most of the Ukrainian elite thought of themselves as distinctly different from their northern neighbors. After the destruction of Kiev, the Golden Horde ruled Muscovy, but Ukraine fell beneath the milder rule of Poles and Lithuanians. Perhaps thanks to that trick of fate, perhaps because it lay closer to the West, Ukraine developed a different aesthetic sensibility and different customs from Muscovy, a different language and a different historical memory. For many centuries, travelers visiting Ukraine were impressed by the region's strong sense of itself. Maximilian Emmanuel, Duke of Württemberg, who traveled through Ukraine in the eighteenth century, could already write of the Ukrainians that 'they want to be a free people, and not subjected either to Poland or Moscow; therefore, they always fight for their privileges and rights.'

Even Russians visiting the region at about that time or even later were struck by the dissimilarities. In 1803, a Russian judge visited Ukraine and left a memoir:

'Here are different faces, different customs, different dress, and a different system; and I hear a different language. Is the frontier of empire here? Are we entering another state?'

Still, while it was clear that Ukraine was different from Russia, it was not, from the point of view of nineteenth-century Russians (and of some Ukrainians), nearly as different as England or France. Both Russia and Ukraine had the same roots, East Slavic and Orthodox; both nations spoke a language the other could usually understand. Nor did Ukrainians seem, in Russian eyes, to have a culture as strong as their own. Because Russians had been conquerors, Russian became a literary language much earlier; in the mid-nineteenth century Ukrainians used Polish as a literary language, and Ukrainian itself still had the status of a peasant tongue. In the nineteenth century, the first works of literature to appear in Ukrainian were often satires, designed to mock the language as much as to celebrate it; until the era of the national poets, Ukrainians who wanted greater recognition often wrote in Russian – Nikolai Gogol is perhaps the best example. There were, of course, Ukrainian folk songs, stories, and legends, much admired and much recorded in the nineteenth century, but these, in Russian eyes, were hardly enough to sustain a national identity: none seemed quite worthy enough, or quite clearly Ukrainian enough, to establish Ukraine as an independent country in the eyes of nineteenth-century Russians, and sometimes in the eyes of Ukrainians themselves.

It was true that the western Ukrainians had a religion of their own: the Greek Catholic Church, the hybrid created by the Union of Brest in 1596. Greek Catholics, sometimes called Uniates, were a perfect borderland mix, loyal to the Pope but celebrating the Orthodox rites. It was also true that the western Ukrainians, under milder Austrian rule in the nineteenth century, and under Polish rule in the twentieth century, developed a more advanced civil society and a more acute national consciousness. But however singular it might have been, the Greek Catholic Church did not represent all of Ukrainian culture, nor did the national awareness of western Ukraine spread quickly east. Most Ukrainians, for better or for worse, were Orthodox in the nineteenth century, and most remained under Russian rule.

But even if the Ukrainians lacked a literary language and religious unity, even if the Ukrainians seemed a peasant nation to outsiders, even if the Ukrainians had been conquered by others – still, by far the greatest obstacle for those who wanted to establish a national identity for Ukraine was the lack of historic certainty. If the Russians were the cultural inheritors of Kievan Rus, the 'second stage' in a line of civilization begun by Rus, who were the Ukrainians? If the Russians were – as the nationalist historian Mikhail Pogodin claimed – the ethnic descendants of Kievans who had migrated north, who were the Ukrainians? The Russian czars had conquered the Polish-Lithuanian Commonwealth in the name of re-creating the unity of Kievan Rus. If, then, Rus was now unified under Russian rule, then what need had the Ukrainians to rebel against it?

There was much argument and disagreement on these points. Some Ukrainians subscribed to the Russian view that the two nations were really one; some disagreed. But toward the end of the nineteenth century, a new generation of Ukrainian nationalist historians and poets came up with a theory that answered all of these questions: the Russians, they claimed, had stolen Ukraine's history.

'Peaceful land, beloved country, O my dear Ukraine,' wrote Taras Shevchenko in 1842. 'Why, my mother, have they robbed you? Why do you thus wane?'

The theft was the theft of the past: Russia had lied, Russia had tried to deprive Ukraine of the legacy of Kiev, Russia had renamed Ukraine 'little Russia' and taken the glory of Kiev, the beauty of St Sophia, the mosaics, and the icons for itself. But the theft could still be reversed. In 1906 the Ukrainian historian Mykhailo Hrushevsky set out to prove that the population of Kievan Rus had not migrated north but rather had remained exactly as it was: that meant that the inhabitants of Kievan Rus were the ethnic forebears of modern Ukrainians. The Russians, he claimed, were quite a different tribe, only distantly related to the rulers of Rus. Muscovy had imported culture from Rus just as Gaul had imported culture from Rome; Ukraine, on the other hand, was the direct descendant of Rus. Ukrainians were the 'elder brothers' of Russians, and not vice versa.

Uncertainty remained. Just as the Russians were never quite sure if they were justified in ruling over peoples more sophisticated than themselves, so, too, were the Ukrainians never quite sure whether they were really different enough from Russians to justify their desire for a separate state. Too often they were willing to let outsiders tell them what they were, as Shevchenko writes again:

> The German would say: 'You are Mongols.'
> Mongols, that is plain!
> Yes, the naked grandchildren
> Of the golden Tamerlane!
> The German would say: 'You are Slavs.'
> Slavs, yes, Slavs indeed!
> Of great and glorious ancestors
> The unworthy seed!

And yet,

> all tongues of the Slavonic race
> You know full well, but of your own
> Nothing . . .

Kievan Rus had a third set of descendants, but to say who they are is not easy. For if the Ukrainians wrestled with national ambiguity, the Belarusians have been defined by it.

In the year 1636, the head of the Russian Orthodox Church returned from a trip to the lands near Minsk. He was shocked: 'In the houses of the Belarus, fathers and sons, husbands and wives, and even lords and servants are often divided between three, or even four faiths. At least one of these is usually Christian. The others recognise either the faith of the Pope, the faith of the Lutherans, the Arians, or the Jews. And jointly they sit at table, eat and drink, and marry one another. And some even jointly pray.'

Belarus – or, as it was known in the past, Belorussia – means White Ruthenia, White Rus. Why the people west of Ukraine and south of Moscow were ever called 'white' is unclear. Some accounts, noting that the Belarusians had not been forced to pay tribute to the Golden Horde, guess that 'white' was associated with freedom, as it is in many Central Asian languages; others say 'white' implied 'West' in some older tongue. Still others speak of Belarusian peasants wearing white clothing. In 1826, scholars claimed to have traced the name not to 'white' but to Bel-bog, a Slavonic deity. Like Ukrainians, Belarusians were once called Ruthenes, but just as czarist Russia invented the name 'Little Russians' for Ukrainians, so, too, did czarist Russia alter the name 'White Ruthenes' (Belarus) to 'White Russians' (Belorossiya) to make the two peoples sound more closely related. 'Belorussia' has troubled Belarusian nationalists ever since. During the nationalist revival of the 1920s, Belarusian scholars tried to replace 'Belorussian' with 'Kryvič,' after an early Slavonic tribe that inhabited the region; in the early 1990s, their spiritual descendants came up with Belarus – a return to 'White Ruthenia' – because they thought 'Belorussia' sounded too similar to 'Russia' and proved too confusing abroad.

They were right to fear such confusion, since the very existence of Belarus has often come as a surprise to outsiders. In 1826 E. Henderson, who published a very stuffy travel book – *Biblical Researches and Travels Across Russia* – came across an example of the White Ruthenian language but could not fathom its origins. He decided that White Ruthenian was a dialect of Russian, and formed his own explanation:

> About the beginning of the sixteenth century, considerable changes were introduced into the Russian language, in consequence of the relations subsisting between Russia and Poland, the progress of the Poles in grammar and lexicography, and other powerfully operative causes, whereby a peculiar Polish Russian dialect was formed, which continues to be spoken to this day by the common people inhabiting the provinces, comprehended under the name of White Russian …

W. R. Morfill, whose tract on early Slavonic literature appeared in 1883, complained that White Russian, as he called it, was hard to study:

It is often very difficult for the philologist when examining the few religious books and others published in early times in the White Russian territory to say exactly what the dialect is. As is always the case where a language is but little cultivated, we get a great many forms. Thus the foundation of the languages of most of these books is Palaoslavonic, but Polonisms abound ...

For anyone discovering Belarus, it was always easy to say what the Belarusians were not: they were not Poles, they were not Russians, they were not Ukrainians. It was much more difficult to define what they were. Lacking a state, they had no kings. Lacking a nobility, they had never even had rebel leaders, as had the Ukrainian Cossacks. Lacking kings and rebel leaders, they had a history of occupation. They had never been independent, but what was worse, they had never tried to be independent, as the Ukrainians had, before the twentieth century.

Looking back on their history from the nineteenth century, just when so many other East European nations were discovering their origins, a tiny handful of Belarus nationalists faced up to this problem. Backing out of the Russian-Ukrainian battle over who deserved to claim the legacy of Kievan Rus, the Belarusians instead decided to enter the Polish-Lithuanian battle over the heritage of the Commonwealth. They pointed out that the Ruthenian language, which had begun as a diplomatic tongue by the leaders of the Commonwealth, was a form of proto-Belarusian. They claimed that the symbols of the Commonwealth – the Lithuanian rider, for example – ought to be their symbols, too. They noted that they had contributed to the Commonwealth's glory, that Belarusian troops had contributed to the great victory over the Teutonic Knights at Grunwald. It was all true enough, but neither of the Commonwealth's other partners, the Poles or the Lithuanians, was ever much interested in acknowledging Belarus's role. 'I must admit,' wrote Czesław Miłosz later,

The Belorussians are still a puzzle to me – a mass of people, spread over a large expanse of land, who have been constantly oppressed, who speak a language that could be described as a cross between Polish and Russian with a grammar systematized only in the twentieth century, and whose feeling of national identity was the latest product of Europe's nationalist movements. But their case brings us up against the fluidity of all definitions; such a mass can easily be transformed from subject to object in foreign hands . . .

Whatever the nationalists said, 'Belarusian' has always been a flexible term. To be Belarusian is to be able to choose one's identity, even to allow that identity to change over time. In a land that was often invaded, at times there were good reasons to be one nationality, at other times good reasons to be another. To speak Polish brought one closer to Europe, but Russian, for many centuries, was the language of power. Polish priests could bring gifts from the West – they had Polish books, Polish Bibles, Polish newspapers – but Russian officials could dispense jobs and privileges. Only from time to time, usually in the gaps between rulers or in the odd moments of anarchy, has being Belarusian proved advantageous to anyone at all.

It may not always be that way. 'From people, even from those who are not our enemies, one may often hear that the ideal of Belorussian independence is a dream that can never materialize,' wrote A. Stankevic, one of Belarus's most distinguished nationalists. He continued, 'Never mind. National ideals of many other peoples were deemed utopian. With time, even utopias have become historical facts . . .'

Both Ukraine and Belarus have made stabs at independence in the twentieth century.

Their first chance came at the end of the First World War. It was 1917; the Russian state had collapsed; a group of socialist and liberal Ukrainians established a Central Council, which dedicated itself to working for a 'federation of free and equal peoples' among the nations of the former Russian empire. The Council sought the help of the anti-Bolshevik White Russians and the support of the Western powers. No help was forthcoming. The Central Council was disbanded by the German Army a few months later. A further attempt to set up a West Ukrainian Republic lasted only as long as it took for Polish troops to arrive; the sovereign Belarusian Soviet Republic, brought into being on December 14, was crushed on December 18 when the Red Army appeared in the hall where the constitutional convention was taking place and simply shut it down. A handful of other attempts, led by various armies (no less than eleven were operating in Ukraine in 1918), came to nothing; attempts to interest the Paris peace conference came to even less. By 1920 both eastern Ukraine and eastern Belarus had been absorbed by the Soviet Union, while both western Ukraine and western Belarus had become part of Poland.

The second chance for Ukraine and Belarus came, oddly enough, in the 1920s. The White Russians, the Poles, and the Western powers at Versailles had not supported either Ukraine or Belarus, although the Bolsheviks did – temporarily – through *korenizatsiia* ('rootedness'), a policy designed to make Bolshevism seem less foreign. In the years of *korenizatsiia*, Ukrainian and Belarusian commissars replaced Russian and Jewish commissars, national universities were established, national literature was encouraged, and books in Ukrainian and Belarusian were printed on a mass scale for the first time. Great Russian chauvinism was vigorously denounced by Lenin himself. In later years, the memory of the *korenizatsiia* era helped the Ukrainians to keep their national struggle going; *korenizatsiia* in Belarus probably saved the Belarusians from dissolving into Russia forever. Inevitably, periods of Soviet liberalization brought new periods of Belarusian, and especially Ukrainian, nationalism along with them.

But Lenin gave way to Stalin, cultural flowering to extermination. By the end of the 1920s, Stalin had decreed that the consolidation of the dictatorship of the proletariat required national self-government to be abandoned in favor of direct rule from Moscow. The Russian language was reinstated as the 'official' language of Ukraine and Belarus; Russian literature was hailed as 'superior' to other national literatures; Russian historiography was brought back to prove the benefits of Russian rule. Ukrainian and Belarusian intellectuals began to disappear in the night; after a time, schoolteachers, priests, anyone who might be considered part of the national elite disappeared as well. In the name of the dictatorship of the proletariat, Ukrainian *kulaks* – wealthy, and sometimes not so wealthy, landowning peasants (or anybody opposed to collectivization, in the end) – also found themselves forced onto collective farms. The collective farms were then allowed to starve to death slowly, while grain was confiscated for distribution in the cities. The peasants had been thought to be the heart, even the soul of the Ukrainian nation. By destroying them, Stalin hoped to destroy any hope of Ukrainian sovereignty.

For Belarus and for Ukraine most of all, the purges, famine, and collectivization of the 1930s were the equivalent of the Holocaust, although they have never been recognized as such in the outside world. Stalin had the census-takers shot, but Walter Duranty, a *New York Times* reporter who never reported the famine (he wanted to curry favor with Stalin and keep his visa; in the end he won a Pulitzer Prize), estimated privately that 10 million had died. The historian Robert Conquest guesses that 11 million died in the Ukrainian famine, and 3.5 million died in the purges and terror that followed, bringing the total to about 14.5 million.

The White Russians, the Poles, and the Western powers at Versailles had not supported Belarus and Ukraine; the Bolsheviks had tried to destroy them. Perhaps that helps explain what happened when Hitler's armies entered western Ukraine in 1941, accompanied by a group called the League of Ukrainian nationalists; perhaps that explains the photographs – the fat-cheeked Ukrainian women welcoming German soldiers with round loaves of bread and salt – and the young Ukrainian men who rushed to enlist. Faced with a choice between two dictators, one of whom had already murdered thousands, the other still unknown, quite a few Ukrainians, and some Belarusians, chose Hitler. This was to be the borderland peoples' third stab at independence in this century, and it ended, like all the others, in chaos and disaster. Afterward, the partisans were chased into the woods or into camps for displaced persons in Germany. Some Ukrainians fought until the early 1950s, but to no avail. Once again the most energetic, most intelligent, and most ambitious Ukrainians went abroad.

After that, it almost seemed as if there would never be another chance. After the war, the Soviet leaders embarked on a new policy toward Ukraine, one that would make the country 'second among equals,' ranked above all other Soviet republics except Russia. Ukrainian prestige was to depend on Ukraine's relationship with Russia; the big brother–little brother relationship, familiar from the czarist era, was revived. The opening of this new relationship was marked in 1954, the anniversary of czarist Russia's acquisition of Ukraine, with speeches, publications, outdoor fairs, and parades. From Khrushchev, Ukraine received the 'gift' of Crimea, 'a token of friendship from the Russian people': as it had in czarist days, Russia was trying once again to hijack Ukrainian history. Taras Shevchenko was enshrined as a national poet – his anti-Russian works were reinterpreted as anti-czarist and therefore pro-Marxist – although his most subversive poetry was banned. His house was made into a monument, where his bust appeared beside those of Pushkin and Lermontov, to prove that he fit well into the Russian tradition. Ukrainian national symbols were subverted, perverted, put to the use of the Soviet state: the Shevchenko Prize, one of the Soviet Union's most prestigious literary awards, was granted year after year to writers who penned 'social realist' portraits extolling the happiness of life under Soviet rule.

But the fate of Belarusian national aspirations was even harsher. If Ukraine was encouraged to establish its identity within the Soviet Union, in Minsk all forms of 'nihilistic nationalism' were discouraged altogether. Belarusian literature was not taught. Belarusian writers were dismissed, because 'Their works are nonpolitical, undated, indeed, they might have been written at any time, even before the Revolution . . .'

City dwellers became ashamed to use the Belarusian language, which was thought to be a rural dialect; Russian became the language of the cities, of the press, of literature. Ambitious people sent their children to Russian schools, spoke Russian at work, read Russian newspapers. Despite its seat at the United Nations, Belarus had almost no independent life of its own. By 1989 there was not a single Belarusian-speaking school left in Minsk.

Only in the late 1980s, when the tectonic plates shifted once again, did Ukraine and Belarus get a fourth chance. This time it would be – at least to start out – without the help of anyone else.

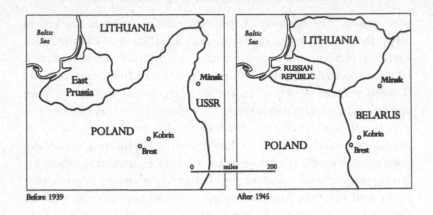

Minsk

After the baroque extravagance of Vilnius, the remote silence of the countryside, and the slow pace of the pastel-colored villages, the suburbs of Minsk came as a shock: dirty concrete apartment blocks lining the highway, muddy courtyards, ancient trams, people scurrying through the long shadows cast by the tall buildings.

The city center wasn't much better. On the morning I arrived, Minsk seemed to be suffocating in its own dirt. Visible grains of black pollution floated through the air, and a thin film of black grease lay over the buildings and sidewalks. Plumes of purple smoke puffed out of the cars, the factories, the chimneys of the apartment blocks, the cigarettes in the mouths of pedestrians. Everywhere there were crowds: crowds lining up for bread, crowds waiting for the broken-down buses, crowds pushing and shoving one another across the wide streets.

I had arranged a meeting. But to get there I had to take a crowded subway train and then a slow bus, picking my way through the puddles and the broken sidewalks in between, passing shops with empty shelves, posters for last year's folk music festival, kiosks where one could buy smudgy newspapers, key chains made of cheap plastic, Soviet candy (grayish-pink sweets, dusty chocolate bars), and an odd assortment of 'folk' knickknacks: wooden spoons, machine-embroidered handkerchiefs, matryoshka dolls. Outside, the breeze brought the bitter scent of cheap coal; underground, the odors of unwashed bodies and old cigarette smoke were almost overwhelming.

The city was disorienting, and its gray surfaces began to bother me. As I walked, the first line of an old joke kept repeating itself in my head: 'Two rabbis are on a train from Minsk to Pinsk, and one of them says to the other ...' Somewhere, I had once seen a black-and-white print of Old Minsk: wooden houses crowded along a river, horse-drawn carriages, Jews with long side curls; perhaps the print had been in a book about the old Polish-Lithuanian Commonwealth, which Minsk had been part of, or in a book about the East European Jews. But it was impossible to reconcile the joke and the print with the city around me, nor could I see what Minsk had to do with Pan Michał and Nowogródek and the many ghosts of Adam Mickiewicz. Except for one or two churches, none of the buildings in Minsk looked at all like buildings in the villages I had just left behind. It was as if a collection of concrete blocks had been plucked out of Soviet Russia and thrust, arbitrarily, into the provincial fastness of Belarus.

Yet Minsk once had been just as I imagined it: a wooden village populated by Jews, a few Poles, a few Belarusian peasants. That was how it was until 1919, when Belarus joined the Soviet Union and the city was chosen to become the republican capital. The purges followed, and the old Polish-speaking ruling class was murdered. Then the Second World War destroyed most of the city's old buildings and old streets, along with most of the city's inhabitants.

Afterward, Minsk had to be rebuilt to a scale suitable to the capital of a republic that was quite a bit larger, thanks to the addition of the Polish territories, and was in possession of its own seat at the United Nations. But as in other Soviet and postwar East European cities, the development of Minsk was planned according to ideological criteria: not only would Minsk become a new kind of city, but Minsk would also harbor a whole new Soviet way of life.

This was the era of steel factories, machinery plants, and power stations, and Minsk got them all: the big, black buildings belching black smoke, the endless assembly lines, the factory floors strewn with bits of steel cable and rubber wire, the busloads of workers coming in for the two o'clock shift. Peasants poured in from the countryside to join them, filling up the new concrete apartment blocks with their cousins, and their neighbors' friends, and their nieces and nephews, just like the peasants in Kraków or Kiev. Within a decade, Minsk had experienced the Industrial Revolution, the Socialist Revolution, the proletarianization of the peasantry, the enlightenment of the proletariat, the enlightenment of the vanguard of the proletariat, the Russification of both the proletariat and its vanguard, and the Communist Revolution: the creation of *Homo sovieticus*, the Soviet Man who knows no history and has no culture.

The inhabitants of Minsk were even cut off from the language of their grandparents' villages: by 1989 there were no Belarusian-language schools in the city. As for the prehistory of Minsk – the jokes about rabbis on the train from Minsk to Pinsk, the polite squabbles of Catholic and Orthodox priests, the competition between the Polish bourgeoisie and Armenian traders – all of that was forgotten, and no one missed it. Hardly any of the city's inhabitants had actually lived in Minsk before the war anyway.

The new Minsk had workers, factories, and a bright future. But because Minsk had no history, Minsk had no soul. Instead of a baroque quarter, Minsk had a reconstructed Old Town, with all the churches turned into restaurants. Instead of small shops, Minsk had ugly department stores where all the products were packaged in the same shades of beige and mauve. Instead of an old market square, Minsk had an imitation of Moscow's Red Square, a wide open space perfectly measured to fit the requisite number of dignitaries and tanks on May Day and the anniversary of the October Revolution. Large, bland, impersonal structures served as public buildings; bronze Lenin statues stood outside every one of them. Everything was too big, as if the architects wanted to remind Minsk's citizens of their own insignificance beside the enormous forces of history which the buildings represented. Everything was ugly, as if no one much cared about the city, as if no one felt connected to it.

In Minsk, Soviet culture had triumphed – but not completely. If the sound of Vilnius had been the loud noise of competing voices, the sound of Minsk was a quieter one: the low murmur of a people discovering, or rediscovering – or perhaps inventing – who they were.

'We are postmodernists,' said Igor softly. His black hair was pulled back from his face. His eyes watered from too much reading. His skin was pale from too much time spent inside. 'Do you know Heidegger?'

I said that I did.

'Do you know Foucault?'

I said that I did.

'Then you must see how Belarus is the perfect postmodern country.' Igor kept a straight face as he spoke, blinking only occasionally.

'I'm not sure . . .'

'Look, postmodernism is about the reappropriation of the past, the making real of false consciousness, the revaluation of values. Until now we have been living here in a false culture, surrounded by mass-produced' – he struggled to translate the right word – 'kitsch. And now it is time to discard the kitsch and replace it with something real.'

Igor was a poet, and a student of English. Most of his vocabulary seemed to come from three sources: English translations of German philosophy, American Beat poetry, and Beatles' lyrics.

'Kitsch,' he repeated. 'They gave us fake peasant culture: mass-produced dolls for tourists, cheap wooden spoons. And all the time they were destroying the real peasant culture, shutting down workshops, telling people to give up carving and join the Communist Party.'

When he wasn't reading, Igor and his friends spent their time in the countryside, trying to find real craftsmen, real Belarusians making real folk art. Occasionally they succeeded: Igor had photographs of artisans, all old men now, who made wooden furniture and cloth. Most laughed at Igor and didn't believe that what they did had any value. Most would give away what they made for nothing.

Igor said that it was now up to the city dwellers to revive Belarusian culture: 'We must sing folk music at intellectual gatherings. We must read folk poetry. We must invent tradition afresh, if necessary, where we have forgotten it.'

Igor's friends' wives also participated in the revaluation of values. They wore homemade aprons and cooked traditional meals, dressed their children in folk costume and studied Belarusian. Igor approved of such efforts. He disapproved, on the other hand, of Belarusians who emigrated.

'Why should I emigrate – why should I go to New York and become a taxi driver? My life can be interesting here. We young Belarusians can be like gods – we can create the world by inventing new words for things. Where else in the world can I do the first translations of Derrida, or write the definitive work on Hegel? Here I can help create a literary tradition, and influence the thinking of the many generations of people who will follow me.'

There were others who felt the same way, he said. One of his friends had translated *Ulysses* into Belarusian, just to see if it could be done; another was working on 'The Waste Land.' Once, it had been the fashion to learn foreign languages. Now everybody – *everybody* – was studying Belarusian.

The apartment where Igor and I were talking was very small – one tiny sitting room, half a bedroom, half a kitchen – and everything in it was cheap in the Soviet way: the linoleum on the floor, the upholstery on the sofa, the thin porcelain coffee cups, the aluminum spoons. But the apartment of a Belarusian nationalist is also a shrine to the Belarusian nation. There was a red-and-white Belarusian flag, a shelf of Belarusian books – histories of Belarus, Belarusian literature – and photographs of significant works of Belarusian architecture. When I looked closer, however, I saw that the emblem in the center of the flag was the man on horseback who is also the emblem of Lithuania; the books were histories of Poland, histories of Russia, histories of Lithuanian Jews; the photographs showed the palaces of Radziwiłłs and Czartoryskis, families better known for the roles they played in Polish history. Everything – the Lithuanian coat of arms, the writers, even the Turkish carpet on the wall – was borrowed from someone else.

Igor didn't deny it. 'That's what I mean: postmodern,' he said cheerfully. 'We borrow from the past of others. We were a part of

Lithuania, a part of Poland, a part of Russia. Our history is theirs. Their symbols are ours.' He shrugged. 'How was England created? How was France created? Just the same.

'Anyway,' said Igor, 'old nations have invented new states before. Look at Israel. Look how successfully the Jews turned their old culture into a new country. The world has already forgotten that they were once stateless, like us.'

I pointed out that the Jews had a bit more written literature and somewhat more written history than the Belarusians.

'True,' Igor admitted. It didn't bother him.

'We must simply write our history, where it doesn't exist.'

At that point he began to question me, very seriously, about modern English poetry. He wanted to keep up, he wanted to know what was new.

'Ted Hughes?'

'No, no,' said Igor, 'everyone knows about him.'

'Philip Larkin?'

'That's old, too.' He looked at me, surprised. 'Don't you know more than that? What about music?' He reeled off a list of unfamiliar jazz bands.

I shrugged. Igor sighed. But we were even on modern novelists: the expression 'magical realism' was new to him.

'Magical realism,' he mused, translating it literally: 'imaginary truth. That is exactly what I would call Belarus: imaginary – but true.'

'Look,' said the scholar, and he opened a book.

It was a reprint of the Bible, Old Testament and New Testament, translated and illustrated by one Francis Skaryna. The scholar showed me the date of printing: 1519.

Francis Skaryna, he explained, had been born in Polotsk, in the eastern half of what is now called Belarus – and what was then called the Polish-Lithuanian Commonwealth – in 1490. Skaryna was educated in Wilno, Kraków, Prague, and Padua. He was acquainted with the Polish king Sigismund, and was present at the Congress of Vienna in 1515, when the Habsburgs, kings of central Europe, married their children off to the Jagiellonian kings of Poland and Lithuania. It was an efficient way to keep the peace: 'Make marriage, not war' might have been the Habsburg motto.

Skaryna was a doctor of medicine, an accomplished printer, a theologian, a linguist, and an expert in the occult sciences, including the Jewish Kabbalah, which was then fashionable among the rabbis of Prague. He was a man of both East and West. His language, called Ruthenian at the time, was a borderland tongue: neither Polish nor Russian, but something closer to the Slavonic language used by the Lithuanian kings, with words of Latin, Czech, and German thrown in. His imagery was mixed as well, the scholar explained: 'Skaryna took the Byzantine order of saints and the Slavic script of the Greek Catholic Uniate Church, and placed them into Gothic and Kabbalistic traditions of allegory.'

The scholar kept pushing his glasses down his nose as he spoke, and kept stroking his beardless chin: these were the gestures of a man who had spent the better part of a lifetime surrounded by yellowed manuscripts and old sheets of music. But Skaryna was the love of his life. 'Nothing in this Bible is what it appears to be at first,' he told me. 'Skaryna had his own ways of conveying God's word, but nothing is what it appears to be at first.'

In one of Skaryna's engravings, Jehovah seemed to be crowning the Virgin. 'Ah,' asked the scholar, 'but why did Skaryna call this print *The Wedding of the Bride and Groom*?' He sat back, satisfied that I would never guess. After a moment, he continued.

'After careful thought, I have uncovered this mystery. In the Kabbalah, God has both male and female traits. Now, you can see in this picture that the Virgin is making the Jewish sign of blessing, holding her third and fourth fingers apart, drawing our attention to Kabbalistic allegory. So in fact this print depicts both the crowning of the Virgin and, allegorically, a marriage: the marriage of God's male and female elements.'

Another engraving showed the Ark of the Covenant being carried by the Twelve Tribes of Israel. 'But look at the flags. These are not the flags of the Twelve Tribes, but rather the flags of three dynasties – the Habsburgs, the Jagiellons, and the kings of Denmark – together with the coats of arms of the Commonwealth's leading nobles. Allegorically it is the Twelve Tribes, literally it is the Habsburgs and the Jagiellons and the Northern Union of Scandinavians who, having agreed not to fight one another, are marching back to reclaim the land stolen by the Turks.' Everywhere, the scholar said, there were multiple references to Christian theology and Jewish magic. Skaryna's figures included a *golem*, the man-robot which a certain rabbi in Prague was once said to have brought to life from clay; a variety of devils; and a parade of symbolic animals.

But it was more than the mixture of images, the quirky combination of Western, Greek Catholic, and Jewish allegory, that the scholar wanted me to understand.

'This,' he stated, 'is a style instantly recognizable to any Belarusian. Show any Belarusian this book and he will understand it. Let any Belarusian see these drawings and he will feel they belong to him. Skaryna is their poet, their artist, and they will recognize him immediately. The Belarusians are like fish who have been swimming beneath the ice. Armies have passed above them, marching back and forth. Poles and Russians have occupied them, colonized them, taught them to speak other languages and forget their history. But beneath the ice, they have preserved a memory of older things. Skaryna is one of them.'

In the special mix of Gothic and Byzantine, Christian and Jewish, Catholic and Orthodox, in the ancient borderland language of Skaryna, the scholar thought he had discovered the thing about Belarus that made it unique – the special, mystical quality, in other words, that made Belarus a nation.

I must have looked doubtful. Belarus lacked so many things – written history books and national traditions, dictionaries and language teachers, even sovereignty: whenever Russia wanted Belarus to sign a treaty, Belarus signed. How could it be called a nation?

'God creates nations,' the scholar told me, 'not men.'

He opened another edition of Skaryna's Bible – this time printed in Russian – to the same engraving of the Ark of the Covenant. 'Compare these two prints. Here, you see that flag up here in the corner? It is empty. Just a flag. Now here' – he pointed to the Belarusian edition – 'you see that the flag is not blank. What is on it? A Star of David, *Mogen David*. So Skaryna included the Jews in his procession of nations; Soviet historians didn't like this idea, so they left them out. But it is nothing new.' Just like the czars before them, the Soviet rulers had tampered with Belarus's heritage, even censoring reprints of a Renaissance Bible to suit the ideology of the moment. Just like the czars before them, the Soviets had changed Belarus's history so that no one knew the truth.

Outsiders like myself were always fooled by these changes, he said. He pointed his finger at me. 'I can see from your questions that you believe their lies. You believe that Belarus is not a nation. You have fallen for their tampering and their burning of books. You do not understand that the past has been altered, that the truth about Belarus has never been told.'

Indignant, he rustled his yellowed manuscripts and bade me farewell.

In one of the farthest-flung suburbs of Minsk lived a man who loved Jews.

'But not you modern Jews,' Vitaly said, pointing at me. 'You do not interest me. Really, you are no different from anyone else.'

Vitaly was not Jewish. Nevertheless, he spoke both Hebrew and Yiddish better than almost anyone else in Minsk. He even taught Hebrew to the few Jews who remained in the city, almost all of whom were now preparing to go to Israel. Still, he admitted, they did not really interest him either. What Vitaly loved were the Jews of the past: the Jews with caps and ringlets around their ears, the Jews in long black coats, the Jewish women in wigs, the Jewish children who studied Talmud and Torah by candlelight, the Jews whose culture once dominated Minsk. He could list the names of their great rabbis, always putting the accents in the right places: 'It was important to them that the names be right, so it should be important to us,' he told me. He knew where they had lived, and pointed to their now nonexistent houses with the respect of a connoisseur. He showed me the overgrown field in the center of Minsk where they had been buried, read to me the faded Hebrew from the handful of stones that remained. He even owned some of their books, as the Jews leaving for Israel were selling their grandparents' Bibles, prayer books, and scholarly works.

Vitaly had known about Jews for as long as he could remember, although he had not always loved them. As a child, his grandmother had told him how the Jews had sacrificed Christian children, using the blood for their Passover matzohs. Then, when he met his first Jew – a little blond girl in his primary school class – he had pulled her hair and called her a 'yid.' She had cried. Later, he felt sorry. But the incident remained lodged in his memory. Why had he done it? What did the word 'yid' mean? Why did people not like 'yids'?

As a young man, Vitaly began to read about Jews. The only books he could find were Soviet, anti-Zionist tracts, histories of the perfidious capitalist imperialist state of Israel. At first he believed these accounts. Books were books; what was inside them must be true. But he also discovered that many of the capitalist imperialist founders of Israel had come from Belarus – some, even, had come from Minsk. From the context, he understood that there had once been many Jews in Minsk. What had happened to them? Where had they all gone?

To learn more, he had to read more. But there was nothing much written about Jews in Russian, at least nothing he could find. Vitaly began to study English and Hebrew – both were, at that time, looked down upon by the authorities. Through studying Hebrew, he began to meet Jews and dissidents. Through studying English, Vitaly met people who laughed at the books he had believed were true, people who knew different versions of history, people who had access to Western books and Western magazines that told different stories about the past. At first he found these people confusing; later he understood that they were right and that the authorities – including his parents and grandparents – were wrong.

The Jews of Minsk: when they had been alive, there had been no lying. When they had been alive, Minsk had been a different kind of city, a better city, a city of prayer and study, not a city of factories and smog. The ancient Jews, they had been better people, more moral people. That was how Vitaly understood it, and that was why he had taught himself the names of their rabbis and the melodies of their prayers.

One afternoon, Vitaly took me to the newly opened synagogue, a small brick building with boarded-up windows and what appeared to be a makeshift extension. The extension turned out to be a sukkah, an outdoor structure that religious Jews build in their backyards during the harvest season. The sukkah was not yet finished, and a handful of small boys were quietly hammering nails into its walls. An enormous man decked out in a skullcap, side curls, and black suit looked on, supervising. 'I have never seen him before,' whispered Vitaly, eyes round.

The man was a Lubavitcher from Brooklyn. He had arrived just a few days earlier.

I introduced myself. He wasn't particularly pleased to meet me.

'American? What are you doing here? You Jewish?'

Yes, I said.

'But not really, huh? When did your family stop being Jewish?'

I stared at him. 'Who said that we've stopped?'

'Haven't you?' the Lubavitcher asked, looking at me critically. 'Jewish girls don't dress like you.'

He turned to Vitaly, who was still staring at him. The Lubavitcher's eyes narrowed. 'You Jewish?' he asked Vitaly in English.

Vitaly shook his head, but said something in Yiddish.

'Where'd you learn to talk like that?' the Lubavitcher demanded, again in English.

Vitaly explained that he had studied Yiddish and that he taught Hebrew as well. He began to recite a prayer: 'Hear, O Israel . . .' The Lubavitcher listened for a minute and then interrupted.

'You a spy?'

Vitaly looked shocked: 'No.'

'They told us there would be spies here in Russia, spies reading our mail, spies listening to our telephone conversations. You might be one of them. How come you know Yiddish if you aren't a spy?'

Vitaly looked at the floor. 'This isn't Russia,' he said, 'this is Belarus.'

'Russia, Belarus, all the same thing. They had pogroms in Minsk, that's all I know.' The Lubavitcher turned back to me. 'You know what I miss here? Kosher hot dogs, that's what I miss.' He shook his head. 'We have to bring all of our food in big crates. Can't eat anything local.'

In English this time, Vitaly asked the Lubavitcher a complicated question about the age of the world: how was it calculated?

'No problem. Read what it says in the Bible, that's what's true. You don't need to read any other books to know it. Science' – he waved his hand in the air – 'all nonsense.'

I wanted to leave, and tugged Vitaly's arm. But he was still interested in talking.

'What are you doing here?' he asked.

'Just trying to bring a little learning to the locals. Teach them a few things before they go to Israel. We're not missionaries here' – he waved his arm, to indicate the synagogue – 'we don't want to convert anybody. We're only interested in our own people.'

'Did you know that some famous rabbis' – Vitaly mentioned a few names, proud of his pronunciation – 'lived around here? I've been to their tombs.'

'That so?' The Lubavitcher shrugged. He turned his back to us and began shouting instructions to the troupe of boys.

We walked away. 'It is living archaeology,' Vitaly told me happily. 'That man – he is a living relic of my past.'

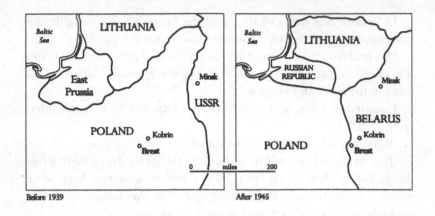

Before 1939   After 1945

Brest

From Minsk, a Russian couple drove me the three hundred kilometers to Brest. He wore gold rings on most of his fingers, she wobbled dangerously on pencil-thin heels. Both of them were very fat, and their dog was fat, too. It sat in the front seat, sniffing at the Christmas tree-shaped air freshener that hung from the rearview mirror.

'I am afraid to leave him at home,' she said, nuzzling the dog's black nose. 'The thieves these days, they will steal anything.'

South of Minsk, the land seemed flat and dry. Long tails made of dust followed the cars on the highway, and there were no trees.

Driving into Brest, we watched the billboards flash by:

LENINGRAD – HERO CITY
VOLGOGRAD – HERO CITY
SEVASTOPOL – HERO CITY
MURMANSK – HERO CITY

and finally:

BREST – HERO CITY

'The Great Patriotic War is still very close to us,' said the woman, putting her hand to her heart. 'It lives with us every day.'

THE PEOPLE'S VICTORY NEVER DIES!
LONG LIVE THE PEOPLE'S VICTORY!

'You cannot imagine what it still means,' and she covered her eyes. As it happened, the Second World War had not touched her. Her father, a factory manager, had kept the family safely east of the Urals.

'We learned of it in school,' she said proudly. 'We had more casualties than all of the other Allies put together: more than England, more than France.'

Twenty million Russian dead is the number quoted again and again. But whether there were twenty and not ten, whether they died from Hitler's aggression or Stalin's stupidity, whether they died at the front or in Siberian concentration camps, it is hard to say. In any case, the number certainly includes Poles, Lithuanians, and Ukrainians from occupied territories who fought against the Red Army in the final days of the battle; indeed, it was mainly the border peoples, not the Russians, who had died to save the Soviet Union.

'The world has not yet repaid us for what we suffered,' she said.

I nodded politely.

They dropped me off at the fortress. 'You must go inside before you do anything else in Brest,' she made me promise. 'It is our scene of martyrdom.'

It would have been hard to avoid: the fortress dominated the town. Its entrance was marked by a vast, five-pointed star-of-Lenin blasted into a slab of rock. Somber military music poured out of hidden loudspeakers. People walked past the fortress entrance on tiptoe, and spoke in whispers inside; it was as if they were visiting a sacred shrine, which, in a way, they were. Past the entrance, a long, imposing walkway led to an enormous sculpture of a man's anguished head and an eternal flame.

The outside walls were red brick and covered with moss. Once, the Brest fortress was linked to a chain of czarist fortresses, all built in Russia's newly acquired western territories in the early nineteenth century. They were used, however, to Russify the natives, not to guard against enemies. The Brest fortress once served as a garrison for Russian occupation troops and doubled as a prison for local nationalists, not unlike Caernarvon, an English castle built to help Anglicize the Welsh.

But the Brest fortress had also played another role in the conflict between Russia and the borderland nations: in the winter of 1917, Trotsky lectured the kaiser's generals on the principles of socialism in the fortress of Brest, and then negotiated his 'separate peace' with them, ending Russia's participation in the First World War. The resulting Treaty of Brest-Litovsk, a great blow to the Bolsheviks, separated the Baltic states, Poland, Belarus, and Ukraine from Russia. Like many border treaties signed in the years after the First World War, it failed to hold. But partially thanks to the Treaty of Brest-Litovsk, Brest remained in Poland until another war and another treaty shifted the city and the fortress back into the Soviet Union. Now both lay just along the Polish-Belarusian border.

Two soldiers walked past me, their metal heels clicking on the stone walkway. I followed them into the exhibition hall. A portrait of Lenin ruled over the entrance, and his spirit was still in evidence: tickets cost only ten kopecks. Thanks to hyperinflation, ten kopecks were now worth a fraction of a fraction of a cent, but no one had bothered to raise the price.

The hallway was filled with czarist military memorabilia, swords, and uniforms. There was no mention of Poland, or of Trotsky, or of Brest-Litovsk. There was no mention of the 1930s, when Brest lay on the other side of the border. Instead, the exhibition of the history of the Brest fortress shifted quickly from the czarist era to the Great Patriotic War – and to the great Belarusian patriots who had given their lives to save Brest for the Soviet Union.

It was an exhibition of staggering proportions. There were portraits of the heroes, and portraits of their wives; a diorama showing where and how they hid in the fortress cellars; quotations allegedly discovered on the walls afterward ('I die for Stalin' and 'I die for the Bolsheviks'); authentic earth from the cellars, scooped up after the war; a day-by-day account of the battle; the remains of the Soviet flag that flew over the fortress. There were models of the battlefield, complete with toy soldiers and toy tanks, knives and forks used by Soviet soldiers, and war posters that featured a big-breasted woman towering over the battlefield. She was *Rodina-Mat*: the motherland personified.

There was even a film, complete with German battle footage. At the end, after the defenses had finally fallen and the last defenders had starved to death, Nazi troops marched into the fortress, their swastika-bedecked flags waving in the air behind them, while the commentary intoned, 'They did not die in vain.' I sat in the back of the hall, just behind a group of French tourists who complained all the way through: their tour leader had forced them to leave Moscow early to see Brest, and they didn't like it. '*C'était un peu – de trop*,' one remarked about the film, twisting the lens of his camera.

But it was in the last room that the exhibit reached its ideological climax. This room had little to do with Brest, or the Brest fortress. Instead, it was dedicated, in the most straightforward manner possible, to the glories of the Soviet Union and to the many advantages that membership in the Soviet Union had showered on western Belarus. One glass case contained samples of food brought by Soviet cosmonauts into space. Another displayed medals and certificates of bravery granted to the citizens of Brest, the Hero City. Others held tributes brought to the fortress by impressed outsiders: a crystal jar from Poland, a medal from Yugoslavia, a model windmill from Holland, nuclear disarmament buttons from America, a glass bull from Spain. In the last cases stood bits of unrelated Soviet kitsch: seashells inscribed with Lenin's sayings, a red glass vase inscribed with the date of Belarus's entrance into the Soviet Union, and plastic models of Belarus marked by red stars.

On the final wall hung a large map of the world. In the dim light of the exhibition hall it seemed to shimmer and shine, and when I drew closer, I saw that dozens of cities – in Europe, America, Africa, the Far East – were lit up by tiny light bulbs. These, a caption proudly explained, were friendly cities, cities whose citizens had sent gifts to the Brest fortress. From Tokyo and Sydney, London and New York, tributes had flowed to Brest, it continued: in Alma-Ata and Mexico City and Paris, people recognized the heroism of the citizens of Brest.

Nowhere did the exhibit indicate that the Soviet Army had originally captured Brest from the Poles. Nowhere did any sign point out that the Red Army had held the fortress for only a few months before they had been forced to defend it from the Germans. Nowhere did any of the displays indicate that the siege of the Brest fortress had, in the end, no military importance whatsoever: by the time Soviet soldiers had starved to death in the fortress's cellars, the Germans had long moved east. But the truth was not important to those who planned the exhibit. The Brest fortress provided a useful focus for Soviet propaganda in western Belarus, encouraging the myth of the Great Patriotic War, of which the annexation of western Belarus was meant to be a logical, legitimate outcome.

I left the exhibit. At the exit, a woman was on her knees, scrubbing the floor with a dirty rag. In the courtyard, the sun was setting over the red brick walls, turning them deep orange. The music had turned from martial to choral. A wedding party – the bride frail and pimpled, the groom stout and mustachioed – was making its way up the steps to the eternal flame. It was a Soviet tradition, this custom of visiting war memorials on one's wedding day; in Leningrad I had once seen a line of newly married couples waiting to have their picture taken in front of a mass grave. But the custom made sense. The state service that had replaced church weddings was bland, and the new couples were simply trying to feel that something immortal, something greater than state bureaucrats, bound them together, even if it was the eternal death of war corpses rather than the eternal life of God.

'Tanya,' one of the men called out, 'come pose for another picture over here,' and he pointed to the plaque inscribed with the names of those who had died defending Brest.

The bride held her bouquet closer to her chest as she moved sideways. The train of her white wedding dress dragged through the mud. The groom stumbled a little, still nervous, as he turned to face the camera. They leaned their heads together, and he gingerly put his arm around his new wife's shoulders.

'Cheese,' said the man with the camera, in English.

No one smiled.

Vasily Ptashitz – the name meant 'little bird' – was clearly a hunting man. The walls of his apartment were bedecked with the carcasses of dead animals. An owl, its glass eyes staring crazily out of its moth-eaten head, hung from one corner; a fox, its jaws snapped shut, stood atop the dining table.

Vasily had caught the post-Soviet nationalist fever, and he believed deeply in every nation's right to have its own state. More specifically, he believed that the Polesians had the right to have their own state. Polesia, he explained, fell between Ukraine and Belarus; Brest and Pinsk were its capital cities.

'The inhabitants of Brest are Polesians,' he told me, 'but they just don't know it yet.' He said that the Polesian dialect sounded something like Ukrainianized Belarusian, or Belarusified Ukrainian, but with a slightly Germanic ring to it. Polesians, after all, were descended from the Iatvigians, the ancient Celtic/Germanic tribe who had ruled the region until the ninth century.

Proudly, he pronounced a few words for me in Polesian: 'Can you hear it?'

I shook my head. It just sounded like Belarusian to me. Distress clouded Vasily's broad face.

'Try again,' he said, and repeated a few more words. To please him, I told him that I could hear the Germanic sound, ever so slightly.

He smiled. This proved, said Vasily, that Polesians were not Slavs. This proved that Polesians still possessed many Germanic virtues: thrift, love of hard work, efficiency, and did not have the faults of Slavs: laziness, drunkenness, slovenliness. 'We are better organized than those Ukrainians and those Belarusians. If they would give us our independence, our economic reforms would leap ahead of theirs.'

I told him he talked the same way as a Lithuanian. The Lithuanians, I said, were fond of stressing their differences from Slavs.

'Yes, of course,' he agreed. 'We have much in common with Lithuanians. The Lithuanians were closely related to the Iatvigians.' Vasily had tried to get some Lithuanian scholars to come and give a lecture in Brest about Iatvigians, but they had refused, he said, sighing deeply.

For Vasily had a problem. People had enough trouble believing in the validity of Belarus; it was almost impossible to get them to believe in Polesia. Vasily had only one fellow freedom fighter in Pinsk, a man who also believed, and he wanted me to speak to him. While I waited, he dialed Pinsk.

'Hello,' said a faraway voice down the other end of the line. 'Hello. If you want to know about Polesian, I can tell you the exact composition of our language. It is 40 percent Ukrainian, 5 percent Belarusian, 5 percent Polish, and 50 percent Polesian. And I can tell you that Polesian culture is 30 percent Ukrainian, 3 percent Belarusian, 2 percent Polish, and 65 percent uniquely Polesian. And I can tell you that the propagation of Polesian language and culture is a healthy phenomenon: the Bolsheviks made everybody speak Russian, and look what happened. Now the Ukrainians and Belarusians will make everybody speak Ukrainian and Belarusian. The result will be worse.'

I said that sounded very reasonable, and asked how independent Polesia's economic policies would differ from those of Belarus and Ukraine.

The voice grew excited, and began talking about joint ventures. 'We want to have a Western Polesian bank, and we also want cultural links with the West. We want free markets, and capitalism. Polesia is richer than eastern Belarus and eastern Ukraine – we have only been under communism for forty years – and we can develop much faster.'

With a click, the voice was disconnected. The Polesian telephone lines from Brest to Pinsk were still weak.

'He is a genius,' Vasily breathed. 'He is our national genius. If only more people knew of him.'

Vasily was not depressed by the great and difficult task ahead of him. 'I think that there is a biological program, written by God, that makes us do certain things. God wants me to be here; God wants me to struggle to create independent Polesia.'

And there would be a reward at the end of his struggles: Vasily showed me a photograph of his cousins in America. They stood, pasty-faced, in front of a white picket fence, grinning at the camera. The cousins had also sent him photographs of a supermarket, a Kentucky Fried Chicken outlet, and the Statue of Liberty. He kept them all in an album.

'But I think Polesia will never be as great as America.' He shook his head sadly. 'You have beat us to it. You have had a head start.'

Early in the morning, someone pounded on the door of my hotel room.

'*Polski? Polski?*'

I had been asleep.

'Polish? Are you Polish? Do you have something to sell?'

Heavy feet stomped away. I opened the door and saw a man going door to door, carrying a thick wad of dollar bills. From a group in one room he bought a leather jacket; from another, a small radio.

The day before I arrived, the Brest authorities had banished the street market, calling it a 'center of crime.' Brest's traders had therefore been forced to move their livelihood elsewhere. Trade, legal or not, was impossible to stop: Brest, a city of several hundred thousand straddling the border, was the perfect entry point for hard currency, liquor, Western clothes, and perfume. Cheap electrical goods, cheap children's toys, cheese, and butter flowed the other way. The trade interrupted the traffic flow throughout the city. One of the few Polish-Belarusian road border crossings lay just to the south, and cars packed with smuggled goods waited for weeks to go through it, jamming the roads around Brest. Because most trains heading east to Moscow or west to Warsaw had to go through Brest, the train station was also mobbed with traders carrying rucksacks and cardboard boxes. Business had even flowed onto Brest's main street, blocking traffic in the center of town. Walking down it, past the Orthodox church, past the statue of Lenin, touts arrived in waves, some buying dollars, some selling amber necklaces, some just wanting a chat, all speaking some form of passable Polish.

Brest had always been a trading city, but it was not always Poles who did the trading. On the contrary: before the war, the population of Brest had been not just heavily Jewish but predominantly Jewish. Brest, the birthplace of Menachem Begin, had been the largest Jewish city in Europe; Catholic Poles had been in a minority.

Now Poles, and people pretending to be Poles, were everywhere. In the villages south of Vilnius, I had met people for whom Poland and Polishness had a cultural draw, almost a mystical appeal. Here in Brest, Poland was a source of wealth, Polishness was an opportunity. A few weeks of black market work in Poland, where the economy was much stronger, was enough to purchase a house in Brest. Polish cousins and Polish friends – who could help Belarusians obtain visas – were therefore in heavy demand. Poles had replaced Jews as the region's traders, and the number of Belarusians who might claim to be Poles was growing.

There was a Polish network operating in Brest, through which Dobrynin found me. Dobrynin was the official leader of the local Polish community, and someone had told him that a Polish-speaking American journalist had arrived in town. Once he had discovered my hotel, my hotel room, and my telephone number, there was no avoiding him.

'Let's have lunch,' he said over the telephone.

I tried to get out of it, mumbling something about other plans.

'Yes, yes, lunch at your hotel. Best restaurant in town. But before that, tell me: What do you need? What can I do for you here in Brest? What can I arrange for you?'

'Nothing,' I said.

'Oh, but we'll do anything. Just name it.'

I told him it was quite all right, I would manage.

'Perhaps if you let me know exactly what it is that you are doing here, I can give you advice?'

I said something about looking at historical houses and he gave up, clearly dissatisfied.

'Just let me know, just let me know and consider it done. We have cars at our disposal – I can arrange a Mercedes – and we have drivers. We have access. Just let me know.' He hung up, reluctantly.

In the morning he appeared in Porsche sunglasses, a gray suit, a black shirt, and a green tie. His wavy hair had been set into a kind of pompadour. He kissed the receptionist's hand, slapped the restaurant manager on the back, winked at the waitress, and got the best table, even though they were all 'reserved.' He ordered the most expensive dishes on the menu – smoked salmon, steak, wine – even though they were all marked 'unavailable.'

'The good life, no?' He winked, and laughed a bit too loudly. He bit into his salmon with zest and began to speak. On many subjects – on the proud history of the Polish Ethnic Community Organization in Brest, on the great friendship between Poles, Russians, and Belarusians – he was eloquent. But he was far more interested in my opinions.

'Who do you know in Brest?' he inquired casually. No one in particular, I said. And a few minutes later: 'What made you come here?' Oh, I said, chance, luck.

I asked him about his family, and watched him go suddenly vague.

'Mother was brought up in the Orthodox Church, you know, but Grandfather was a Polish nobleman . . .' He changed the subject. Jealously, he complained about the Poles born in Brest who went to study in Poland and never came back. The Polish Ethnic Community Organization helped arrange it.

'They get a monthly stipend, one hundred dollars,' he said. 'So much for a student!'

I told him it wouldn't be easy to live on a hundred dollars in Warsaw.

'More than a factory manager gets here,' he grumbled.

Finally Dobrynin gave up asking questions, and got to the point. He had an excellent business idea, he said, and he wanted me to be part of it. After months of thinking about it, he had dreamed up a way to make a profit out of being Polish, a real profit, more than what these so-called students got. He had decided to start a business researching the ancestry of Poles whose families had come from the Brest area. Across a plateful of caviar he handed me a stack of leaflets advertising the idea.

'Now, my dear, if you could just see fit to publish this in your newspaper, you would do me a great favor. There must be lots and lots of Poles in America who would pay a bundle to have the head of the Polish community here carry out a little research for them here.' He grabbed the waitress by her chubby elbow. She squealed. 'How about some coffee?'

Later, back at his unfinished, unfurnished rectory, I told the local Polish priest about meeting Dobrynin. He rolled his eyes.

'Ah, so you have been visiting our friend.'

In the last days of the Soviet empire, he said, Russian operatives, trained in Moscow, had mysteriously appeared in various parts of the Soviet Union, fluently speaking the local languages and attempting to form ethnic organizations. It had certainly been true in Lithuania, where local Poles had opposed Lithuanian independence; it was probably true in Ukraine and in Uzbekistan, too, for all the priest knew. Moscow was not trying to halt the various national revivals, but the Russians did prefer to know what was going on, to have their man as local leader, to use the new ethnic groups to the Soviet Union's own advantage.

'It's not what Dobrynin does that bothers me, it's what he doesn't do. We had a Polish conference here and he "forgot" to tell people about a commemorative event at the Polish cemetery. We celebrate Polish anniversaries and he "forgets" to put up the posters. Now it's money, money, money. Maybe whoever paid him in the past doesn't pay him anymore.'

The priest sipped his cognac. He was a short man with black hair and black eyes. His face had an odd sensuality about it; his lip curled slightly when he smiled. He knew that he lived on the edge of civilization, and he liked to tell battle stories. Out here on the frontier, he was waging his own personal war against shysters, crooks, stooges, and most of all, against the ill-mannered and the ill-bred.

'So I saw a group of teenage boys standing on the steps of the church, smoking cigarettes. And I said to them, "What will people think? Don't you know it's bad manners to stand here and smoke?" And they said, "We don't care, we are Russians." And I said, "Aren't Russians human, too?" And they just shrugged and said, "We are Russians." And that was the end of the conversation.'

He shook his head.

'All I can say is that whatever they told you in Minsk, no one around here knows if he is Belarusian, Polish, Russian, *tutejszy* – it means "local" – or what. They just have no real identity at all, like those teenagers, or they choose an identity for personal gain, like Dobrynin. Slowly, some people are coming to me because I give them a language with poetry and grammar, and I give them a faith with real values.'

He sipped his cheap cognac with the relish of a connoisseur.

'But slowly. Very, very, very slowly.'

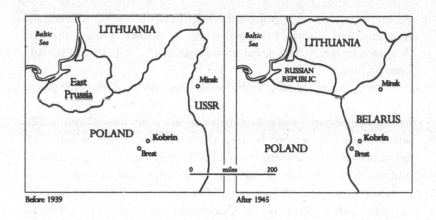

Before 1939

After 1945

Kobrin

It was a Saturday morning, and still dark when the bus left Brest for Kobrin. I had to stand: all of the seats were filled with traders heading for rural markets, their boxes filled with stale chewing gum and Brand X soda, fake blue jeans, and car parts. Through the window I saw pinpricks of light coming from small farmhouses, and the outline of trees.

Like everyone else in the Polish-speaking provinces of western Russia, the nineteenth-century inhabitants of Kobrin had been forced to serve in the czar's army. The life of a conscript was terrible – long marches, no food, no sleep, beatings and jail for those who disobeyed. People would do anything to get out of it: shoot holes in their feet, swallow poison to become ill, break their arms and legs.

Instead of mutilating himself, my father's father's father, born in Kobrin during the late-nineteenth-century reign of Czar Alexander III, ran away to America. He smuggled himself across the border to Prussia and made his way onto a ship sailing for New York, arriving at Ellis Island sometime in the first decade of the twentieth century. From New York, advised perhaps by one of the Jewish charities, or driven perhaps by some desire of his own, he made his way to Ensleigh, Alabama, and later to Bessemer, where he opened a shoe store. In Bessemer, he married my great-grandmother, who was also (it is said) from Kobrin.

After that, my great-grandfather rarely spoke of his birthplace. Occasionally he mentioned 'Poland' – that was what most of western Russia's inhabitants still called their country – but never Kobrin. My father doesn't remember hearing the name at all, and it took my grandmother some months to recall it. Perhaps my great-grandfather had no fond memories of Kobrin. Or perhaps Kobrin was just the past, and therefore best forgotten. That was the way most of his generation felt about immigration. Once arrived in America, they wanted to become American, and lost interest in whatever had happened before. If one knew what was best, one was careful not to tell the children anything about it, lest they somehow grow up foreign.

It was still early when I arrived in Kobrin, and a mist had descended, wrapping the houses in a thick bandage of fog. The bus stopped first near the new town, where low, concrete houses huddled together for warmth. Most of the traders got off: the market, it seemed, took place in the bus station parking lot. The bus then bumped its way down the pockmarked streets toward the older part of Kobrin. I got off in what would have been the old market square and was immediately hit by a wave of strong odors: mildew seeping from the houses, bread from the bakery, stale beer, and diesel fuel.

A middle-aged woman emerged from one of the shops. I stopped her and asked for the synagogue. She looked at me, surprised.

'Synagogue?' She shook her head and walked on.

I stopped a man in a cloth cap and put the same question to him. He thought for a few seconds. 'That way,' he said, and pointed down a street lined with low wooden houses. I followed it, but saw nothing that looked like a synagogue. The Catholic church stood at the end of the road – perhaps that was what he had meant.

An elderly woman was scrubbing the steps. 'Synagogue?' She, too, had to think before answering. 'I was not born here. You must ask the priest.'

'And where is the priest?'

'He comes back tomorrow.'

She returned to her scrubbing but then looked up.

'You might try Boris Nikolaevich. Boris Nikolaevich knows about Kobrin.'

I wandered down another street. At the movie theater, a poster showed a Technicolor cowboy in an ill-fitting hat. I found the house of Boris Nikolaevich among a clutch of other wooden houses; a man with distinguished white hair and glasses opened the door.

Boris Nikolaevich was a descendant of Russian officials who had come to Kobrin to do the bidding of the czar. He knew how to read French, and in Kobrin he had the reputation of a man who knows about the world. Proudly, he told me of his collection of French stamps. 'No one else has anything like it,' he said.

I asked him about town records, births, deaths, and so on. 'Of course we have them,' he said. 'All the way back to 1945.' Before that it might get tricky, he said. Everything had been burned during the war.

While he spoke, he cleaned his fingernails with a penknife and complained about the price of potatoes: 'Last year they cost fifteen kopecks for a bushel, now they are one and a half rubles.' Potatoes, he said, had become a form of money. People traded potatoes – bags of potatoes, boxes of potatoes – for things like sugar and paper, which were scarce.

Life hadn't been much easier in Polish times. Before the war there had been unemployment, and the best jobs went to the Poles, not to the Russians. That was why his brother had emigrated to France, in 1932.

'I almost left, too, but I was on a starvation diet then; I was not in good enough health.' He mentioned a famous doctor; had I read his book about the benefits of fasting?

'Even now I fast for one day every week, and last month I fasted for two days every week. In my life I have fasted for more than a thousand days. That is why I am so healthy. Would you believe that I am eighty-seven years old?'

It was true, he looked much younger. I calculated backward. He had been born in 1904. As a child he might, just possibly, have run into my great-grandfather on the street.

I asked him about the Jews in Kobrin.

'Yes, I remember them.' Boris Nikolaevich sat back in his chair. More than half of Kobrin's eleven thousand inhabitants had been Jewish in 1939, he said. The Jews ran all the shops. Practically all of the doctors were Jewish. In the center of town, all of the buildings were owned by Jews. The houses on this street were owned by Jews.'

'They were good neighbors,' he said, sighing.

Go on, I told him.

'On June 23, 1941,' he said, the Germans came to Kobrin. On June 24, the Germans had rounded up 150 Jews, taken them outside of town, and shot them. Once in July and once again in August they did it again: each time 150 Jews, just people picked up off the streets. But then the Polish partisans began to fight in the woods around Kobrin, and the Germans had to find other methods. In October and November they began to organize ghettos. There were two: Ghetto A for richer Jews, Ghetto B for the poor.

'I worked in the town library,' said Boris Nikolaevich, shaking his head. 'Before the war, most of my colleagues were Jews. I told them to run away, to go to the forests with the partisans, but they wouldn't believe me. They wouldn't believe me, and they all went to Ghetto A. When the Germans sent the Jews of Ghetto B to Babi Yar, one of them – he had sat right beside me for years – poured benzine all over himself, lit himself with a match.'

His family had also known a man called Goldberg. Goldberg and his friends had hidden in his mother's barn. Everything was fine for a few weeks, but Goldberg and his friends forgot to talk in whispers: 'One night, our neighbors heard them arguing, and they knew they had to go, it was too dangerous. Goldberg had six gold coins. He told me that if a German caught him, he would buy his way out. Until now, we don't know what happened to him.'

Boris Nikolaevich shrugged. But he didn't want me to think that no one in Kobrin had fought back. During the war, the Nazis had knocked down the Jewish cemetery and put a stable on top.

'One of the peasants who worked for the Nazis as a stableboy asked me to help him get poison: he wanted to poison the horses. I was friendly with the pharmacist at that time, so we did it. The Germans were perplexed. Why were their horses dying? They brought in veterinarians to say what the problem was. The veterinarians did some examining, and after a whole day they announced to the Germans that the horses had not been poisoned. But the Germans were still suspicious, and they brought in another set of veterinarians. These said that the horses had indeed been poisoned – it came out that the first doctors had been Czechs, and therefore were not trustworthy. Afterward this peasant, my friend, ran to the woods and joined the partisans. Nobody suspected me.'

One or two of Kobrin's Jews had come back after the war, but nowadays a mixed lot of people lived in the town. A few Poles, a few Russians. The local people spoke a dialect that was really Ukrainian, not Belarusian. Kobrin, he said, was Belarusian by accident. But what was the difference? Ukraine, Belarus – what did it matter anyway?

I asked him about Applebaums, or Apfelbaums, as they might have been then.

He shook his head. He remembered no one of that name. Maybe, *maybe* a Rosa Applebaum in his primary school, but no one after that. My eye drifted up to the print on the wall behind him. He followed my gaze.

'It is Goya – you know it? I like Goya a lot.'

The print was *Reason Asleep, Dreaming of Monsters*.

I bade him good-bye. 'You'll find the synagogue on this street – you must have passed it on your way here.' He pointed the way.

I traced my steps backward, this time walking more slowly, stopping and looking at each of the wooden houses, one by one. I passed a garden where a young woman knelt, digging something in the ground, and a house painted a surprising shade of pink. They gave nothing away, they told no stories. They provided no more access to the real past than the Lubavitcher in Minsk or the fortress in Brest.

Finally, I found the synagogue. It was a large yellow building surrounded by overgrown shrubs and set back from the road. A long cable reached up to the round window where the Star of David used to be; metal beer barrels, crates, and the entrails of trucks had been strewn about the courtyard. The entrance was locked and barred with barbed wire. A sign hung from the gate: BREWERY.

I started to climb the fence but thought better of it.

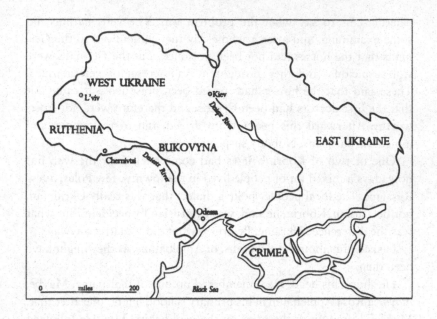

A Memory

During one of the long, end-of-summer days I spent in Vilnius, I discovered, by accident, a Ukrainian linguist. He was a small, dark man, with a torso so full of energy that he bounced in his chair as he talked. He had lived in Chernivtsi and Minsk, Uzhhorod and Kiev, he had married a Lithuanian woman, and his head was filled with the languages of the borderlands: Ukrainian, Russian, Belarusian, Polish, Lithuanian, the dialects of Ruthenia and the Bukovyna, Romanian, German, a bit of Turkish, and now English.

'This is the first time in my life that I have spoken English with a real English person,' he told me. 'Let's drink to that.' He poured out two glasses of sweet Armenian cognac and grinned.

We spoke of various things, of Poles and Lithuanians, of the mutual dislike between Baltic and Slav, of Belarusians and their new sense of nationhood:

'They seem as drunk, a little, without real orientation, flying in air, in space, in a space where things are not finish. Yes,' he said, 'in a space where things are not finished. Have I said it right?'

I told him that he had.

'Let's drink to that, too,' he said, and gently sipped his cognac.

He was learned and loquacious and enthusiastic on nearly every subject, he was ready with a fast answer to every question, he had jokes and stories about every borderland nation. It was only when I turned him to the subject of Ukraine, his own nation, that he began to stumble, just a little bit, to speak more slowly, to hesitate. Finally he stopped altogether.

Go on, I said. What about Ukraine?

'Well, I have problem with Ukraine. Yes, problem – or do you say a problem? A problem. You see, I do not know what people mean when they say Ukraine. There are many Ukraines. There is Kiev, central Ukraine, the heart of the Kievan Rus from which we were descended – oh, they speak the most lovely, the most pure Ukrainian in Kiev. There is eastern Ukraine – Donetsk, Xharkov, Dnipropetrovsk – which has been sadly Russian for so many years, so many years that the language is even lost, they speak a bastardized Russian there, a kind of slang. Then there is the Black Sea coast – Crimea, Odessa – conquered by Catherine the Great, called by her Novorossiya, New Russia, settled by her courtiers. They also speak Russian, but by history, by right, Crimean Tartaria belongs to Ukraine: we have so many connections there, so many of us are descended from the Tartars, you know.'

He began to pick up speed again. 'Then there is the northern Bukovyna – and the beautiful town of Czernowitz, now called Chernivtsi – and southern Bessarabia – land of the Gaugaz, the Turks. Those regions were taken from Romania at the end of the last war, and there they speak Ukrainian and Moldovan and a kind of mix of the two, such a language, I say, such an interesting language! And western Ukraine (here I mean L'viv, L'viv, of course), which was once Polish – why, you could probably get away with speaking Polish there, no one would notice you were speaking a different language. No one would notice! And, of course, Ruthenia – Transcarpathia – owned so long by Hungary and then Czechoslovakia. How can I explain to you about Ruthenia? How can I express it? You have to know it for yourself, you have to go and stand in one of those long Ruthenian villages, the ones that stretch up right into the mountains, go and stand there and you will know it is different. Listen to the language there – it is not my Ukrainian, it is not Kiev Ukrainian, just listen to it! It is Transcarpathian Ruthenian!

'All of this variety, all of this variety, but they tried to knock it out of us. We are all Soviet people now, *Homo sovieticus*. They concreted us together – yes, is that right, concreted? – they concreted us together and told us to speak Russian. Ideology for this Marxist movement, it had to be completely simple, and absolutely primitive and absolutely contrary to everything that had gone in the past. Bang, they eliminate everything and tell us we are all the same, they tell Ukrainians that a Soviet Ukrainian is a Soviet Ukrainian and there is no more story. They teach us Russian, they tell us to forget these silly dialects. They teach us to be Ukrainian in a Soviet way.

'So now we have democratization, and democratization goes with new nationalism, it is inevitable. We have new Ukrainian nationalism. We are a society that is to such an extent destroyed that we needed the simplest ways to pull people into the process, and the simplest way is national revival. But I am afraid . . .' He stood up and paced around the room.

'I am afraid that this nationalism will be unifying in a bad way. Our people will not recognize the value of their differences. They will want all to be the same, they will want Ukrainians to be the same. And then some will oppose this, some will feel Ukrainianization, this is a bad thing. But the Ukrainians, they know only one model, the Soviet model, and that model said that strength lay in unity. But strength is in the differences. Variety, that is the beauty of Ukraine. Variety, that is its treasure.'

Here the linguist reached a pitch of excitement – and then suddenly gave up. He threw his hands into the air: 'Everything I say . . . I try to be as clear as possible . . . but this English, it is not native, you know, it is not native.' He collapsed back into his chair, frustrated.

I told him that I understood him perfectly. He sighed, and poured another glass of cognac.

'It is very hard, yes, very hard to understand. We are not a new nation like Belarus, you see, we are a very old one. We are a very old nation, but never ever in our history have we had our own state. It has been our fate always to exist beneath the rule of others. And so it has been our fate to be described by others. I am afraid that because of this we will let outsiders tell us we are unified, we will accept this Soviet idea of unity because we do not know ourselves. Real Ukrainians do not have a picture of themselves, so we will not have the confidence to be various, to allow our different dialects to flourish. But even I, even I am sometimes at a loss when I am asked to talk about my own country, to explain what it looks like, what it is.

'You see, sometimes I say to my nearest, to my nearest people, to my Lithuanian friends, sometimes I tell them: You don't know the world that I come from. You don't know this Ukrainian dirt, this kind of mud that we had in the village where I grew up, and Ukrainian flowers, Ukrainian smells. But I cannot convey it, it is impossible to describe. I once asked a friend, an artist, to help me describe it, and he could only say, "a Ukrainian village smells ... different." I can't even say anymore right now, because it requires a different mood, a different kind of conversation, a less learned one.

'It is true, though, it is true that I am a little bit of an outsider. Yes, I am Ukrainian, but I am also an outsider in Ukraine.'

What did he mean by that, I asked.

'It is my name. You see, I have a Turkish name. It is not a Ukrainian name. And I have some Turkish blood – you see, I have dark skin. During the war, my aunt and my uncle hid me and my brothers in their cellar. They hid us. They hid us because the neighbors might think – because of our Turkish name and our dark skin – that we were Jews. So I am like a Jew in my own country. Since my Jewish childhood, I see my own country as if I were an outsider.'

And that, he said, was the most Ukrainian thing of all: to read the history of your country as if you were reading it through an outsider's eyes. It was the fate of borderland nations always to know yourself through the stories of others, to realize yourself only with the help of others.

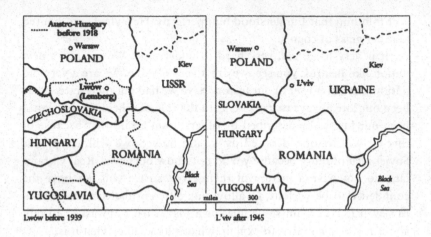

Lwów before 1939   L'viv after 1945

L'viv/Lvov/Lwów

Let others go travel where they can, where they want,
To Venice, to Paris, to London,
But I, from Lwów, will never leave home,
Mother, may God punish me if I do!

For where do people live, as well as they live here?
Only in Lwów!
For where do songs wake you and send you to sleep?
Only in Lwów ...

— *Polish folk song*

On the road going south to L'viv, I stopped in Kovel and bought sweet black grapes from a Georgian trader. His face was darkened by a swarm of bees. Rhythmically, he swatted them away with his purple-stained hand, as if he were keeping time to music.

No guards or gates marked the border between Belarus and Ukraine, but the roads began to improve when we crossed from lands that had been ruled by Russia in the nineteenth century into Galicia, which was under Austro-Hungarian rule at the same time. The old border between Russia and Galicia had been out of use since Poland was reconstituted in 1918, and out of memory since the whole region had finally fallen to the Soviet Union in 1945. But it was easier to see than the new border between independent Belarus and independent Ukraine, which was still unmarked. As the bus rumbled on, the trees grew taller, the fields broader, the houses sturdier. Austro-Hungary had managed its land better than Russia, and it still showed.

Austro-Hungary had also left a different architectural legacy. Entering L'viv – Lvov, Lwów, Lemberg (it meant 'lion's mountain') – was like returning to civilization. The concrete grays and muddy browns of Belarus were gone, replaced by the white of marble steps, the bright yellow of churches, the red brick of libraries and museums. Oil street lamps glowed brown in the evening, casting chocolate shadows across the cobbled streets. The opera house ruled over the city like a dowager who has lived in a grander era and tolerates – but just barely – the indignities of the present.

Austro-Hungary: it had been a mixed bag of nations held together by the silken bands of custom, the portrait of the emperor, sturdy houses, and squat churches with golden altars. In their time, the Habsburgs were thought oppressive. Yet they are the only rulers of western Ukraine who still inspire nostalgia. The Poles are remembered as petty dictators, the Russians as tyrants, but in L'viv the Habsburg era is still recalled with fondness. Perhaps that is because the Habsburgs encouraged Ukrainian national ambitions; attempting to weaken Polish influence in the region, they encouraged Ukrainian political parties, Ukrainian parliamentary deputies, Ukrainian newspapers. Perhaps it is also because, in retrospect, the Habsburg empire no longer seems terribly serious. Whatever territorial ambitions the Habsburgs once had no longer matter, whatever cruelties the empire inflicted on its subject nations look mild in the light of what came afterward. Austro-Hungary was never to blame for the horrors of the Second World War or its aftermath. Compared to Soviet rule, the Habsburg legacy in Galicia seems benign.

But there were many other national legacies to be found in L'viv. On my first trip to the city, in the long-ago days of Brezhnev and the stable ruble, time and weather had prevented me from seeing much of L'viv, aside from the cemetery. Now, in the strong autumn sunlight, I could see that the past – the Habsburg past, the Polish past – was still very much in evidence. The past was there in the German names engraved on the sewer lids, in the faded-out paint on the old Polish bank, in the cracked windows of the synagogue, in the Italian glaze on the tiles in the courtyards of the big family houses, in the chipped gilt on the altars in the churches. The past was there in the city's central park, where men in brown suits and felt hats sat on benches beneath the tall trees and talked to one another in low voices, sometimes stopping to watch the games of chess that were played in the park all day and all night, too, when the weather was good. The past was there in L'viv's old market square, in the baroque houses, blackened with age, which gazed scornfully at the unimaginative town hall, a nineteenth-century upstart which stood in the center. The lion of St Mark was carved over the entrance to number fourteen, the old Venetian consulate. Number six had once been the property of King Jan Sobieski, who defeated the Turks at Vienna and saved Christendom from the infidel. Another king, the ineffectual Michał Wiśniowiecki, died in number nine.

In the cathedral, plaques and marble vases dedicated themselves to Hoffmans and Tarnowskis. Colored tiles, laid out in the pattern of an Oriental carpet, covered the floor and the walls of the nave. On one tomb, a man dressed as a Polish nobleman (Turkish trousers, blouse, cape, and saber) slept on a stone pillow with a stone hourglass by his side. On another, an armored knight lay with his helmeted head on his hand. *Trompe l'oeil* flowers lined the pillars, light streamed through the windows. Outside and around the corner stood a private chapel, built in the seventeenth century because the cathedral had already run out of space for all the rich men wanting to erect eternal monuments there. Amber panels lined the walls, and a relief of the Last Supper showed Jesus breaking bread in a L'viv drawing room. The inscription dedicated the building to 'George Boym E Pannonia,' a wealthy Hungarian merchant. Just nearby, sunlight spilled onto the gravestones in the courtyard of the Armenian church. The spidery script shone dark against the white stone, like a secret code suddenly revealed.

The past was to be found even in my hotel, which was quite different from the Intourist monstrosities I had found in most Soviet cities. Built by an Englishman at the turn of the century and named for

St George, the hotel held traces of his taste. My room had high ceilings, French windows, a threadbare Persian rug, and a wash basin that bore the inscription 'Manchester, 1903.' Brass signs hung over the doors to the public washrooms: 'Gentlemens Toilet' and 'Ladies Room.' The central staircase was festooned with cracked mirrors and Greek columns, and it smelled faintly of sewage. A slovenly maid sat at the top and wrote something down in a little black book whenever anyone came in or out. That was Soviet, but it was Habsburg, too.

It thrilled me at first, this evidence of a lost civilization, the way the evidence of the past had thrilled me in Vilnius and the lands around Nowogródek. But after a while I began to be wary of it. L'viv was part of the borderlands, and the same historical breaks, the same mass murders, the same shuffling of peoples back and forth across borders had affected the city like all other borderland cities. Although the preservation of the old architecture meant that one didn't, at first, feel the lack of continuity so much, the city's lazy grace was deceptive. When a mollusk dies, the shell remains, beautiful but empty of life. It can be inhabited only by a different animal, one that knows nothing of the former owner; perhaps L'viv was like that.

While the city's past might have been many things – Polish, Habsburg, or just simply borderland – its present was Ukrainian. There were Ukrainian faces on the buses in the morning, Ukrainian signs on the shops. Ukrainian had not been the city's main language before the war – it fell third, behind Polish and Yiddish – but Ukrainian was the city's main language now. As I walked around the city, half imagining the past, half seeing the present, I tried hard to listen to the sounds that the new Ukraine was making.

'Skandal!' screamed the newspapers.

'You've heard about our scandal?' asked my Polish friends Irena and Władek.

'You ought to be writing about our scandal,' a local politician told me, almost proudly. 'Our scandal is the biggest in Ukraine.'

Over lunch in the restaurant of the Grand Hotel – a few hundred yards and several generations away from the George – Marta told me her side of the story. The restaurant was new: the walls were freshly painted, the tablecloths were clean and white, the cups and saucers were free of cracks and chips. It was also empty, and our waiter tiptoed fearfully up and down the dining hall like a guest who fears himself to be unwelcome. When Marta asked him to recite the wine list he stuttered, and forgot which were red and which were white.

'Bulgarian red,' she said crisply, not waiting for him to finish, and handed the menu back.

'You cannot imagine,' she said, turning to me, 'what it took to rebuild this place. To train these people. And see how much farther we have to go!' She shook her head vigorously. Not a strand of blond hair moved out of place. Her hair, like her long red nails, had been lacquered to perfection.

Marta had been born just after the war, in a displaced persons' camp near L'viv. Almost immediately afterward, her family had made its way to America, like so many others. Those of the postwar Ukrainian diaspora were a special breed: unlike those who crossed the Atlantic earlier, they had more recent memories of an almost-free Ukraine, they had more optimism, they had fought in guerrilla bands against the Red Army. Abroad, in America and Canada, they flourished, speaking their language, building their churches, and publishing little magazines full of nostalgic poetry and angry prose – preserving a version of Ukrainian history different from the one taught in the Soviet Union. Marta had grown up surrounded by the songs and legends of a country she had never known, and she had always dreamed of going back. She had worked, she said, as a Ukrainian-American travel agent, leading tours of Ukrainian-Americans back to places like L'viv. 'Smalltime stuff,' she said, wiping an invisible speck of dust from her impeccable white suit. But in 1989, when things began to change, she began to think of bigger projects, bigger goals. At about that time, a man called Gennady Genschaft drifted into Marta's field of vision.

Genschaft seemed to have connections. He understood the confusing world of hard currency regulations, permission slips, and disappearing telex reservations that riddled the Soviet tourist bureaucracy. He seemed able to procure hotel rooms, to reserve buses, to arrange catered meals. If I can't do it, he told Marta, nobody can. Feeling more confident about Ukraine, Marta began to make plans. 'I said to myself, my children are grown up. I have a nice house. I have a comfortable life. I've achieved most of what I wanted in life. Why not do something for other people now? Why not do something for Ukraine?'

The waiter, his hands shaking ever so slightly, brought us two bowls of bright pink borscht. He laid them carefully on the table, turned, and walked away, clutching the two spoons he had forgotten to give us.

'This hotel,' Marta told me, 'it was not going to be just any old investment.' Western Ukraine might have been defeated, but now the rebuilding could begin. What L'viv needed, Marta told herself, was one hotel, one beautiful hotel, one hotel that businessmen and tourists could stay in, one hotel that would lift the city's profile and make it a place that people would want to visit.

It was important that L'viv recover its glory, Marta said. L'viv had played a special role in the Ukrainian independence movement. Post-Soviet Ukrainian nationalism had not been born in Kiev, after all, but in the West, the lands that were Polish before the war and Austro-Hungarian before that. In the late 1980s, when *glasnost* began, it was western Ukraine that began to encourage a free press, and it was western Ukraine that elected former dissidents as parliamentary deputies and nationalist local governments. The blue and yellow Ukrainian flag appeared in West Ukrainian villages long before it appeared in the East, and politicians from western Ukraine were always the most fervent advocates of independence. L'viv was the capital of western Ukraine, and it was here, in L'viv, that Marta wanted her hotel to be. Together with Genschaft, she drew up a plan. Marta would be the director; he would be the main partner; and Halych, Inc., their new company, would restore the old Grand Hotel in the center of L'viv, just across from the opera house.

Work began. Marta gave Genschaft a notarized letter permitting him to carry out company transactions in her name. Marta paid Genschaft a salary. Every month she came to examine the hotel's progress, while Genschaft arranged for stonemasons and carpenters, paint and carpets, chandeliers and furniture. Genschaft made sure that the cornices on the ceilings and the plaster around the doorways were completed correctly, that the parquet floors were restored; Genschaft arranged for the roof to be covered with old-fashioned tile. By the time it was finished, the Grand Hotel was a small miracle. Each of its rooms had new furniture, new fixtures, and satellite television. Downstairs, the hotel had a restaurant, a bar, a conference room. It had clear running water, its own generator in case of power cuts. Nothing like it could be found anywhere else in Ukraine, Marta's Ukrainian-American tour groups marveled.

The waiter returned with the spoons. 'Sorry, sorry,' he kept mumbling. Marta, intent on telling her story, ignored him. He slipped the spoons beneath the soup bowls and scuttled away.

'People tell me it is a wonderful thing I have done for Ukraine,' she said.

After a few months, Genschaft told Marta that the company really ought to form a joint venture: joint ventures were tax-free for five years. She agreed to write a letter to the mayor of L'viv, asking permission to form the joint venture, but she did not make formal application. Nevertheless, when she next returned, she discovered that the joint venture had been founded: Genschaft had become the majority shareholder.

'My signature appears on the documents,' she told me. 'My signature appears, and I wasn't even there!'

Marta began eating her borscht. Just then, the waiter appeared with the second course: boiled chicken and rice. 'Put it over here,' she told him, gesturing toward the next table, which was empty like all the others.

In the meantime, she said, Genschaft had received political asylum in America.

'Political asylum?'

'Yes, yes.' Marta pushed her soup bowl to one side. 'He is – you know – Jewish. They get permission to emigrate. His family are in America.'

There was no point in arguing with Genschaft in L'viv if he was in America, so Marta took a copy of the joint venture statute back to America. There, a Ukrainian-American attorney told her that the document might be invalid. Marta called Genschaft in Philadelphia and arranged to meet him. He failed to appear. Instead, he flew back to L'viv – and Marta followed him.

When she arrived, she found Genschaft sitting in the director's office of the hotel. She tried to lock him out; he broke the lock. She shouted lawsuits. 'Go ahead,' he told her, 'let us see which one of us will win a lawsuit in this city.' Marta went to the mayor, screaming corruption, newspapers, the American embassy, the Ukrainian-American community.

The mayor shouted back. Why was she in business with Genschaft anyway? Marta, the mayor said, had told everyone in the city that Halych, Inc., was an American company. And here was this Russian Jew, running everything!

Marta looked up from her chicken. 'If everyone thought it was a bad idea to do business with Genschaft, why had no one told me?'

Calming down, the mayor agreed to do what he could to stop Genschaft from taking control of the hotel. He annulled the joint venture for thirty days and held an investigation. Genschaft offered Marta $300,000 to leave. She refused. Or, he said, she could pay him $900,000 to leave. She refused again.

'Nobody,' said Marta, 'nobody can buy me off. I am not here just to make money. I am here to create a legitimate Ukrainian business. I want this hotel to be honest. I want people to do things the right way here, the American way. Ukrainians also want to be honest. They are tired of corruption, tired of being cheated. Ask the staff. The staff are praying that I will not leave.'

Marta grabbed the waiter, who had come back to refill the wine.

'Are you happy working here?'

The waiter looked confused. Marta repeated the question, in Ukrainian. The waiter broke into a confused smile.

'Yes, yes, happy,' he said.

She turned back to me. 'Then, the final straw: last week, Genschaft was arrested for kidnapping the son of the mayor. He and his friends held him for several hours, trying to force the mayor to change his mind.'

She looked up. 'The law must triumph. I will see to it. The law must be enforced.'

I went to see Genschaft. He was ensconced in the director's office in the back of the hotel, and he winced at the sound of Marta's name.

'Crazy lady,' he said in Russian. 'Crazy lady. She tried to lock me out of my own office.'

Genschaft was a handsome man, well coiffed, well fed, and sleek like a prize stallion. He wore a gold watch and a gold bracelet, a cashmere sweater, and neat gray flannel trousers. I looked at his feet and saw that he wore fine leather shoes, the first I had seen anyone wear in the former Soviet Union.

'Sit, sit,' he said. 'What can I get you? Coffee? Tea? Brandy? Whiskey? I have some Armenian cognac, if you would like.'

'Tea,' I said. He looked disappointed, but he pressed a button under the table. A girl in uniform, one of the waitresses from the hotel restaurant, opened the door and stuck her head around it.

'Two teas,' Genschaft commanded, and I heard her scuttle back down the hallway. He turned to me.

'You see,' he said, 'Marta has put money into this hotel. She helped to start it. But whose idea was this in the first place? Mine. Whose connections got us the lease? Mine. Who found the wood, the tile, the carpets, the furniture? I did. You think you can just walk into a shop and buy things like that in this country? No. You have to barter. You have to know people. You have to know how to get things done.'

The girl came back with the tea. Genschaft poured two large spoonsful of sugar into his and waved his arm around the office. 'I built this hotel. Without me, this hotel would not exist.'

The joint venture was perfectly legal, he claimed: he had done nothing wrong. Marta had given him a notary act, permitting him to sign contracts in her name. Marta had even given him blank sheets of paper with her signature at the bottom. The only reason she was protesting now, said Genschaft, was because Marta had wanted more profits for herself. 'She is like a child who has done something wrong and wants to take it all back. She has made a mistake and wants to start all over again. And now she will organize the government against us.'

I asked Genschaft about his American citizenship. How had it been possible to emigrate and then to return so quickly? I had thought it was illegal for someone who had been granted political asylum to return to his or her country of origin so quickly without losing the right to return to America.

He waved the question away. 'I received permission to emigrate from the Soviet Union, where I was persecuted for being Jewish. Now I have returned to Ukraine, which is a different country – so, you see, I have not come back to the same place ...'

His voice trailed off. I looked at him, feeling sorry for all of the authentically oppressed people in the world who are unable to get visas to America. Genschaft must have guessed my thoughts. He leaned forward:

'You realize, of course, that Marta and all of her people have turned on me because I am Jewish and because I speak Russian. They think they can turn popular sentiment against me. Ukraine for the Ukrainians, they say, but it is all nonsense: these Ukrainian nationalists are simply angry that people more clever than themselves are making money in this city, and they want to stop us from doing it.'

Marta's nationalism had infected the local government, he said, bringing them around to her side. 'The mayor has frozen the bank accounts of my hotel, but the mayor refuses to see me. What can I do? I call him, he refuses to speak. I write to him, he fails to write back. Last week, we brought his son, Nazar, in here to help. Nazar works for a friend of mine: Levon Enokyan, a wonderful businessman, by the way, you ought to meet him. Anyway, Levon and I sat Nazar at this table, gave him a little brandy, made a telephone call to his father. Next thing we knew, the police had arrived. Next thing we know, they are accusing us of kidnap!'

Genschaft's eyes narrowed when he spoke of the mayor and his cohorts. 'Those little people,' he said. 'All they can do is shout slogans, they've never run a business, they've never managed companies. They are incompetent. They know nothing. They should leave the conduct of business to those of us who know about business. People who have spent their lives in Siberian camps should not be running governments. And if they break their own laws to give the hotel back to Marta – they will be sorry.'

Quite unexpectedly, Genschaft smiled.

'*Miami Vice* – that is my dream,' sighed Iaroslav.

Iaroslav was a crime reporter for a L'viv newspaper. He knew all of the L'viv mafia, and many of them knew him. Many thought, even, that he was one of them. 'They tip me off when they know there is going to be a crime carried out by a rival group, they want me to spill the beans to the police.'

Iaroslav knew a different L'viv from the one I knew, and he showed me a new set of sights. He took me first to see a strip of dirty sidewalk near the monument to Adam Mickiewicz. A group of men in windbreakers and imitation Adidas loitered there, leaning against street benches. Every so often, one would approach another, whisper something or exchange something, and then drift away. It was the criminal exchange, very different from the commercial exchanges that took place in the park near the opera.

'An assassination can be arranged here for fifty dollars,' he explained. 'And a theft can be arranged for thirty. But most of these people are just arranging exchanges of goods that are illegal to export.' These included quite mundane things – wood, for example, and roof tiles – as well as oil, precious metals, and a mysterious substance called red mercury, which was, he claimed, criminal slang for plutonium. Shipments of illegal goods were driven around Ukraine in ten-car convoys protected with automatic weapons.

Iaroslav also walked me through what would have been a prewar suburb, a neighborhood filled with squarish, plastered houses, a style the Polish middle classes had once loved; it reminded me of the prewar Warsaw suburbs. We passed one house surrounded by a high wire fence; a German shepherd on a long chain was tethered in front. That, Iaroslav explained, was the home of Levon Enokyan, chairman of LV Holding, L'viv's biggest company.

'You know him?'

'I don't know him yet,' I said.

Iaroslav was an admirer. 'He is the best businessman in the city, the only Armenian who has really made it here.'

We stood outside the gate, listening to the dog bark. After a while, a man in dark glasses appeared on the doorstep and slowly began walking in our direction.

'Let's go,' said Iaroslav. 'It's a security guard.' We walked quickly away, passing a blond woman driving a new Mercedes.

'His second wife,' said Iaroslav.

On the way back into town, Iaroslav told me that he had been invited to a party that LV Holding gave to mark its first year in business. The city, he said, had seen nothing like it before. Perhaps people did these sorts of things in Moscow, but not in L'viv.

'They got all of these people from Moscow – oh, rock stars, a famous Russian footballer, an Olympic athlete – and they flew them down here on a *private plane.*'

A private plane, in the former Soviet Union, is an almost unheard-of luxury. 'Then they brought them from the airport on a *private bus.*'

Ownership of a private bus is almost as great a privilege.

'They served caviar, sturgeon, plates of ham and cheese, different kinds of wine – more food than anyone here had ever seen. All of the city government were invited – the mayor, the presidential representative, the city councilors. I could see them sitting there, speaking Ukrainian among themselves, watching the Russian performers from Moscow, growing more and more jealous: it was obvious that LV Holding has more power than all of them put together.'

The conversation turned back to crime, criminals, and criminal reporters. 'Maybe Sicily,' said Iaroslav. 'Maybe Sicily would have more interesting stories than those I have to write here.'

In his wood-paneled office on the top floor of what used to be the Galician Senate, Ivan Hel, one of L'viv's city councilors, tried to speak, first in Polish, then in Russian. He was a stern, strong man, with wide shoulders, a white beard, long white hair, and deathless eyes shaded by white eyebrows. The thick cross he wore around his neck hung all the way down to his large stomach. He was an imposing figure, and yet his face lost something of its granite security as he stumbled and slipped in the languages of Ukraine's former rulers. Finally he gave up.

'You'll just have to listen carefully. It's so close to Polish.' And as he switched to Ukrainian – Galician Ukrainian – his voice became clearer and his dignity returned. Every so often, when I failed to understand something, his assistant gently intervened.

Ivan Hel's father had been born blind, but the Virgin Mary of Calvaria restored his sight at age three. The miracle had touched Hel, too: during his term in the Soviet Army, he wore his father's crucifix beneath his uniform. The crucifix could have been discovered in that godless place, but the Virgin preserved him, prevented anyone from noticing.

Afterward, Hel resolved to work for her and for Ukraine, her step-child, and never to remove the sign of her grace. So the crucifix followed him into basement rooms where the secret printing presses were kept; into the police stations where Russian officers hurled abuse; into the meetings beside Shevchenko's grave, where the Ukrainian national movement was born. The crucifix followed him into Brezhnev's labor camps after a wave of arrests sent most of Ukraine's intelligentsia to Siberia. Finally, the crucifix had followed him into free elections: the Virgin had given Ukraine back to the Ukrainians, and Hel was proud to say that West Ukraine, and L'viv in particular, had led the way from the beginning.

The story of Marta and the Grand Hotel made him sad, very sad, however. It showed how immature Ukraine still was, how she was still not a real nation.

'When Moses took the Israelites out of Egypt, he made them wander for forty years in the desert in order to lose their slave mentality. Generations passed before men felt themselves free again. We also need generations before we will feel ourselves free men,' he explained.

For Ukraine to grow up, the nation's leaders had to undertake a program of Ukrainianization, Hel explained. Children needed to be taught Ukrainian history, Ukrainians had to be promoted to high government positions, Ukrainian literature had to be read and celebrated.

It sounded, I said, like the *korenizatsiia* of the 1920s, when the Soviet Union sponsored similar programs.

'No, no,' said Hel vigorously, 'this is totally different.' The new wave of Ukrainianization was also to have an economic component. Institutions had to be created: a central bank, a post office, a diplomatic service, an army. Trade with Russia had to be directed elsewhere. Factories and state enterprises were to be Ukrainianized along with schools and universities. They would have to learn to buy all of their raw materials from Ukraine, not Russia; they would have to learn to sell their products to Ukraine, not Russia.

I told him that many factories in America buy their raw materials in other countries and sell their products in other countries.

'But that is all very well for America. You have already had your forty years in the desert.'

Fighting the mafia was also part of Ukrainianization, Hel explained. A good, clean Ukrainian state could not tolerate these criminals who had sprung up, apparently from nowhere, during the Soviet Union's last few years of life: 'When there are new structures and bad laws, these people rise to the surface. This is a very dangerous time for us. We must prevent these kinds of people from gaining power.'

But these semi-corrupt businessmen were the only businessmen around. I put it to Hel that stopping them meant stopping free enterprise altogether. He disagreed, rather violently.

'Free enterprise? These people do not even have the interests of the Ukrainian state at heart.' They were not, he said, lowering his voice, even Ukrainians. Everyone knew that the mafia were Russians and Jewish.'

Hel clasped his hands together.

'The old KGB and the mafia, they are bound together like this. And they are all controlled by Moscow. They will sell us to Russia again if we are not careful. They will bind our economy to the Russian economy and corrupt our state if we do not stop them.'

As I walked out of Hel's office, a man approached me, very agitated.

'You know the Reuters correspondent?' he asked me.

'What?'

'The Reuters correspondent,' and he mentioned a name. 'I heard you tell the mayor's secretary that you are a journalist, so I thought you might know him. He is in Moscow, he came here and left a tape recorder. I want to give it back to him.'

I looked at the man, and he glanced away from me.

'A tape recorder?'

'Yes,' he said quickly, and then changed the subject. 'I see you were talking to Mr Hel.'

'I was.'

'You are wasting your time. Mr Hel cannot help you. He knows nothing about this city. If you want to know about this city, you should talk to important people, important businessmen. In fact, you should meet the leader of my company' – his voice dropped to a whisper – 'Levon Enokyan. He is the chief Armenian businessman in L'viv.'

I said I would be very interested to meet Mr Enokyan. 'But how did you happen to be standing here just now?' I asked him.

Momentarily, he seemed startled by the question, but then he waved it away. 'I am trying to get an export permit,' he explained. 'These people – these amateurs – they change the rules every week, it is impossible for business. Last week I had an export license, this week they took it away. Now I must reapply.'

I thanked him and took down his telephone number. Later I told Iaroslav about it, and he laughed.

'Aha,' he said. 'They are on to you. They think you might have influence, they think you will write their side of the story. But don't worry – they would never hurt a foreigner. They will never hurt Marta, they will never hurt you. They know it would bring in police from Moscow or Kiev, you see, instead of just the locals whom they can bribe.'

I drove to LV Holding in the back of a white Mercedes. The driver, who had picked me up in the city center, kept apologizing for being late.

'We like to treat Levon's friends the right way,' he explained.

From the outside, the company headquarters were not impressive. The offices were on the fourth floor of a shabby office block, on the outskirts of L'viv. But there was a reason: all city property still had to be rented from the city government. Given that LV Holding was not in favor with the city government, this office block was the best they could do.

Inside, one felt immediately how the company differed from a Soviet state enterprise. No less than three clean-shaven thugs in neckties were waiting at the door to search my bag. 'Security,' one of them mumbled. If they went to the trouble, one had to assume that there was something to protect. A woman wearing what appeared to be a white tennis dress led me down narrow hallways past people running to make their next appointment, and into an anteroom where the telephones never stopped ringing. The bored secretaries, underemployed clerks, and clean desks that marked the offices of a Soviet state enterprise were nowhere to be seen. A man walked in, looked me up and down, and extended his hand.

'Averkov,' he said briskly.

'Ania,' I replied. He nodded, and walked out again.

After a few minutes, the woman reappeared. 'Mr Enokyan is waiting,' she said in English, and led me through the door into a large room lined with Turkish carpets. A large black safe stood against one wall, and an Armenian Bible graced one of the side tables. The chairman sat at a big oak desk, talking on the telephone. He wore an expensive suit, a heavy gold watch, gold bracelets, and yet another pair of fine shoes. As I entered, he put down the telephone.

'Mafia! I hate that word,' Enokyan shouted in answer to my first question. 'Mafia! Whenever something in this country goes wrong, these nationalists need someone to blame. First they blamed the Communists. Then the Communists left. Now they blame us, new businessmen. Am I responsible for the bread lines? No. Am I responsible for the cheese shortage? No. Who is responsible? These petty Ukrainians!'

The telephone rang again. He picked up the receiver, barked an order, and put the receiver down again. 'What else can I do for you?' he asked, suddenly polite. 'Coffee? Tea? Cognac?'

Enokyan had been born in Armenia, and drifted into L'viv sometime in the 1970s, 'to study,' he said. He had never finished his university course, however. Instead, he said, he had begun to do business in what was then the shadow economy. Back in the days when all private business was banned, he had been involved in 'some underground manufacturing and trade.' Although people went to jail for it, few Ukrainians really considered such activity to be criminal. Underground entrepreneurs were pillars of the Soviet system, distributing goods where the state failed to do so. And as soon as it became possible – after Gorbachev passed new laws on 'cooperative enterprises' – he and a partner opened a restaurant and a shop that sold goods on commission. Business boomed.

But business boomed, in the eyes of some, suspiciously quickly. LV Holding, a group of twelve companies, now claimed a monthly turnover of more than $2 million, a lot of money in a city where the average monthly salary hovered around $10. The sources of the cash also seemed to be peculiarly diverse: LV Holding bought goods abroad and sold them in Ukraine, traded steel and textiles across what used to be the Soviet Union, held interests in dollar shops, casinos, and hotels. Enokyan told me that he was also talking to Americans about bottling soft drinks and assembling cars, and to Israelis about making chemicals.

But it was pointless to talk about whether LV Holding was operating legally: laws were so confusing in Ukraine that anyone engaged in business activity on that scale was breaking one of them, and taxes were so high (75 percent of profit for trading companies) that almost anyone who paid them would go bankrupt. The regulations served the purposes of the state, not of the businessmen: every law, every license was an excuse to take a bribe, and every tax prevented businessmen from making too much money. But while it wasn't fair to criticize businessmen for breaking bad laws, that was not quite what Enokyan had been accused of.

'Mafia,' Enokyan dismissed the charge. 'It is just a slur put about by the Ukrainians. It means that we are competition for them, and they don't like it.'

Competition was the right word. Recently, the L'viv district leaders had offered a joint venture deal to a Ukrainian-Canadian, a returning émigré whose interests the city had wanted to promote. LV Holding sent in a counter-offer, which they claimed was far more lucrative for the city. Embarrassed, the city leaders withdrew planning permission for the project altogether – and LV Holding had suddenly encountered unexpected obstacles in its efforts to get export licenses.

The episode with Nazar, the mayor's son, was part of this competition, too, Enokyan explained.

'Nazar – he is a nothing, unimportant.'

'Why did you hire him?'

Enokyan shrugged. 'I felt sorry for him. Anyway, Genschaft asked me to ask him to help us get in touch with his father, and Genschaft is my friend – I always help my friends. Next thing I know, we are being accused of kidnap. Kidnap! Me! Always law-abiding! I haven't slept for four nights, I've been awake worrying about it.'

Enokyan got up from his desk and began to pace around the room. For the first time I saw that he was a rather short man: short with broad shoulders.

'Andrei Sakharov once said that stupidity creates evil. Here, in L'viv, stupidity is creating evil. Here – look,' and Enokyan retrieved a newspaper article from his desk. 'Look what it says: "Levon Enokyan put the government to shame, showing off his ability to give to charity." I gave hundreds, thousands of rubles to orphanages, old people's homes, veterans' homes. What have they ever done for the poor of this city? Nothing.'

He threw the newspaper down on the desk.

'You want corruption? I'll tell you about corruption. Every one of those so-called nationalists, every one of those petty governors and mayors and city councilors, every one of them is stealing as much as they can and as fast as they can, because they don't know what the next election will bring. Their salaries are risible, their wives want them to bring home food for their children. What can they do except steal? Examples – I could give you hundreds.'

Enokyan sat down again.

'Do you mind? I'm not feeling well.' He swallowed a pill and waved me out of the room.

The Mercedes took me back into the center of town. On the way, the driver stopped to show me LV Holding's private hotel, used only for clients of the firm. The hotel was in a prewar villa, used until recently as a Communist Party guest house for distinguished visitors – the driver said he didn't know how LV Holding had managed to get hold of it. Inside, the fixtures were in perfect order, and there was satellite television, just like at the Grand Hotel. In fact, the furniture looked just like the furniture at the Grand Hotel, the bathrooms looked like the bathrooms at the Grand Hotel, the floors had the same kind of parquet as those at the Grand Hotel.

It occurred to me that I had never asked Genschaft about the nature of his business with Enokyan.

Before I left, I went to see Marta again, and listened to the latest installment: the case had been further complicated by the possibility of elections. Someone was passing leaflets around the city listing Genschaft, Enokyan, and other local businessmen with Jewish and foreign-sounding names as 'anti-Ukrainian elements.'

Meanwhile, the Grand Hotel remained empty. Foreign investment into L'viv remained low. From week to week, inflation was going up, city services were deteriorating. Energy prices were going up because of Ukraine's conflict with Russia. In central L'viv, the water only ran from six to nine in the morning and from six to nine at night. One afternoon I found my friend Irena at home, weeping: the water had not come on that morning, and she was afraid it would not come on at all that day. Alas, a city official told me, he was unable to increase the supply of water because the peasants in the countryside refused to cooperate with government edicts and would not allow a new reservoir to be built on their land. Was that true? Or had someone with commercial interests in the area bribed the official not to increase the supply of water?

When I went to see the mayor the next day, he said that his son Nazar had come home from his famous meeting with Enokyan and Genschaft very upset. I asked the mayor whether the police would be able to prove the charge of kidnapping.

'I don't know,' he said simply.

The next day someone said that Nazar was now working for another company, one that had mysteriously been exempted from export duties.

Much later I heard that Marta's investment in L'viv had led to at least one tragedy. Marta had returned to America, leaving one of her Ukrainian relatives, an older man, in charge of her business affairs in L'viv.

While she was away, the man was shot in the street. The assailant was never found.

Months afterward, I ran into Marta in a restaurant in Kiev.

'I am still fighting for the Grand Hotel,' she told me. 'I will not give up on the Ukrainian people.'

Woroniaki

For the last two miles, the car followed a track that was slowly turning from dirt to mud. The rain was falling harder, and deep pools of dirty water appeared whenever the road turned down a hill. Finally, the long village stretched out into nothing: there were no more houses, only trees. We could drive no farther as great heaps of mud, dead branches, and rocks barred the road.

'No,' said Liudmyla, 'this is where we begin to walk.' Władek, Liudmyla's son, groaned audibly. He covered his head with a piece of newspaper and motioned for me to do the same. He was a soft man, with white skin and a sentimental face. His eyes shone with faint embarrassment: he was sorry he had brought me to this place. Woroniaki was less than a hundred miles from L'viv, but it felt far from civilization.

'Irena will shout at me for bringing you here,' he said, shaking his head and thinking about his wife.

Liudmyla didn't hear her son and wasn't bothered by the same sentiments anyway. She was in her element. Despite the cold rain, she wore no stockings beneath her black skirt, leaving her bare feet clad in plain brown shoes. Her hair, unusually dark for a woman in her seventies, streamed uncontrolled down her back. She was of a peculiarly Ukrainian type: neither peasant nor city woman, she contained within herself both the superstitions of the past and the skepticism of her own time. She had studied to be a doctor, yet she told fortunes with cards. She listened to Western radio and knew something of foreign countries, yet she crossed herself quickly when she met foreigners, to ward off the evil eye just in case. Her children lived in the city, taught music, and read books, while she kept them supplied with homemade jam, home-picked apples, potatoes, and cabbage.

'Up,' she said, 'up this hill over here. This is the way to the farm.'

Liudmyla had first come to live in Woroniaki because Władek's father had played a silly prank.

It was just at the beginning of the war, before people knew how bad things were going to get. In those early days, when Poles thought defiance a daring thing, Władek's father and a gang of fifteen-year-old saboteurs stopped a train and stole the food meant for German officers. They were caught the next day, drunk on Riesling and sick with Belgian chocolate. The Gestapo clapped them into jail.

Władek's father was lucky. Instead of shooting him on the spot, the Germans sent him to a farm, just west of Graz, in Austria. It was hard work, but the rich food, the neat fields, and the trim houses were like nothing he had ever known. Good fortune also introduced him to Liudmyla, a Ukrainian laborer on a neighboring farm. He was drawn to her flat cheekbones and gray eyes, the softened consonants in her accent, and her long, loose limbs: these things spoke to him of the East, of home.

The time passed quickly, their war was quiet. Only toward the end did they hear the whine of bombers and the sound of distant gunfire. That was when Władek's father knew it was time to go home.

Others were staying in Austria, frightened by the terrible stories of tragedy in the East. But the pull of Galicia was strong, and Władek's father enchanted Liudmyla with stories of Polish wealth and prosperity. So together they followed a long, circular route, traveling by slow-moving freight train across the low hills of Croatia, by wagon cart through the black forests of Romania, and then by train again, north to Galicia, to the tiny village of Woroniaki. Along the way they stayed in refugee camps filled with people like themselves, displaced people trying to go home, or trying not to go home, leftover Jews with big eyes, confused Poles, Russians afraid to go back to Stalin's camps. By the time they arrived in Woroniaki, it was no longer Poland. Woroniaki, like L'viv, had been permanently ceded to Ukraine.

His youngest brother saw Władek's father and Liudmyla first, and his eyes opened wide when he saw Liudmyla and heard her speak. 'She's not a Pole!' he crowed, and ran back up the dirt road to the house on the top of the hill, shouting the news all the way.

('It was this road, this road right here,' said Liudmyla. She stopped in front of an oak tree. 'This was just about where he saw us.')

On their first night in Woroniaki, Liudmyla and Władek's father slept on a bed of straw, surrounded by new relatives. The cottage was tiny and damp, with a thatched roof and thick stone walls. It was different from the wooden houses she had known as a girl in Donetsk. The people were different, too. They were fiercely Catholic, whereas her own family, softened by the years of famine and Soviet repression, had already lost its Orthodox faith. These Poles mumbled prayers to the saints whose portraits hung in the corners of the cottage, wielded rifles against Ukrainians and Russians who crossed over onto their tiny plot of land, and went barefoot in the summer. On the evening of their arrival, Liudmyla had tried to wash her hair, but it was a Sunday, and the family frowned on it.

On her insistence, they moved out. Liudmyla got an inspector's job in Zablocko, a town near Woroniaki. Władek's father began to work in the mill. They got married in the registry office. The Catholic priest wouldn't marry an Orthodox woman who had traveled, even in wartime, with a man who was not her husband.

'Hypocritical little man he was,' Liudmyla sniffed. 'Hit the bottle almost every day.'

Soon afterward, the Poles of Woroniaki began to leave: Woroniaki, it was said, was going to become Ukraine. Władek's father's brothers left, his uncles and his cousins: all were going to the rich, new lands of Silesia, the German territory given to Poland in exchange for the lost lands of the East. But Liudmyla would not leave. Woroniaki was no longer Poland, but it would be Ukraine, and she was Ukrainian. They would do well to stay there, she told her husband. With her clean Ukrainian blood and Soviet childhood, they would do better in Woroniaki than the locals, mixed-breeds, half-Poles with suspicious politics. And it was so.

Władek disagreed. 'Biggest mistake my father ever made,' he said. 'We would be in Poland by now if he hadn't stayed.'

We had reached the top of the hill. It had stopped raining, but the sky was still iron gray. The tiny house where Liudmyla had spent her first night in Woroniaki was still there, now covered with a tile roof instead of straw. A girl in a headscarf stood in the front yard.

'Is your mama home?' Liudmyla asked. 'Tell her we are from the family who used to live here.'

The girl stared, first at Liudmyla, then at me, saying nothing. She ran inside. A minute later, an older woman emerged from behind the low wooden door.

'Don't mind her,' she said, speaking Ukrainian, 'my grandchild is deaf and dumb. Come in.'

The house was tiny and dark. A porcelain stove stood in its center, and a sickly-sweet portrait of Jesus, his eyes turned up to heaven, hung over the big bed in the main room. A young woman sat beside the bed. Her shirt was open; an infant sucked at her breast. She looked up at us, unembarrassed, and smiled a smile full of gold teeth. Władek turned his head away.

The men, she explained, were at work in town. The women – the grandmother, the mother, the child – ran the farm. They fed the geese, collected the eggs, and waited for the men to return.

They were Ukrainians from a village on the San River, in southeastern Poland. During the war, the big house on the estate where they lived had burned down. The older woman said she remembered seeing the flames as a child.

'So high they were, so high.' She shook her head at the memory.

After that, the partisans had come. On one night there were Germans; on the next night there were Poles; and on the third night there were Ukrainians, led by the rebel Bandera. They thought the fighting might never end. So when they were told to go to Woroniaki – the

Polish Communists had wanted all Ukrainians to return to Ukraine – they went. The commissars had assigned them to the childhood home of Władek's father, since he and Liudmyla were already living in the town, and the others had left.

At first there was nothing to eat. 'We had to make borscht from grass,' the old woman said.

They had thought to stay a year or two, but they stayed forty.

During all that time, they had never stopped wanting to go back. Things got easier with time, but never as good as they had been in Poland. The family were Ukrainians, true, but the little house on the San River was their true home, and they thought of their old garden every spring when the weather was good. But they had no way to know whether these things still existed, whether other people lived there now.

'Poland,' said the nursing mother. 'Poland. Is it as rich and beautiful as they say?' She lifted the child from her breast and placed it carefully on the bed. Calmly, she buttoned her work shirt back up to the top button, pulled her sweater over her shoulders, and adjusted her scarf. She had never been to Poland, but again and again her mother had told the story of leaving Poland and coming East after the war. It was a legend now, like a tale of expulsion from paradise.

'They came back once, the people in this house,' said the grandmother. She meant Liudmyla's brother-in-law.

'The man told us how much he wanted to return. The man said he hoped someday to buy us a house in Sanok so that he could come and live out his life right here. We hope he will do it.'

Liudmyla shook her head. 'They have the biggest house you ever saw in Silesia. It is all made of stone, with carvings over the door.'

'But it is not their home,' said the woman. 'This is their home, and my home is in Sanok. I am waiting to return to Sanok.'

For forty years she had been waiting, she said. Forty years, to go home.

For forty years, Władek's relatives, the Poles from Woroniaki who lived in Silesia, had been waiting to go home, too.

The young mother returned, holding a bottle without a label. Carefully she poured a pinkish liquid into five dark green glasses. The fresh smell of flowers filled the small room.

'We made it from roses,' she said.

Drohobych

From L'viv I rode south in the back of a new car, through wooden villages and deserted spa towns, over and around the low foothills of the Carpathians. After a time, the mountains themselves appeared, sharp and distant. The town of Drohobych sat at their feet like an acolyte, gazing up at their purple silhouettes on the horizon.

I got out at the Church of Our Lady. It was tiny – from the outside it seemed like a child's toy, not a real church at all – yet perfectly formed. An onion dome topped each of its four towers. An intricate pattern of wooden leaves and flowers had been carved on the door, and the church's roof and sides were covered with evenly shaped wooden shingles. Each piece of wood fit smoothly into the next; not a single nail had been used. The builders, like medieval monks illuminating parchment manuscripts, must have constructed the little church as an act of devotion, and must have experienced the long process of carving its joints as an act of prayer.

With a great show of effort, the church warden, a young man with a beard reaching down to his chest, struggled with a heavy iron key against the heavy wooden door until it opened. Inside, the smell of old wood and earth mingled with the leftover scent of incense.

Once the door had shut again, the warden held up his lantern.

Frescoes, invisible before, appeared on the dark wood of the ceiling like stars emerging from the evening sky: the devils and dragons of Revelations were rejoicing at the end of the world. A man on horseback blew his trumpet to mark the arrival of Judgment Day. Saints boiled in oil, hung from trees, stood shot full of arrows. On one side, wailing sinners huddled together before the flames of hell. On the other, the good and righteous stood beneath a ladder, waiting to ascend to heaven. Above them all, an implacable Christ ruled on a throne, His head surrounded by a golden halo. His flat-faced disciples sat beside him, each one staring straight ahead.

The frescoes were the work of a professional, a man with an artist's interest in the possibilities of the human body. Yet they were not the solid, heavy creatures of the baroque imagination that were usually found in this part of the world. They were composed of fine lines, faint colors, thin shadows. Christ was an ethereal being; He might float away at any minute, taking His disciples and His saints and His revelations with him. He looked like the temporary god of an uncertain place.

The artists and architects of the church had come down out of the mountains to Drohobych in the Middle Ages, when this part of Galicia was made wealthy by the salt trade. When the wealth disappeared, the artists and architects went away again. The bearded warden held his lamp higher – we had one last look at the frescoes – and then he blew it out.

'Now they are fading into the wood,' he told me. 'They are fading back into the wood, and soon the church will fade back into the forest with them.'

*

Civilization had failed in Drohobych more than once.

'Let us say it bluntly,' wrote Bruno Schulz:

> The misfortune of that area is that nothing ever succeeds there, noth-
> ing can ever reach a definite conclusion. Gestures hang in the air,
> movements are prematurely exhausted and cannot overcome a cer-
> tain point of inertia. We have already noticed the great bravura and
> prodigality in intentions, projects, and anticipations which are one of
> the characteristics of the district. It is in fact no more than a fermenta-
> tion of the desires, prematurely aroused and therefore impotent and
> empty . . .

Born in Drohobych in 1892, Bruno Schulz was small and sickly.
His eyes were sunk deep into his head, his skin was too pale, his limbs
were too thin, his head was too big for his body. He was Jewish, at a
time when that was a liability for a writer, and his talents seemed
minor, especially to himself. As an adolescent, he moped about in the
shadows of his family's squat house and sat in the sunlit patches of
their overgrown garden. He watched girls walk by but was afraid to
speak to them. He meditated on his collection of stamps ('I opened it,
and the glamor of colorful worlds, of becalmed spaces, spread before
me'), on the weather ('their fur coats, soaked with wind, now smelled
of the open air'), on the seasons ('each spring begins like this, with
stunning horoscopes reaching beyond the expectations of a single season'). For most of his life he taught art in a secondary school for boys
and quietly produced caricatures of his fellow citizens: absurd men in
pretentious bowler hats, cowering before haughty women in furs and
high heels. But he also translated Kafka's *The Trial* into Polish, and he
published two collections of stories and a thin novel.

In his fiction, Schulz wrote about the people who lived in Drohobych. He wrote about his father, a man who 'shrunk from day to day,
like a nut drying inside a shell,' shriveling finally to the size of a cockroach. He wrote about Adela, the beautiful servant girl who ruled
over the house and the shop like a dictator. He wrote about Eddie, the
obese neighbor, and Dodo, the imbecile relative, and the cinnamon
shops, where you could find 'Bengal lights, magic boxes, the stamps
of long-forgotten countries, Chinese decals, indigo, calaphony from

Malabar, the eggs of exotic insects, parrots, toucans, live salamanders and basilisks, mandrake roots, mechanical toys from Nuremberg, homunculi in jars, microscopes, binoculars' and all of the other mysterious things that came from the world outside Drohobych.

Schulz also wrote about the city itself, with its changing seasons, its patchwork of streets where a child could get lost at night, its strict rules and secrets. Drohobych was then suffering from an economic depression which followed in the wake of the great Galician oil boom, an explosion of prosperity which began at the end of the nineteenth century, when prospectors discovered oil in a cow pasture. In its wake, the oil rush left sturdy houses with wide porches, big gardens, and heavy facades, houses filled with large families, men with bank accounts and solid wool jackets, women with long skirts and fashionable hats. The families read newspapers from Vienna, books printed in London and Paris, and they felt themselves to be part of the wider world.

Yet the boom had come too easily. In its wake the town remained haunted by its own lack of substance; Drohobych was too far away from anywhere to be certain of anything. In Schulz's stories, the houses of Drohobych are always melting beneath the lushness of their gardens, things and people are disappearing without explanation. Even the town's new wealth seems lightweight, imitation, 'suspect and equivocal': 'In that city of cheap human material, no instincts can flourish, no dark and unusual passions can be aroused . . .'

Schulz survived the Soviet occupation of Drohobych, from 1939 to 1941, but he failed to survive the Germans. A Gestapo officer conceived a liking for his drawings, and protected him; another Gestapo officer, hating the other, didn't approve. In 1942 he shot Schulz in the street while the writer was carrying a loaf of bread home from the market.

After the war, Drohobych found itself on the Soviet side of the border. The substantial people and the large families vanished completely; newspapers no longer arrived from Vienna; the wider world receded into the distance. Ivy climbed the walls of the sturdy houses, eating into the stone a little bit more every year. Termites infested the wooden beams, mold rotted away the foundations, weeds slowly choked the walkways. The streets cracked and the cobblestones chipped. The town sank, as Schulz had said it would, into the vegetable lushness of its gardens. The Jewish cemetery disappeared beneath a housing development.

I found Schulz's house. It was simple and wooden, 'one of those dark houses with empty blind looks, so difficult to distinguish one from the other.'

Not sure of the number, I asked a sad-faced woman emerging from the door whether this was the house of Bruno Schulz. She shook her head.

'Never heard of him,' she said.

'Already for some time,' Schulz had written, 'our town had been sinking into the perpetual grayness of dusk ...'

Outside the town's Catholic church, I met a Pole. He was short, with short arms, short legs, and the squashed, orange face of a peasant. He wore an ill-fitting jacket of poor brown cloth, dusty shoes, and black trousers without a hem, and he was agitated. He couldn't speak clearly, his sentences had no proper endings. He had lost his tenses, lost his sense of time.

'You should come and see,' he kept saying. 'It is there, it is there to see. Everyone has seen it. The blood ran all the way down the alley, there where we lived. Our garden was full of it. They have dug them up now, they have found them, you must come and see, but I shouldn't take you there, oh, terrible, terrible, you should come and see.' As he spoke, the present and the past kept running into one another without logic, descriptions and pleas melded into one another without sense; he wanted to show me something but would not explain what it was.

'Blood in the garden,' he said, 'blood came into our garden.'

He began walking, running almost. 'Come, come, they have dug them up,' he said, 'they have pulled them out again.'

He led me down one of the long streets that led to the outskirts of town, turning right and then left and then right again. After a while, we were not far from the place where we had started. But the little man kept walking, easing his way down a back alley, stepping gingerly over the autumn squashes and gourds growing in the patches of garden behind the houses. He stopped, finally, beside a wooden fence.

'Over there they are,' he said, 'there is where the blood came from.'

I climbed over the wooden boards, hopped lightly over to the other side, and saw what the people were looking at.

There was a hole in the ground, a pit – perhaps twenty, thirty feet deep – and some men with crude spades were digging in it. Every few minutes one would extract a bone, a piece of cloth, a brass button. He would shout up to another group of men who were standing around the edge of the pit. The onlookers, mostly children, would cram their heads forward to see; the men at the top of the pit would spread their arms wide to hold them back. Then, with a great show of bravado, one of the men would reach down to get the object, dust if off with his handkerchief, and carry it gingerly over to a long, hand-fashioned table nearby.

On the table, the fruits of this archaeological labor had been subjected to a macabre form of organization. Yellowed human skulls were stacked in piles, the bigger ones to the left, the smaller ones – perhaps the skulls of children – to the right. Some, with bullet holes in the forehead – and one with the head of a metal ax still neatly inserted into the back – were displayed prominently in front of the others. Beside the skulls, leg bones and arm bones had been sorted into groups and carefully stacked, one on top of the other, like children's building toys. Near the bones stood piles of dried organs, livers and lungs, hearts and bits of muscle, also carefully sorted according to type and kind. Next to them were the brass buttons, the soldiers' buttons, the ladies' shoe and dress buttons, and then the leather shoes, the riding boots, the silver crucifixes, the noblemen's swords, and the multitude of coins – from the Third Reich, the Second Polish Republic, the Soviet Union – that spoke of the confusion of those times.

The pit was in the center of town, just behind what used to be the Austrian courthouse. In the fall of 1939 and the winter of 1940, the building had been the headquarters of the NKVD, Stalin's secret police, the predecessors of the KGB. The NKVD had wanted to ensure that communism would take hold in Galicia. Systematically, they began to single out certain people – the wealthy and the well-bred, owners of large farms and of farms just scarcely larger than garden plots, army captains and priests, ladies who ran church choirs, young men who taught school. One by one they were taken into the court-house, shot or axed in the back of the head, and dumped into the pit beside it. Most were Poles. Drohobych's Jews met the same fate two years later.

Behind the table, a local biology teacher in a white apron presided over the gruesome display.

'This is the scientific way,' he said. 'This will enable us to study our discovery. We all knew what we would find here. Now we must ana-lyze it.'

He modestly admitted that he himself had hit upon this method of categorizing the find, and casually picked up the body parts, moving them from one pile to the next. His apparent lack of horror lent him a certain authority; around the site, people – casual onlookers and diggers alike – gave way to him, moved aside to let him pass. Because he seemed to know what to do with this terrible treasure, they bowed to the schoolteacher's greater authority and let him stack the bones in orderly piles; after a few minutes, I saw that they were also afraid. It was impossible to know what it meant, to discover a pit of bodies in the ground, impossible to guess what it might bring. Civilization had returned to Drohobych only recently, and it was possible – indeed, probable – that the city might fade back into the earth once again.

Across the Carpathians

From Drohobych, I hitchhiked.

A soldier in a green army truck took me over the mountains. The road followed the path of the oil pipeline. The pipeline was called *druzhba* – it meant friendship. '*Druzhba, druzhba*, like me and you,' he said. He thought this was very funny. I got out at the next crossroad, and a factory manager in a battered Lada took me the rest of the way.

The factory manager was named Markus; he had been born in Uzhhorod in the 1930s, when Uzhhorod was still part of Czechoslovakia. He had grown up during the war, after Uzhhorod had been occupied by Hungary. Ruthenian was the language of his childhood, but at school he had learned to read Hungarian and to pray in Old Slavonic. He knew words in many languages. To say 'yes' in Ruthenian you said *eino*. In Russian you said *da*. In Ukrainian you said *tak*. In Slovak you said *ahno*. It proved, he said, that Ruthenians were closer to Slovaks than to Eastern Slavs.

His name, he claimed, was Italian; his family, he claimed, were descended from Roman legionaries. He had five brothers.

The eldest married before the war, moved to Budapest, and was never heard from afterward.

The second brother joined the Czechoslovak Army, and, after the liberation of Prague, made his way to Canada. No one had been able to write to him throughout the long, difficult Soviet years, but just recently Markus had received a letter. Maybe, soon, maybe this brother would be able to visit Ruthenia. Maybe Markus would be able to visit him.

The third brother had been a captain in the Czechoslovak police but was forced to join the fascist Hungarian Army during the war. He died fighting the Allies, and the family didn't know where to find his grave.

The fourth brother joined the Red Army, helped to liberate Prague, and came back a hero and a Communist. He now lived in Kiev.

Markus, the youngest, had been born sickly, and missed out on the war altogether. But he sang me a wartime song, a Ruthenian song about a sea gull that had lost its way in the mountains:

Oh, sea gull, you are far from home, Ruthenia is so far from the sea . . .

But he had never seen a sea gull.

In Uzhhorod, the houses were the square village houses of eastern Hungary, each with its own kitchen garden; its own cow; its own chicken; and its own vine, pregnant with strong, white grapes. On the hill was a Hungarian castle, its turrets worn down by the wind, and a church built by Maria Teresa, who was said to have loved her Ruthenians above all other people.

Markus invited me for dinner. He said that Ukrainians would never show such hospitality. He said that Ukrainians were like wolves, they gathered only in packs, in mobs, at rallies. They never invited one another to dinner. All over the world, he said, good nations had been placed next to bad ones. Thus had Ruthenia – tiny, good, forgotten Ruthenia – been placed next to evil Ukraine.

*

A farmer with blackened skin drove me up the mountain to Mukachiv. He told me a story about Czar Peter of Russia.

Czar Peter of Russia, he said, was not yet known as Peter the Great on the day he first marched into Mukachiv, and the eighteenth century had not yet begun. But Czar Peter was already a man to be reckoned with, and he arrived with a grand entourage: boyars and hussars, water girls and prostitutes, horses, mules, and dogs. The Hungarian aristocrats – for it was they who ruled Mukachiv at that time – jumped into action. The Russian court had to be sheltered properly, so the grandest landlords gave them the castle. The Russian court had to be fed properly, so the peasants provided goats and wild rabbits, honey and fresh bread. The Russian court had to be given drink, so the nobles commanded the monks to bring bottle after bottle of the strong, clear white wine they kept stored in the cellars near Mukachiv, then called Mukhachevo.

Czar Peter was impressed. On leaving, he pronounced himself more than satisfied, and he ordered his servants to procure for him a bottle of Ruthenian wine every month, to be sent by special courier to the temporary court at the new city of St Petersburg, just so he could experience, once again, the taste of Ruthenian sunlight.

I repeated the story to the caretaker of the wine cellar at Mukachiv. He shrugged. He didn't know if it was true. Perhaps yes, perhaps no. Perhaps it was just a story.

The caretaker was a faded man, with a dry face and tired eyes. He was a Ruthenian – 'whatever that means,' he said, and shrugged again – but he spoke softly accented Russian, stumbling over the difficult words. He was suspicious. He didn't want to show me the wine cellar. It was Saturday, he said, it was forbidden to foreigners. I told him I wanted to export wine to Poland. His eyes lit up. 'Export' was the magic word.

We walked down a long, narrow stairway. I reached out to touch the walls, and they were damp, as if it had been raining underground. The air was sweet, touched with the faint smell of rotting grapes.

At the bottom, the floor flattened out and the rows of giant wooden barrels, each one taller than a man, stretched out as far as I could see.

They went on for more than a mile, the caretaker said, but there were not as many as before. The barrels, made with the wood of local birch trees, were meant to last twenty years. Most of these had not been replaced since the war. Some had lasted thirty years, some fifty. They leaked, they let in air, the wine didn't have quite the same flavor anymore.

Anyway, only one in ten barrels was full; every year there were fewer and fewer grapes. It had started with the anti-alcohol campaign – Gorbachev told people to cut down the vineyards, and they had obeyed. Then there was no more central planning, no reason to keep making anything. Soon there would be no more wine at all.

At the very bottom, the caretaker took out his cigarette lighter and held it up against the wall to show a crude carving in a script that looked almost runic. A date, 1557, was carved in Roman numerals, and there were two signatures: Fathers Stefan and Dominic. Beyond that, the caretaker said, nobody could read the inscription.

His voice dropped to a whisper: 'It is a mystery. It is an ancient language. Nobody can decipher it.'

I looked closer and saw that the language was Latin.

Once upon a time, a steam train had linked Uzhhorod, the capital of the Ruthenian province in Austro-Hungary, to Czernowitz, the capital of Bukovyna Province in Austro-Hungary, a distance of a mere few hundred miles. The train had continued to work even after 1918, when Uzhhorod became the capital of the Ruthenian province of Czechoslovakia and Cernăuți (Czernowitz) became the capital of the Bukovyna province of Romania. But ever since 1945, when Uzhhorod and Chernivtsi (Czernowitz) had been united at last in the Soviet Republic of Ukraine, the train no longer connected the two cities.

In Uzhhorod they said that two of Stalin's generals were at fault. In 1945 the generals had conquered eastern Czechoslovakia, they had conquered Romania, and they were celebrating by drawing the border between those countries and Ukraine.

The night was dark. The forest was still. A map lay on the table, and a bottle of vodka stood in the center. 'To your health,' said the first general to the second general. 'To your health,' said the second general to the first. They began to drink, and they began to draw. As dawn broke, they were still drinking, but the map was finished.

It was a fine map. Czechoslovakia had a new border, which no longer included Ruthenia, its eastern tail. Romania had a new border, this time without Bukovyna, its northern slice. Ukraine's border had expanded so that now Ukraine had a foothold on the far side of the Carpathian Mountains. Everything about it was perfect – everything, that is, except the border between Ukraine and Romania, which wavered just a bit. Or rather, it wavered quite a bit – back and forth across the old Austrian train tracks.

Because the tracks lay on both sides of the border, the train was useless. That, at any rate, was the way that people in Uzhhorod explained the absence of a train to Chernivtsi.

It was impossible, they said, to travel between Uzhhorod and Chernivtsi, between two Ukrainian cities which had once been two Habsburg cities. No one would dream of driving all the way there from here, on those bad roads, across the Carpathian Mountains. No one, that is, except two Hungarians: Kalman and Istvan.

Kalman and Istvan: mirrored sunglasses and leather jackets. Kalman: slender and narrow-waisted, with the flowing blond hair of a *belle époque* dandy. Istvan: very tall, very dark, broad shoulders, and big hands. There had to be two of them, they told me, because one could encounter bandits on the road. Before leaving, they pocketed the fee: fifty dollars, cash. It was more than I had spent in the previous month. But the drive would be worth every penny, Kalman said, and proudly showed me his Ford.

There was only one problem: no gasoline. No gasoline for sale anywhere. No legal gasoline, no black market gasoline, no gasoline. Don't worry, Kalman said, we are Hungarians, we know how to do things. Soviet Hungarians know how to do everything in the Soviet system, we are the only people who have beat it. Just outside of town, Istvan stopped the Ford beside a small huddle of wooden shacks, caravans, and army tents – a Gypsy camp. Crazy-eyed horses with bones jutting out from their sides grazed in the muddy field beside. The air was drenched with the not unpleasant odors of smoke, fire, and cooking meat.

'The smell,' said Istvan, making a gagging noise. 'I hate their smell.'

Kalman pushed open the car door, strode over to one of the shacks, banged his fist on the scrap-metal door, and disappeared inside. A few minutes later he emerged with a small, dark man.

'You carry these,' he told the man, and handed him two large metal cans. Kalman disappeared into the shack again, this time with Istvan in tow.

The man carried the cans over toward the car. He looked at me, narrowed his eyes, lit a cigarette, and said nothing. After a while he took out his cigarette, threw it down, and stamped on it. Then he lifted up one of the cans, and poured its contents into the car.

Kalman and Istvan emerged again.

'You can go now,' Kalman said to the man. The man looked at me again, turned, and walked away, carrying the empty gasoline can. Kalman stored the other, full one in the backseat of the car.

We drove off.

'Made me leave a deposit for the can,' said Istvan. 'Gypsy bastards.'

'Gypsy bastards,' agreed Kalman. They muttered oaths to one another in Hungarian.

Past Mukachiv, the road climbed upward through brown hills and green pastures. The mud had washed into the asphalt, and the asphalt had washed farther downhill. The Ford bounced and splashed from pothole to pothole, and after a while the road seemed to lose some of its logic. It twisted and turned for no apparent reason, passing villages and tiny farms. For a while it ran through vineyards; then, as it grew steeper, the vineyards were left behind. Neat orchards, their trees sprinkled with hard green apples, tiny pears, and darkening plums, took their place while the square, spare, Hungarian village houses gave way to the rambling wooden houses that belonged to the mountain people.

In the high Carpathians, each valley speaks a different dialect, and each village has its own architecture. We passed through a region where the inhabitants paint pictures on their walls. At every turning, a girl and a boy, or a boy and a cow, or a farmer, presumably the owner, was depicted on a barn or a shed in flat, primary colors. A few miles later, the villagers stopped painting pictures, but instead built all their houses with high, pointed roofs designed to keep off snow in winter. A few miles after that came a village in which every inch of wooden space on every inch of house was covered with carvings – leaves and snowflakes and geometric designs. Each house seemed to compete with the next, each seemed to want to be more elaborate than its neighbor. One house stood alone on a hill above a village and was completely covered in tiny mirrors that picked up sparks of sunlight, glittering and shimmering like a jewel cut to exotic proportions.

'There's the border,' said Istvan, abruptly switching back into Russian. 'Look, you can go across.'

A thin wire fence ran just alongside the road, without a guard or a knot of barbed wire in sight.

'What for?' said Kalman. 'Nobody wants to go to Romania. Worse there than here.'

There was silence again. We passed a house whose walls, door, and roof were covered with what appeared to be aluminum foil.

'What do you do?' The question was for Kalman.

Kalman gave a low laugh. 'I trade.'

Istvan grinned. 'I work with cash,' he said. 'I am engaged in the purchase and sale of foreign currencies.'

They were black marketeers. Both spent a good deal of their time crossing back and forth between Uzhhorod and Hungary.

'But it's hardly worth it anymore,' said Kalman. 'You used to do good business bringing in videos, bringing out machine parts. But the trains are so expensive now, they are pushing black marketeers out of jobs.'

Hungary was tough. Wages were low, prices were high, it was hard to get work there. All of the Soviet Hungarians – and there were still a few thousand – were trying to emigrate, but it wasn't easy to land on your feet. At least in Uzhhorod, a little money still went a long way. If you had a few dollars, you were living well.

I noticed for the first time that Kalman had an enormous black eye. 'What happened?'

'There were two of them,' he said, and laughed again.

Now and again the road crossed back and forth across the train tracks. While passengers could no longer use the Uzhhorod–Chernivtsi train, the state companies who imported Hungarian products into Ukraine were free to do so. Four times we had to stop for a train; four times Istvan slumped over the wheel.

'Soviet bastards,' he said.

'Soviet bastards,' Kalman agreed.

We passed through Khust – spelled 'Huszt' in Hungarian – a town that attained fame briefly, not long after Hitler divided Czechoslovakia into pieces at Munich in 1938. At that time Sudetenland became part of Germany. Bohemia and Moravia became German protectorates. Slovakia remained independent but under the leadership of a pro-Nazi government.

Ruthenia, the far eastern tail of Czechoslovakia, became an autonomous province led by a Uniate priest, Monsignor Voloshyn; Khust, a Ruthenian city, became the center of a large and expensive propaganda project. From Khust, Hitler hoped to incite the Ukrainian population of Poland into rebellion. Teachers trained in Berlin's up-to-date schools of modern Fascism and Nationalism poured into Khust to give lectures on the great Ukrainian fatherland. Ukrainian and Nazi symbols were displayed; a Ruthenian Storm Trooper regiment called 'Sich' was organized; flags were waved, slogans were shouted, and there was a call to arms.

But by March 1939, Hitler had grown bored with the whole scheme. He had bigger and better ideas. So he signed Ruthenia over to the Hungarians. In 1939, the Hungarian Army moved in, and the peasants of Khust went back to tending their sheep.

We passed near Mikova, the village where Andrei Warhola and Julia Zavacka once lived, in the early years of the twentieth century. Andrei was a farmer, wealthy by local standards, with a house and a horse and his own pasture. One day Andrei saw Julia bringing in wheat from her father's fields and was struck by her beauty.

'Who is that girl?' he asked a woman standing beside the field.

'She is my daughter, Julia, and she will become your wife,' the woman answered.

No one had asked Julia, but the size of Andrei's house and his horse and his pasture had already won her mother over. That was enough: Andrei and Julia married soon afterward, sometime around the year 1908. A few years later, Andrei slipped over the Polish border and made his way to America, having promised to send Julia money for the passage.

Nine years passed. Andrei got a job in a Pennsylvania coal mine, and then another job as a construction worker; he lived in a part of Pittsburgh called Ruska Dolina, the Ruthenian Valley. He was to send money for Julia's passage, but it never arrived. In 1921 Julia borrowed money from her priest to join her husband.

They had a surprisingly joyful reunion, which produced three sons.

All grew up to become successful. Paul sold scrap metal for a living. John worked as a clerk at Sears, Roebuck. Andrew, although sickly as a child, went to college and studied graphic art. Julia never learned English properly, but she supplemented the family income by making imitation flower bouquets out of soup cans and crepe paper. On Sundays she prayed at the Greek Catholic church.

Later in his life, Andrew became Andy, and dropped the vowel from the end of his last name.

'I come from nowhere,' Andy Warhol used to tell people.

We passed through Slatinski Doly, the village where Jan Ludvik Hoch was born in 1923. According to legend, Slatinski Doly was so poor that its inhabitants could not afford a cemetery: either they emigrated, or their corpses were eaten by birds. Young Hoch did his best to make ends meet. He studied at the local yeshiva; worked in his mother's garden; and, when the moon was full, helped his grandfather smuggle horses and cattle into Romania. He was too bright and too ambitious to stay in Slatinski Doly, however, and when Ruthenia became Hungary in 1939, Hoch made his way to Budapest – whereupon he disappeared.

According to one story, he met a group of Czech soldiers heading for France and went with them, via Zagreb and Palestine.

According to another story, he joined the Czech Army, fought Germans and Russians in Eastern Europe, and then retreated via Bulgaria and Greece.

According to yet another story, he led Czech volunteers across Hungary and into Yugoslavia, where he was arrested, tortured, and beaten up by the Nazis, escaping death thanks to the intervention of the French ambassador.

In any case, Hoch emerged from the war with a new name: Robert Maxwell. Forty-five years later, he had accumulated a vast media empire – Canadian newspapers, British tabloids, the New York *Daily News*, Israeli press, Hungarian press, scientific publishing houses, and innumerable media trusts – as well as £3 billion in debts that he could not hope to meet. Having tried everything – he even stole from the pension fund of his own workers – he threw himself over the side of his yacht, and was buried with honors on the Mount of Olives in Israel.

We came to another village, where the houses were suddenly bigger. They had wide, pentagonal roofs and high doorways.

'Germans,' said Istvan, 'this is a German village.'

It was not impossible – Saxon farmers had lived in this part of Europe since the Middle Ages. Since the war, West German governments had been helping them return to Germany proper.

After that, Kalman and Istvan stopped talking. The pine trees cast longer and longer shadows until finally there was no light at all. The road seemed endless, and the bouncing of the car seemed as if it would never stop. Every so often, Istvan would jerk the car suddenly sideways to avoid hitting an old man on a bicycle, or a dog.

'Peasant bastards,' he swore in Russian.

'Peasant bastards,' agreed Kalman.

We drove like that, silent and slow on the bad road, for many hours. Only after dark, when the mountains receded, the land flattened out, and we left the besequined villages behind did Istvan and Kalman brighten up. In Kolomiya, once one of the great, remote Jewish cities of the East, an enormous synagogue dominated the center of town.

'Jew bastards,' said Kalman.

'Jew bastards,' agreed Istvan, and he drew the car to a halt. 'We stop here,' he said.

'But we're not there yet,' I said.

'But we've run out of gasoline,' said Kalman. 'We will stop here and sleep. Either you sleep with us, or you sleep somewhere else.'

There were no hotels in Kolomiya, and it was well after midnight; we had driven one hundred fifty miles in sixteen hours.

'Okay,' I said, and went to sleep in the backseat.

Kolomiya was at the heart of what the Poles used to call 'Polska B,' meaning inferior Poland, underdeveloped Poland. In the morning I went into a bar, asking for coffee. The proprietor looked at me oddly and handed me tea.

'*Kofe – nyet,*' he said.

Inexplicably, there were dozens and dozens of taxis in the central square. I left Kalman and Istvan to hunt for gasoline and bartered with one of the drivers to take me to Chernivtsi. Once we had agreed on the price, he drove quickly out of town.

We were out of the high Carpathians, but the land was still low and hilly, and much emptier than it had been farther north. For an hour or so, I stared out the window: the land seemed sandy and infertile. I had left the Ukrainian black earth behind.

Then, quite suddenly, the driver slowed down.

'Chernivtsi is far, very far,' he said. He didn't know if we had enough gasoline to make it. He shook his head, edged the car to the side of the road, and switched off the engine. The empty farmland surrounded us like a desert.

'I thought we had agreed . . .'

I looked at the driver, and he stared back. He was very dirty, with black marks behind his ears, black lines around his collar, black fringes on his sleeves. His bald head shone with grease. Slowly he turned the key in the ignition. The engine gave a low growl in response. He turned it off again and leaned back against the far door. His eyes widened.

'If you don't want to pay, you could get out here' – he gestured out the window at the empty fields – 'and walk.' But as I reached for my wallet, he grabbed my hand and put it back.

'Just kidding,' he said, and began laughing maniacally. He turned the key once again, and the car, an ancient Mercedes, rattled and burped and picked up speed once again.

I noticed that the driver had blue numbers tattooed on his knuckles: 7–8–4–6.

'Jail,' he said. 'I was young and stupid.' He would not elaborate.

He was a Ukrainian, but proudly claimed to speak not a word of the language. 'Russian only, Russian only,' he repeated.

'What nation are you?' he asked.

Cautious, afraid to appear too rich or too foreign, I replied, 'Polish.'

'Polish! I thought you were American.' Now, there was a decent country, America. Big, progressive, exciting – not like Ukraine. Ukraine was slow and backward. Learning Ukrainian was a waste of time. He had more important things to do, like trying to migrate to Germany. He had been there once. Everyone there had a Mercedes, but not an old Mercedes like this one: a new and shiny Mercedes.

'Stores full of things,' he said, and spread his arms wide, leaving the car to steer itself into the wrong lane.

'Just kidding!' he said and laughed again, pulling the wheel back and forth, to the left and to the right, so that the car squealed in pain. We narrowly missed an oak tree.

To make up for it, he made a long detour to Khotim.

'Polish,' he explained, slamming the door of the car.

I had seen the monument to the Battle of Khotim (Chocim, as the Poles called it) – in the little parish church in Nowogródek, the nine headless men with their heads rolling on the ground beside them. But of the castle I had known nothing.

Then suddenly there it was, rising up tall and silent on the river-bank, an unexpected apparition, like a castle in a storybook. Khotim was high and white, with thick walls, sturdy turrets, and wide crenel-lations. Genoese architects had originally built it for the Turks, and there was certainly something Italian about its graceful round towers and high windows. Among the falling-down cottages Khotim was awkwardly out of place, like a high-born lady who suddenly finds herself living in the slums. The castle was so well built that the death of the Polish Commonwealth, the splintering of the Ottoman Empire, the collapse of Austro-Hungary, and the demise of the czar had failed to topple it. I climbed as far as I could up the crumbling stairway. From the tower windows, the broad Dniestr seemed to lie on top of the green farmland like a thin blue string.

Unmarked and unremembered, the castle at Khotim still guarded the old border between Poland and the Turkish Empire. It was the end of the old *kresy*, the outer limits of the old borderlands.

'I'd wreck it,' said my driver. He kicked a heavy black boot against one of the walls. 'I'd wreck it all, sell the bricks. What good is it to anybody now?'

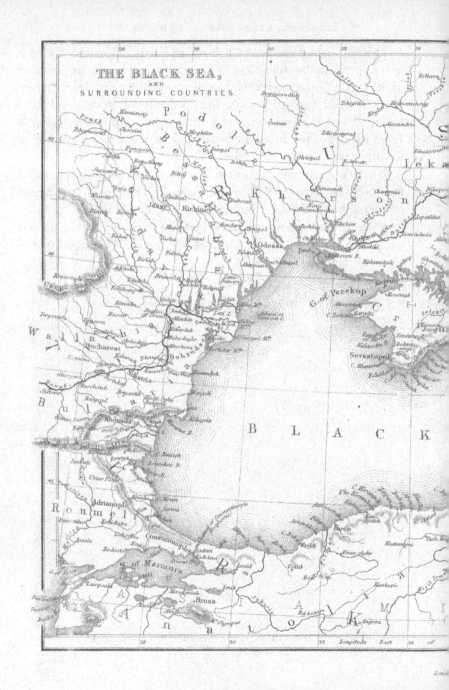

William Hughes, 'The Black Sea, and Surrounding

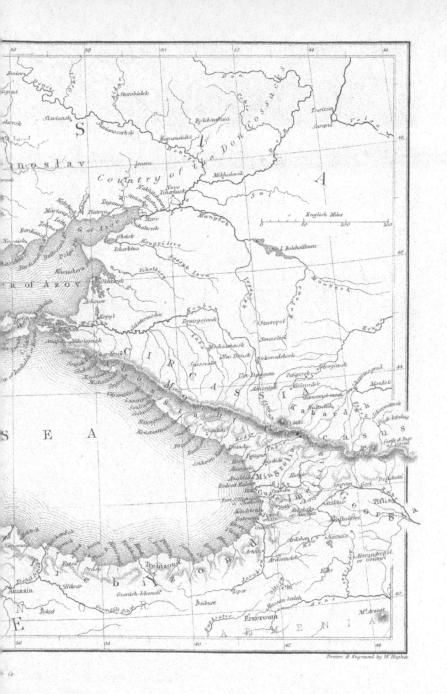

Countries', c. 1840–44.

PART FOUR
Island Cities

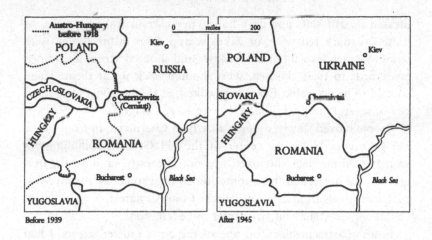

Before 1939   After 1945

Chernivtsi/Czernowitz/Cernăuți

As for the Bukovyna, it was cut off from everywhere, a
meaningless fragment of territory for which there could be
no rational explanation.

– A. J. P. Taylor

Properly speaking, the lands of the Bukovyna belong not to central
Europe but to the Balkans. In Chernivtsi, the region's capital, the
façades were Habsburg, but the colors and the warm winds hinted of
something else: in the morning, I felt as if I had crossed an invisible
line and entered the South.

The air was overhung with the odor of rotting fruit and overripe,
overabundant vegetables. Weeping willows dangled their long arms
down into the streets; flowering vines twisted themselves around telephone wires and Italianate balconies, up through cracks in walls, and
into doorways. Even the faces of the people had changed. The girls
were small and dark like Sicilian girls, and they dyed their hair a
brassy red or let it hang in long black braids down their backs. Some
of the men had brown skins and shirts open at the collar, some were

dressed in stiff suits and gray hats. They carried walking sticks, or bottles of dark red wine, or cakes wrapped up in boxes tied with string. Women leaned out of windows and shouted across linen-lined courtyards to their children, who shouted back up at them. There seemed to be no traffic. Everyone walked, as if Chernivtsi were not a city of several hundred thousand but a large village.

People moved slowly, thought slowly in Chernivtsi. In front of the old Deutsches Haus, the center of the old German community, a woman told me that Chernivtsi was not interested in all of the new politics, the noise, and the commotion coming sometimes from Moscow, sometimes from Kiev, sometimes from Bucharest.

'Down here,' she said, 'we prefer to be left alone.'

In an apartment block on one of the city's quieter streets, I had lunch with a teacher, a friend of a friend. His plump wife served me local wine, and we looked out into the courtyard, where the pigeons slept in the shade.

He shrugged when I asked his nationality. 'My mother was Jewish, my father was Ukrainian. I speak and write in Russian.' It didn't matter in Chernivtsi, he said. So far, nationalism wasn't hurting anybody here.

They had thought of leaving, the teacher told me, but had decided against it. 'It is peaceful here – it is too late for us to go anywhere. We will read books about the world instead. Now we can get good literature from the West. Why should we need to go there?'

His wife nodded. 'It is too late for us to be different,' she said.

The city seemed caught in a vacuum, reluctant to move – and perhaps it had always been that way. In the Middle Ages, the duchy of Bukovyna had been a distant and not especially well-governed Polish province (Polish noblemen tried, unsuccessfully, to enslave the Moldovan peasantry), but by far the most memorable early conquerors of the Bukovyna – and of Chernivtsi, its capital – were the Ottoman Turks. Though they had left long ago, their influence remained: it was like an underground current, the exotic subconscious of the city. Their presence manifested itself in the Turkish arches and cupolas and patterned tile floors of the Orthodox churches, in the riot of colored marble and stone that covered the walls of the university – an enormous building designed by Joseph Hlavka, the architect of the Vienna Opera – and in the darker skins of the people and perhaps in their lethargy as well.

Since then, the city had changed hands several times more, yet it never fully belonged to anyone, and it never lost its slow, peculiar, out-of-the-way character. In 1775, the Ottoman Empire ceded the Bukovyna to the Habsburgs, as compensation for the emperor's mediation in the Russo-Turkish War. In its new incarnation, Chernivtsi became Czernowitz, one of the legendary German-speaking cities of the East, an outpost of empire, always suspect, and slightly shady. Czernowitz attracted criminals and hucksters, people who couldn't fit in anywhere else. The city's humor remained cynical and skeptical; Czernowitzers never succumbed to imperial pomposity.

The city's loyalty to Vienna was constantly under review. Austrians who went to settle there often went native, retreating to the wild isolation of their country estates to fish, hunt, grow their hair long, and jabber away in the Ukrainian and Romanian dialects of their peasants. Jews who took up residence in Czernowitz were mocked for their provincialism and their guttural Yiddish by Jews elsewhere. The Poles and Hungarians who drifted there were always suspected of possessing criminal instincts. Reputedly dirty, remote, and overconfident in the way that provincial capitals often are, Czernowitz became the butt of Galician jokes:

> A Czernowitzer says to another Czernowitzer, 'Where did you get such a nice coat?'
> 'In Paris.'
> 'Really? How far is Paris from Czernowitz?'
> 'About one thousand miles.'
> 'Such a province and they do things so well!'

In 1919, Czernowitz changed hands again. Renamed Cernăuți, the city became the capital of Bukovyna Province in the Kingdom of Romania. According to Romanian myth, the ancient Dacians – the ancestors of the Romanian people – had originated here: the Bukovyna was thus said to be the cradle of Romanian culture, the birthplace of the Romanian nation. But Cernăuți itself went right on speaking

German until the Second World War, and the city scorned the brash nationalism of the Romanian leadership as an aristocrat would scorn the advances of a *nouveau riche*. For twenty years the city could hardly be bothered to change the Habsburg double eagle for the Romanian coat of arms on public buildings. 'In fact,' writes the novelist Gregor von Rezzori, who grew up there:

> The Romanian interlude was hardly more than a fresh costume change in a setting worthy of operetta. The uniforms of Austrian lancers were supplanted by those of Romanian Rosiori, infantry wasn't worth noticing much anyway, and the whole transformation was given no greater weight than the one accorded the changing scenery at the municipal theater between *Countess Maritza* and *The Gypsy Baron* or *The Beggar Student*.

For purposes of his fiction, Von Rezzori invented an imaginary version of Czernowitz, which he called Czernopol: a place of fluctuating nationalities and peoples. Like Czernowitz/Cernăuţi, Czernopol was mutable. No matter how often its national colors changed, no matter whether it was subjected to Germanization or Romanianization, whether the flags on the town hall were raised and lowered, whether stamps and coins and police uniforms were revised, the city's Romanian Hungarian Ukrainian Polish Jewish German essence – Von Rezzori calls it 'demonic' – seemed capable of outliving any empire. Czernowitz remained a place where different nations could survive alongside one another no matter which one was in charge. Czernowitz, people told themselves, would always be able to absorb its conquerors.

After the Second World War change came again. The Soviet Army invaded the Bukovyna and annexed it to Ukraine. Cernăuţi was rechristened Chernovtsy, or Chernivtsi to Ukrainians. Russification and Ukrainianization replaced the Romanianization which had replaced the Germanization which had replaced Ottoman rule. As before, stringent language rules were imposed; the speaking of Romanian was forbidden. But this time, the city was isolated, too. The railway lines to Vienna and Bucharest (and even Uzhhorod) were cut. Germans were deported. Romanians were deported. Ukrainians and Russians were moved in from outside, to give the city a more Soviet character.

Always remote, the city became almost impossible to reach from the outside world. The roads from Kiev and Moscow, hardly used in the past, were poor and hard to travel. L'viv and Kishinev, the nearest big cities, were hardly any less provincial, and they were far away, too. Like a hibernating animal, Chernivtsi dropped out of sight.

In the evening, the professor's wife poured tea out of a cracked English teapot and lit the candles on the mantel, just beneath the portrait of her husband's father. Her face shone round and rosy in the light.

'He was a real gentleman,' she said. She spoke Russian, but pronounced the word 'gentleman' in English.

'And a real Russian,' her husband said. 'My father was brought up to love the Russian language.' Both fell silent. We looked up at the portrait. A thin man with graying hair, wearing a black suit and thick black glasses, stared back at us. The face contained no expression, and the eyes gave away nothing. Born in St Petersburg, the professor's father had been a member of the last generation of true Russian intellectuals, a friend of the poets and writers who filled St Petersburg salons at the turn of the century. As a young man he studied at the university, dabbled in theosophy, discussed art for art's sake, and was once introduced to the poet Anna Akhmatova. His short poems were published in a small newspaper. When the Revolution came, he found the Bolsheviks to be in poor taste but couldn't bring himself to leave the land where Russian was spoken. To stay out of trouble, he changed his specialty from modern literature to ancient Slavonic, moved to Moscow, and began to teach the history of Russian grammar at the university. Like the others, he stopped publishing, then stopped writing, then finally stopped pronouncing poetry out loud.

He was not alone: by the time the purges began, the great Akhmatova herself no longer put her poems on paper. Instead she committed them to memory, and asked friends to keep them in their heads as well. The professor's father was even more careful: he wrote his poems in his head and told them to no one. To prevent himself from uttering any dangerous words, he fell silent, and by this method he lived through the purges and the war.

Inevitably, the authorities suspected him of harboring private thoughts, and they decided to test him. Sometime at the end of the 1940s, they asked him to denounce a certain Jewish linguistic specialist who was promoting cosmopolitan thinking in his work.

The professor's father refused. Instead, he brought his talent for poetry out from wherever he had hidden it and made a moving little speech. A Russian professor had nothing, no specialists to assist him, no books, no paper, no pens, he said, but he could have one thing. He stood up straight.

'A Russian professor can still have some pride,' he said, and he refused to denounce his colleague.

The three university directors who heard this speech turned around and denounced the professor's father as an enemy of the people. Not long afterward, they discovered that a post in Russian language and literature had just been made available in Chernivtsi, which had recently been acquired from Romania. The authorities planned to colonize the city with Slavs, to root out the Romanian influence: you will help, they told him, to return the Bukovyna to her Slavic roots. Silent as always, the professor's father packed his bags and left.

Chernivtsi could hardly have been more different from Moscow. The university was nearly empty. The German professors had escaped or died in camps; the Romanian professors had moved to Kishinev, where it was still permitted to read and write the Romanian language. The Russians were mostly army officers and engineers. For several years, the professor's father was the only teacher of literature in the whole university. He kept to a strict diet of Tolstoy, Dostoevsky, and Pushkin, and after a while the authorities left him alone. He wrote nothing, not even a poem in his head. The speech had been his last poetic effort.

Exile had killed off his desire to write.

No one came to see the professor's father – people were afraid of a man who had been banished. No one came to supper, no one wrote, no one called him, no one played with his children at school. Only after many years in Chernivtsi did they begin to have acquaintances, but they never had friends.

'My beautiful mother,' the professor sighed, 'she was not happy.' The professor's mother was the offspring of Swedish merchants who had come to St Petersburg at the behest of the czar, but she counted Polish and Ukrainian nobility in her family tree as well. She never worked – she said she didn't think it proper – and in the heat of the Balkan summer afternoons she sat facing the wall, her eyes closed, dreaming of cold places and snow.

Occasionally a piece of news from the outside world reached them. Two of their gentler St Petersburg colleagues, they learned, had been murdered in bed by the KGB. A cousin had been sent to America to study engineering at state expense and, on returning, was taken to a camp and shot as a foreign spy. An uncle was accused of Ukrainian nationalism and expelled from the country. His children died in Siberia.

In the fifties, a friend from St Petersburg days came back from the camps. Originally, he had been sentenced for ten years. On the night before his release, his guards gave him a slap-up meal and a bottle of vodka. Afterward he went back to his bunkhouse, reeling and stumbling and shouting that he was going to murder Comrade Stalin as soon as he was free. Another inmate reported him to the camp authorities on the following day. So in the end he was not released, and he served another fifteen years.

'You can't trust anyone,' he said, telling the story to the professor's father over tea one night.

The professor's father agreed, and toward the end of his life he spoke less and less. He stopped reciting the poetry of others, stopped repeating the lines of Akhmatova and Mandelstam, even to himself. He never spoke of St Petersburg or of Moscow. To the end of his life he remained afraid to use the telephone. He never told his son that, if history had gone a different way, he would have been called a prince, as he thought the subject of aristocracy in general and titles in particular too risky to mention. But he brought up his son to love the Russian language just as he did, and when he retired, his son took over his chair at the university.

The professor looked up at the portrait again. His wife fingered the gold butterfly brooch on her jacket.

'Two weeks before he died,' said the professor, 'I caught him burning books. I was horrified – I grabbed his shoulder, told him to stop – but he said they were books of poetry, which he no longer needed.'

For a Russian from St Petersburg, the Bukovyna had been exile: it was a place that had never been described by a great Russian writer. There was no poetry to be found in Chernivtsi's foreign facades, no beauty in the people speaking odd languages on the street.

And yet for the professor and the professor's wife – she was also the daughter of exiles, army people sent to the city against their will – Chernivtsi was quite the opposite.

'It is different here,' the professor told me, 'more civilized than Russia.' To him, the Bukovyna was a borderland, but it was a European borderland. Chernivtsi's architecture, once called provincial by the Galicians, seemed to the Russian couple like evidence of a civilized past. Chernivtsi's German and Jewish traditions, once considered suspect by the Austrians, seemed to them like sophistication. Chernivtsi was far from Moscow, far from Kiev, far from everywhere, but it was possible to live well in Chernivtsi.

'Just look at this flat,' said the professor's wife. 'Nobody lives like this in Russia.' And it was true. They had three large rooms, a marble fireplace, real Danzig cabinets – dark wood, with heavy carvings – and a Biedermeier sofa. The water went off several times a day and the electricity was weak, yet the apartment had space, parquet floors, high windows. While we spoke, their son was in the next room; it was possible for him to sit and read and not to hear us. The apartment was a place to live, not a place to hide in, not like the cramped concrete blocks of Moscow.

Yet they feared the future. They feared Ukrainian nationalism; they feared Romanian nationalism; they feared expulsion.

We don't know Russia, they said. We have no family there anymore, they are dead or have disappeared. Our roots are here, our son is born here – he has never been to Russia. He speaks Ukrainian at school. We spoke Ukrainian at school. We don't feel like conquerors.

'We believe in independent Ukraine – Ukraine must be independent – we do not want to keep Ukraine in Russia,' said the professor, almost pleading. 'We believe Romanians should have rights here. They believe this is Dacia, this is where Romania originated – let them have a home in Dacia, too.'

'We are victims, too,' said the professor's wife. 'All nations suffered in the Soviet Union, but Russians suffered, too.' They both sipped their tea. 'We are not oppressors,' the professor's wife said again. 'We are natives now.'

The Bukovyna had absorbed its conquerors once again.

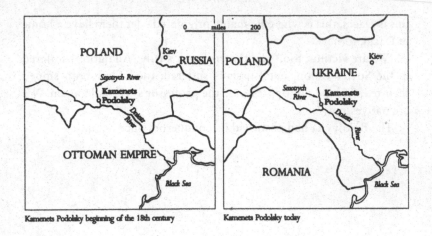

Kamenets Podolsky beginning of the 18th century

Kamenets Podolsky today

Kamenets Podolsky

'Who has built this place?' asked Sultan Osman, leader of
the Turkish troops, when he saw Kamenets Podolsky for
the first time.

'God has built it, using the wondrous methods of nature,'
replied one of his men.

'Then let God himself storm it,' said the sultan, and
ordered his men to retreat.

– From a nineteenth-century Polish guidebook

Along its course from the Carpathian Mountains to the Black Sea, the
Dniestr River is joined by many tributaries. Most of these are undram-
atic streams, but the Smotrych River is an exception. On its way
toward the Dniestr, the Smotrych drops into a canyon lined by high
cliffs. At the same moment, the Smotrych also spawns an island. On
the top of that island, high above the water, sits the magnificent town
of Kamenets Podolsky.

I saw the town for the first time the same way that most people did
for many centuries – from the *Most Turecki*, the Turkish Bridge, one

of two built by the Poles, which link the island with the land around it. Kamenets had once been considered the perfect fortress, and from the bridge it was easy to see why. The river below was swift and filled with rocks; the bridge was narrow, easy to defend. From the city walls, boiling oil could have been poured onto the heads of attackers who tried to climb the cliffs. From the castle, crossbows could have been fired at the armies below.

Kamenets has no founding date. The island has probably been inhabited since the beginning of human time: bronze arrowheads and the bones of Slavic nomads have been found nearby, and in the layers of rubble that lie beneath the city itself there are, it is said, things still older. The first written records of Kamenets appear in accounts of the Mongol invasions of the thirteenth century, when all the towns of Kievan Rus fell to the hordes – except Kamenets. The fortress came under Polish rule in 1396, and during the fifteenth and sixteenth centuries Kamenets stood in the Commonwealth's first line of defense against the Turks, against the Tartars, against rebellious Cossacks. Nearly every other Polish city was sacked during the Swedish invasions – but not Kamenets. The fortress was like a lucky charm: the nation that owned Kamenets knew it had at least one city that would always be safe.

In the annals of Poland and Lithuania, Kamenets glitters with luck and confidence. The castle, considered impregnable, was the scene of glorious balls. The Kamenets market, safe from raiders, was filled with the goods of Persia, Armenia, Turkey, Muscovy, even China. Kamenets was a frontier town, an outpost of civilization in the Wild East. Missionaries and priests flocked to the city, hoping to win more converts to the true faith and prevent the locals from sliding backward as well. By the mid-seventeenth century, no less than eleven churches stood around the central square.

But even a perfect fortress must be defended, and as the Commonwealth grew more anarchic, its fighting spirit declined. In 1672, during the reign of King Michał Wiśniowiecki, one of the least competent monarchs ever to preside over the Commonwealth, Sultan Mehomet IV vanquished Kamenets. Fewer than two hundred infantry were on hand to defend the citadel from attack. The heavy cannon were useless: gunpowder had not been supplied. The Turks crossed the river, scaled the cliffs, climbed over the walls unchallenged, and sacked Kamenets for the first time in its history.

The loss of Kamenets shocked the Polish aristocracy: it was a warning sign, an indication that something was deeply wrong.

'The churches, my Lord, have been changed into mosques and they will sing the Koran in the very place where we have sung Mass,' wails one of the Polish knights in Sienkiewicz's version of the catastrophe. Inspired by the defeat of Kamenets, the Poles call out to the hero, Jan Sobieski: 'Salvator!' They elect him king, whereupon he rallies the knights to defeat the mighty Turkish Army just outside the walls of Vienna. It was a glorious moment: in the Vatican there is a painting of Sobieski triumphant, a vast panorama of victory. Kamenets was recaptured a few years later.

But the damage was done. Poland had been fatally weakened by the Turks, the Swedes, the Muscovites. Sobieski died, anarchy returned, the partitions began, and Kamenets again fell, to Russia, in 1793.

After that, something odd happened to the city. Kamenets had always lain on an important East–West border; now it sat in an unimportant southern corner of the Russian empire. Kamenets had always been a safe haven for traders, but Russian bureaucrats cut off the trade routes. What use is the perfect fortress if it has nothing to guard? What use is a city on an island if there is no longer any need to protect the islanders from raids? The Poles slowly drifted away. The Jews were expelled from the city, allowed back in, and expelled again. A tiny group of Armenians remained to care for the Armenian cathedral, with its collection of thirteenth-century liturgical books. But Kamenets had lost its reason to exist. Walls sagged, potholes grew wider, houses fell down. A nineteenth-century guidebook records that the castle contained 'a bakery, a clothing warehouse, and a steam bath.'

The arrival of the Soviet Union changed nothing, except that Stalin closed the Orthodox churches as well as the Catholic ones. In 1941 the water and rocks that had preserved Kamenets so many times over so many centuries failed to protect the city from German bombs, and the narrow houses in the very center of town disappeared. Afterward the town authorities tried to grow trees in the central square, but failed:

so many centuries of rubble were buried beneath it that nothing came up except scrawny shrubs. The square remained, a gaping hole in the center of the old city.

Kamenets was a city on an island, and what was once an advantage now seemed a curse. Perhaps this was why the city kept reminding me of Venice. Kamenets and Venice had both risen to become great trading cities in the Middle Ages; Kamenets and Venice had both grown decadent in the eighteenth century. Now, the Venetians are slowly deserting their city's waterways for the modern comforts of the mainland, and so, too, are the inhabitants of Kamenets drifting away from the city's island heart and into the surrounding farmland. Just as they measure, year by year and inch by inch, how much Venice is sinking, so, too, should it be possible to measure, month by month and week by week, the decay of Kamenets, the erasing of the features on its statues, the wearing away of its stones, the erosion of its streets.

Like Venice, Kamenets was an odd, uncomfortable city to explore. The streets and the stone houses were dry and dusty; there were hardly any trees. In one back alley, a woman with yellow paper skin ducked inside when she saw me coming. A man sitting beside a vine-covered wall stared when I walked past, but said nothing when I bade him good morning. Laundry hung from the ancient walls, and garbage lay in the streets. Most of the townspeople had pulled themselves inside themselves: perhaps the knowledge of their once strong city's vulnerability to attack had made the inhabitants of Kamenets suspicious of the outside world.

Each of the eleven churches had deteriorated in its own way. All lost their icons, their paintings, their altarpieces, and their wooden pews; most lost their records of births and deaths, their communion chalices, and their stained glass. Some, stripped of steeples, wooden doors, and sculpture, no longer looked like churches at all. Secretly, someone had buried the mixed-up bones of the purge victims in the crypt of the Dominican church. The Trinity church, stripped of its wood paneling, became a state archive. The Franciscan church lost its roof; the statue of St Francis that once graced its portal plunged to its death in the churchyard, where it still lies, face down in the mud. Yet the churches still stood, a monument to another era.

Only the Kamenets cathedral still seemed to possess its sense of self. It is a unique building, an unusual monument to the easy-going morals of Kamenets's past. E. Henderson, the leader of a mid-nineteenth-century Bible Society expedition into Ukraine, recorded his first reaction:

> We were filled with no small degree of surprise to find the following Arabic inscription over the door of the stair-case:
>
> THERE IS NO GOD BUT GOD, AND MOHAMMED IS THE APOSTLE OF GOD. What agreement there could be between the pulpit of a church, professedly Christian, and the watch-word of Islamism, we were at a loss to conceive; but the Bishop soon unravelled the mystery, by informing us, that the church had formerly been a Mohammedan mosque . . .

The inscription is now gone and the frescoes have been white-washed, leaving the walls curiously bare. But the minaret, built by the Turks during their short occupation, still stands; and on the top, the Virgin still stands astride the Islamic crescent moon.

In Kamenets I stayed with Sveta and Yelena. Sveta was a student at the pedagogical institute, the only body of higher learning in the city. Yelena was her teacher, and they shared a flat crowded with dusty furniture and the works of minor Russian writers.

Sveta had the pinched face of a small rodent and a nervous, unhappy laugh. She was probably in her early twenties, but looked older. It was hard to imagine her as an adult, as a mother, or as anything but someone's assistant. She seemed to have remained stuck in permanent adolescence.

'I have never been anywhere,' she told me. 'And I do not think that I will go anywhere.' She smiled fiercely and blinked.

In exchange for room and board, she cleaned the flat, helped with the shopping and cooking, and gazed out the window. She seldom did much else, because it was hard to get good books in Kamenets, and good newspapers were impossible to find altogether. There were no cinemas, no theaters, no restaurants. Anyway, Sveta was frightened to leave the house alone in the evenings, and she was frightened to ride a train. Her family lived in a village, and she seldom saw them. She had few friends, so all of her instincts for love and companionship were directed at the small body of Marsik, an unpleasant black terrier with a high-pitched bark.

'Here, Marsik!' Sveta would shout, getting down on all fours to talk to it. 'Here, Marsik! Hello, Marsik! How are you doing?'

Sometimes the dog would respond, looking up at Sveta and whining loudly.

'What do you want, Marsik? What do you want?' she asked him, and then waited for an answer. When none was forthcoming, she asked again.

'What do you want, Marsik? Tell me what you want.' Then she would shake her head, take Marsik outside, and give him a bone or a piece of cheese.

In the morning, Marsik would wake up, leap onto Sveta – she slept on the sofa in the sitting room – and begin to yap. Sveta would reply with happy cries of greeting. Then she would wash quickly, dress in the dark, and run out the door to take Marsik for his morning walk, her tinny voice echoing in my ear.

'Come, Marsik. You want a nice walk, don't you, Marsik. Come on!'

Once, when I instinctively put my hands to my ears to block out its sharp barking, Sveta glared at me.

'He is hungry,' she said, defending him. She did not speak to me again that day.

Yelena was the physical opposite of Sveta, with high cheekbones, blue eyes, pure white hair, and wide shoulders. Where Sveta darted about, Yelena moved slowly, in the manner of some great animal. Years of teaching had left Yelena with the habits of a perpetual lecturer. She rarely ended a sentence without repeating the last few words once or twice, and she always kept her voice several decibels louder than necessary.

'Da, i eto vsyo,' she would say at the end of every story. 'Yes, and that is all.'

Yelena was Ukrainian, but her surname was Polish and her family had spoken Russian for four generations. Her mother once lived in a town house in the center of Kiev, but the family lost everything in the

Revolution. Yelena had grown up in the Crimea, like Nabokov, after her family fled south.

Now, Yelena belonged nowhere – Kamenets was as good a place as any, or as bad a place. Whereas the young Russian professor in Chernivtsi had seen his exile as a saving grace, as a way to preserve his idea of civilization, Yelena saw her exile as pointless. 'After me, there is still Sveta. But after Sveta – there will be no one. We live on an island, and we are an island, Sveta and I.'

Asked about her work, Yelena closed her eyes in an expression of boredom. 'Our institute,' she said, 'it is a bad institute. It is a very bad institute. We prepare our teachers to be nurses, in case there is war. We lecture our teachers about Marxism-Leninism. We do not teach them how to teach. The professor of atheism has just renamed himself the professor of religion, and he is delivering the same lectures, over and over again. Yes, and that is all.'

Asked about her pupils, Yelena winced. 'Our pupils,' Yelena said, 'they are bad pupils. They are silly girls from the countryside who come to Kamenets to get married. They know nothing when they arrive, they pay no attention while they are here. They fail their courses, and they come to me, and they beg. They say, please give me my diploma. Please, I am pregnant. Please, I must have a diploma to get a job. Please, if I fail I will have to move back to my village.'

Sveta objected. 'Some work hard,' she said.

'One or two like you can't change the system,' Yelena snapped. 'Go and make some tea.'

Sveta resisted, her hands shaking a little.

'I think there is something to do,' she squeaked. 'We can do our best. We can try and study and learn and improve ourselves.'

Yelena glared at her.

'You are foolish,' she said bluntly. 'What do you think will happen when you try to teach well, try to educate your students? What if you work hard, study things on your own? Your colleagues will become jealous, they will destroy you. They will drive you out of your job. No one is allowed to be better than anyone else. No one is allowed to be better than anyone else. Yes, and that is all.'

Sveta looked at the floor. Yelena turned back to me.

'Our city,' she resumed her lecture, 'our city is doomed. Our city will sink back into the river under the weight of its own stupidity. Do you see anyone caring for the churches? Is anyone repairing the road? Last year three ancient houses slid down the rocks, into the water. Is anyone trying to stop it from happening again?'

Sveta scampered from the room.

It was odd: here, in a city built by Poles, ruled by Ukrainians, was a Russian problem. Too sophisticated for their environment, Sveta and Yelena were not sophisticated enough to escape. Too well-educated to enjoy the company of the locals, they were not well-educated enough to find ways out of their isolation.

'If only we could go to Moscow,' sighs Irina in Chekhov's *Three Sisters*.

'If only we could visit Paris or London,' sighed Yelena.

But it had all been predicted: the collapse of Kamenets, the coming of Russification, the end of civilization. It had all been predicted by Zygmunt Krasiński, a Polish poet, a contemporary of Mickiewicz. The setting of his famous play, *The Undivine Comedy*, is clearly based upon Kamenets:

> On the granite island stand the castle towers, naked, hammered into the cliff by generations past, joined to the rock like a human breast joined to the spine of a centaur. High above them, a banner waves, alone against the grey-blue sky ...

If the castle is the Kamenets castle, the plot is also a Kamenets plot. In a queer prefiguring of Marx, the *Undivine Comedy* depicts an aristocrat, Count Henryk, defending himself on the ramparts of the Kamenets castle against an atheistic revolutionary named Pancras.

> *Bread! bread! bread! shout the revolutionaries:*
> *Death to the nobles! death to the merchants ...*

At the end of the *Undivine Comedy*, the mob sacks the castle and murders Count Henryk. Krasiński hints, not very subtly, that the play is really about the fall of Poland, the rise of Russia, the death of an older European civilization and the coming of a new one.

Chekhov described the mood; Krasiński provided the explanation.

'People like you and I, Sveta, we are no longer needed here anymore,' Yelena said.

'People like you and I, Sveta, no one listens to us anyway anymore.'

In the silence, the radio crackled.

'Here, Marsik,' said Sveta finally. 'Come here, Marsik. Yes, Marsik, would you like to go for a walk? Would you like that? Yes?'

The dog wagged his short tail.

'Would you like that?'

Marsik wagged his tail again.

'Yes, we will go for a walk,' said Yelena, rising slowly. 'Come Sveta, come Ania.' Her voice became imperious. 'It is time to go for a walk. It is time to go for a walk. Yes, and that is all.'

We left the flat, walked across the bridge and into a park laid out by a Polish prince long ago. The trees in the park leaned over sideways, groaning with age.

Yelena and I walked in front. Sveta walked behind, pulling Marsik along on a leash. But in the cool air outside the flat, their anger at one another subsided. We walked down a path and up a steep incline. Sveta let Marsik off his leash and he trotted ahead, barking at a squirrel. We turned to look at the view.

From the hill, the town looked unreal, like a movie set created to suit a director's vision of a medieval fortress town. Perched on the rock, high above the water, the cathedral minaret stood out black against the gray sky.

'Yes,' sighed Yelena. 'Yes, and that is all.'

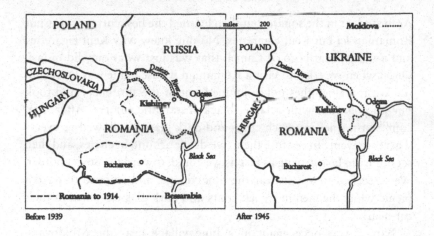

Before 1939   After 1945

Kishinev/Chişinau

The sorrows caused to this poor country by its division will
continue, because the operation is not yet complete.
— *J. G. Kohl speaking of Moldova,*
Reisen in Südrussland, 1846

Moldova is wine country. From the back of an elderly bus, I watched
women in kerchiefs and men in broad hats spread out across the low
hills, trimming their vines, picking their grapes. Not far from Kishinev, the bus passed through a village where all of the houses were
painted blue. It was odd: just a few years earlier I had passed through
another village where all of the houses had been painted blue. That
village had also been in Moldova, but in Romanian Moldova, just on
the other side of the border, near the city of Iaşi.

At that time, the Soviet Union was still intact, Ceauşescu was still
in power, and Iaşi seemed remote and peculiar, like the end of the
world. I stayed in a vast hotel where there were no other guests. The
hotel staff kept moving me and my companion from room to room,
the better to record our conversations. We changed money with an

Arab student in the square, but then learned the best currency was not Romanian *lei* but Kent cigarettes. No one knew why Kent cigarettes and not, say, Marlboro or Camel; that was just what one did in Iași. Once, when we tried to visit a Romanian whose name was known in the West, plainclothes police jumped out of the shrubbery and took our photographs with a large, black Instamatic camera. After that, comic-strip spies in trench coats and dark glasses followed us everywhere we went. To confuse them, we drove around in circles, and then set out from Iași, driving as fast as we could, toward the Soviet border. We screeched to a halt near the blue village, and stopped to have a picnic while the men in trench coats and dark glasses sulked in their car nearby.

Now I was once again in a blue village near the Moldovan–Romanian border, but on the other side, in what had been Soviet Moldova and was now independent Moldova. By my calculation, Kishinev therefore lay one border beyond the oddest place I had ever been.

Like Chernivtsi and Kamenets Podolsky, Kishinev had always lain on the edge of empires; unlike those cities, however, none of Kishinev's rulers had ever thought enough of the city to make it beautiful. Chernivtsi had its lovely squares and Kamenets its astounding castle, but Kishinev had nothing. As we drove through the city I kept looking for something which would give Kishinev a character one could pin down: a notable building, a market square, a memorable street. But most of the buildings had no value in themselves. They were merely provincial monuments, distant echoes of more important buildings in more important cities.

Czarist Russia had ruled Kishinev and all of northern Moldova, the region it called Bessarabia, from 1812 until the First World War. Yet czarist Russia had bequeathed the city nothing more than a weak imitation of the Nevsky Prospekt in St Petersburg: one long street, a few shops striving for elegance, a bank with a statue of Commerce on its pediment. Nor had the long Ottoman reign left much behind except a few Turkish flourishes in the Orthodox church, an otherwise undistinguished building shaped like an overgrown barn. It had been converted into a museum of the Communist Party; now it would be converted back. But it never had been, and never would be, a great religious monument.

There had once been a Moldovan aristocracy. One nineteenth-century traveler to the city describes attending a dinner where he was 'greatly struck with the rich and gorgeous appearance of their oriental dresses. The Boiars, or nobility, affect great state and maintain, within the sphere of their influence, a degree of austere and despotic authority, little short of that displayed by the Turkish Pashas ...'

Yet they left almost nothing to the city in the way of architecture either.

It was true that Kishinev had been destroyed by the war, that many of its more gracious buildings had fallen victim to German or Romanian bombs. But even the new, postwar buildings lacked any sort of style. Minsk, after all, had also been destroyed, and Minsk had been carefully, thoroughly rebuilt. Who could forget the hideous buildings, the windswept plazas, the towering monuments to Stalin's glory in Minsk? Kishinev, on the other hand, was not even especially ugly, and certainly not as memorably ugly as Minsk. Since the war, Kishinev's Soviet rulers had done little more than remove the bag of money from Commerce's hand and throw up some standard concrete tower blocks. One searched hard for real hideousness in Kishinev.

The only buildings that caught the eye in Kishinev were the few remaining rows of single-story pastel-colored houses, indistinguishable from the single-story pastel-colored houses I had seen in Vilnius, in L'viv, in Drohobych: they were the houses of the Jews. The Jews may have been the only people ever to have cared about Kishinev. Yiddish still has its own Bessarabian dialect, and Yiddish literature has its own Bessarabian genre. Kishinev sticks in the Jewish memory the way it sticks in no one else's memory, but the Jewish love for Kishinev was not returned. When Kishinev is mentioned in history books, it is often for the viciousness of its anti-Semitic pogroms.

Perhaps the absence of an identifiable style in Kishinev came from the number of times the city had changed hands. Before the twentieth century, Kishinev was Moldovan, but sometimes Polish, sometimes Turkish, and sometimes Russian. In the twentieth century, the Versailles Treaty gave Kishinev and all of Bessarabia to Romania; the

Soviet Union invaded Bessarabia in 1940; the Germany Army invaded Bessarabia in 1942; the Soviet Union returned in 1945. But such a history is not unusual in this part of the world.

Perhaps, in fact, the lack of character is somehow intrinsic to the place; perhaps it dates back to Stefan the Great, the most revered of all Moldovan kings. During his late-fifteenth- and early-sixteenth-century rule, Stefan found himself caught between the Ottoman Empire and the Polish-Lithuanian Commonwealth. Both were demanding allegiance, both wanted his land. Stefan the Great solved the problem by constantly switching sides. Sometimes he joined the Poles to do battle against the Turks, while at other times he kept his distance from the Poles and sent diplomatic missions to Constantinople. Once he burned the cornfields of his own people to keep the Turks at bay.

Fickleness was Stefan the Great's most notable trait; shiftiness and mutability are Moldovan qualities. Whereas changing regimes had never altered the basic character of Chernivtsi – the city had merely ignored its rulers – Kishinev adapted to each new leader with alacrity. With each regime, the city changed its tone, repeated new slogans, and did as it was asked once again.

Stalin must have known of this Bessarabian fickleness, for it was Stalin who tried to break the province, once and for all, of its ethnic and linguistic attachments to Romania. By his command, the region was renamed the Soviet Republic of Moldova. By his command, the Latin alphabet, normally used by Romanian speakers, was declared illegal, and the Cyrillic alphabet was adopted in its place. By his command, new dictionaries included newly invented Moldovan words ('cloth-to-tie-around-the-neck,' for example, instead of the older word for 'necktie') never before heard in the Romanian language. By his command, history was rewritten to stress Moldova's historic divergence from the rest of Romania, Moldova's closeness to Russia, Moldova's Slavic affinities. In the 1950s, Soviet commissars removed the sword from the hand of the statue of Stefan the Great, which had long stood at the entrance to Kishinev's central park; later, they even moved the statue of Stefan away from the entrance and into the back of the park.

The ruse almost succeeded. Moldova did, after all, have an identity and a sense of itself which differed from that of Greater Romania, and a history which differed from other provinces of Romania. Soviet education built on this separate identity: a whole generation of schoolchildren grew up writing in Cyrillic and reviling Romania. There was, in fact, little opposition to this state of affairs. Many Moldovans simply went along with the new regime, just as they had gone along with Russian and Turkish regimes in the past. In another generation or two, it seemed that memory of Romania would be lost.

Yet even Stalin's plans were foiled by Moldovan mutability.

In 1990, as soon as it became possible, Moldovans, first a few, and then many more, began agitating for change. A law was passed, the rules were broken. Almost overnight Moldova switched back to the Latin alphabet. Within a few weeks, posters with Latin letters on them appeared all over Kishinev. Within a few months, the statue of Stefan the Great appeared again at the front of the park, sword and all.

Fickleness, changeability, even shiftiness won out in the end. To some, it seemed as if forty years of the Soviet Republic of Moldova had never happened; to others, it came as no surprise when, a few years after that, the wind blew differently and the Moldovans began leaning in the Russian direction once again.

'Your typical Romanian?' Nico thought for a moment. 'The typical Romanian loves children. The typical Romanian hates violence, adores music, and works hard. He is very intelligent. He loves flowers. He is kind to women.'

'Is that all?'

Nico thought again.

'And of course, he is very proud of being Romanian. Pride is one of our national traits, along with honesty and generosity, of course.'

Nico came from Bucharest. He appeared to have been taught so many lies that he had adopted his own version of the truth. Romanians, he believed, were an exceptionally virtuous people. Romanians were unusually free from guile. Others – Communists, Ceauşescu, Russians, Hungarians – were constantly taking advantage of the innocent Romanian nature. Bessarabians, his theory continued, were the most innocent of all the lamblike Romanians. That explained how the Russians had been able to press Bessarabia, against her will, into the Soviet Union.

A peculiar combination of hysterical patriotism and righteous anger seemed to have driven Nico to Kishinev, where, he said, the most beautiful part of the world's most beautiful nation still remained under the yoke of oppression. He worked as an agency journalist, but this, he said, was just his job. Really, what he hoped to see in his lifetime was the reunification of Moldova and Romania: the re-creation of Greater Romania.

'Bloody Russians,' he would declare, nearly spitting; at other times he would wax eloquent about the glories of the Bukovyna and Bessarabia, about the ancient Romanian character of Odessa, about the unpleasantness of the Hungarians in Transylvania and about the unfair hand that Romania had been dealt after the Second World War.

Yet there was something odd about Nico's fiercely held opinions and national pride. They clashed: they didn't fit the rest of his personality, which was best characterized as gently feminine. Nico walked with a slightly mincing gait and spoke with a lisp. His small hips were wrapped in tight French blue jeans, a watch jangled around his wrist like a bracelet. He carried his notebooks and camera in a leather bag, slinging it over his shoulder as a woman might. He laughed too loudly, opening his mouth too widely and then shutting it too quickly, for fear someone should notice his crooked, grayish-colored teeth. Even his hatred of Russians seemed somehow affected and self-conscious.

'Goddamn Communists,' he said, curling his lip and lisping slightly.

Nico attached himself to me, announcing that he would show me around, introduce me to important people in Kishinev. For a day or two, we walked up and down the city's central streets, where Nico, curiously enough, knew very little about the history of the buildings.

'All of our great monuments were ruined during the war,' he explained. 'Kishinev was the real victim of the war. Kishinev was damaged far worse than any other city.'

What about Warsaw, Berlin, even Minsk, I asked him.

'Those places,' he told me, 'know nothing of war compared to here.' Yet he was very vague on the question of what the prewar buildings had looked like.

Nico took me to see the statue of Stefan the Great. Stefan's stone eyes were wide open and staring, his eyebrows were thick and arched. He wore a pointed crown and a fur mantle, like a king in a fairy tale. I asked him about Stefan's glorious deeds.

'He was very important,' said Nico vaguely. 'He lived ...' and Nico bent over the plaque beside the statue to find out, 'in the fifteenth century.'

We went to the Orthodox church, where small, energetic, elderly ladies were scrubbing the floors and hanging new icons on the walls.

'Goddamn Communists stole the old icons,' explained Nico. But he hung about the entrance of the church and seemed nervous, as if he were afraid to go inside. Perhaps he had never learned to pray.

I asked Nico about the Yiddish writers who still lived in Kishinev, and he grew vague.

'They don't matter,' he assured me. 'Only Romanian matters here.'

Yet he didn't seem to know Romanians either. He promised to arrange meetings with friends – and then failed to do so. He set up a lunch with a prominent nationalist – who never appeared. He made phone calls and was tremendously helpful with a visa problem – yet never arrived on time. But he did ask carefully about who I was seeing, where I was staying, what I wanted to do in Kishinev. And when I said I was going to Tiraspol, the 'capital' of Transdniestria, he immediately agreed to accompany me.

Transdniestria: it is one of the few places whose Ruritanian name matches the Ruritanian cliché. Transdniestria is a thin strip of territory, measuring just a few miles at its widest point, that has belonged to the Soviet Union since the Revolution. Transdniestria has never been part of modern Romania. From 1917 until the Second World War, Transdniestria, small though it was, went by the name of the Soviet Republic of Moldova. Moldova itself was still part of Romania; the idea was that the mere existence of a nominal Soviet republic would entice the other Moldovans, and perhaps the rest of the Romanians as well, into the Soviet Union.

After the Second World War – after the rest of Moldova had been incorporated into the Soviet Union – Transdniestria served a similar function. Russian-speaking and Russian-dominated, Transdniestria was, in effect, a Russian colony within Moldova: it existed in order to encourage the rest of Moldova along the path of Russification laid out by Stalin. Thus it came as no surprise to anybody that when Soviet Moldova declared its intention to break away from the Soviet Union in 1990, the leaders of Transdniestria declared their intention to break away from Moldova and to join Russia. Nor was it surprising when Russian nationalists agitated upon their behalf. Created by the Soviet Union in order to irritate and provoke the Romanians, Transdniestria continued to irritate and provoke the Romanians even after the Soviet Union had disappeared.

Nico and I set out from Kishinev early. We drove past the enormous fortress where the Swedish king Charles XII took asylum after suffering a crushing defeat at the hand of Peter the Great in 1709.

'Those were the days when Moldova really mattered,' Nico explained. 'Those were the days when Romanians had real power.'

He grew similarly eloquent when we passed a group of peasant women, struggling to pull a bale of hay across a bumpy field.

'Our Moldovan peasants,' he said, 'cannot be compared with any others.'

But Nico's light mood soured when we reached the Dniestr River. Broad and almost blue at Khotim, here it had shrunk to a narrow brown stream. A Soviet flag flew from a tall pole at the border post, although Moldova had declared independence from the Soviet Union a year earlier. Two young men with machine guns guarded the crossing, although Transdniestria's independence from Moldova had not yet been recognized.

On the Transdniestrian side, the landscape was already different. Transdniestria had been part of the Soviet Union for forty years longer than the rest of Moldova, and its countryside was more spoiled, its houses more slovenly, its roads more rocky than those of Moldova proper. We passed a sign: 'Our Strength Is In Our Unity.' We passed another sign: 'Glory to Labor.' Both were written in Russian, as were all the names of shops and streets. Nico pursed his lips in a parody of grim determination and began muttering dramatic oaths under his breath.

'Look,' he snarled. 'Commies. I told you they were Commies.'

He was right: in Tiraspol, the capital of Transdniestria, the Soviet Union lived. An enormous bronze statue of Lenin stood in front of the city hall. Red flags, uplifting slogans, hammers and sickles decorated the other official buildings; the streets were still named after the October Revolution, the Five-Year Plan, and the Victory over Fascism; people still stood in lines for bread, wearing their expressionless faces like masks, just as they had in the past. It was like stepping onto a film set. The Communist symbols seemed almost quaint, reminiscent of gas streetlamps or horse-drawn fire engines; these were things one would expect to see in a town that somehow had been preserved from the effects of time.

At the Transdniestrian government headquarters, a group of young men – boys, really – in would-be military costume lounged about the entrance. One sported an American Army camouflage jacket, another wore a rough imitation of Cossack boots and dark sunglasses. A third carried a machine gun, a fourth sat at a makeshift desk and wrote down the names of visitors in a small black book. It was easy to see what motivated them: it was fun to dress up and stand in front of an important building. No doubt it was better than going to school or going to work. No doubt one felt part of something important, one felt one had power.

The would-be Cossack blocked our path. I explained that we had an appointment with the president of Transdniestria.

'Impossible.'

'Why is it impossible?'

'The president of Transdniestria is not here.'

Nico intervened.

'This is a foreigner,' he said. 'She has an appointment with the president of Transdniestria.'

The Cossack looked confused. He turned, and consulted with his colleagues. Finally, the one carrying the machine gun turned around and ran up the staircase, past the oversized statue of Lenin, past the

Soviet flag. He disappeared into a dark room above. The others sat, looking off to the side.

We waited for a bit.

'Smoke?' The Cossack flicked an American cigarette lighter.

'Yes, thank you,' said Nico, simpering. We waited for a bit longer. The Cossack looked at the floor, shamed by this lack of military precision.

Eventually the boy with the machine gun came running back down, panting. 'The press spokesman will see you,' he said.

We followed him back up the stairs, down a long hallway, and through a series of anterooms. I had been in dozens of office buildings like this – every Communist country had them. In each room, a portrait of Lenin hung on the wall; a secretary sat surrounded by telephones at a wide desk; a window looked out onto an identical building across the street. In the Soviet Union, the most important officials always had the most telephones, for the same reason that the most important officials often had faxes and copying machines in their offices, even though it meant that their secretaries could not use them. At the same time, the officials' shelves were empty of books, papers, and filing cabinets. Technology was power, but the appearance of activity was weakness.

The boy with the machine gun left us sitting beside a secretary who seemed less than pleased to see us. She looked up from her magazine, sighed deeply, and picked up the receiver of a red telephone.

'Guests are here to see you,' she mumbled into the speaker, and returned to her magazine.

We waited for a few more minutes. The secretary closed her magazine, and turned her chair to face the window. Over her shoulder I could see that she was filing her long red nails.

At last a voice rang out from behind the high wooden doors. Nico leaped to his feet.

'Enter,' came the voice from inside.

We pushed open the doors, and there, at the far end of a long table, sat one of Gogol's *chinovniks*: a Russian bureaucrat. His face was shapeless, his chin lacked definition, his hair was scant, his eyes were beady, his clothing was bland. Like the prefect in *The Government*

Inspector, he spoke neither too loudly nor too quietly, neither too much nor too little.

'The president,' he pronounced, 'is having his birthday. Unfortunately, he will not finish with his celebratory lunch until this afternoon, and I am afraid' – he smiled weakly – 'that he will not be in quite the right mood to receive visitors.'

As if on cue, an echo reached us from a distant room: applause, cheers, the clinking of vodka glasses. The press spokesman smiled again.

'Background, only background. I can give you only background,' he said, and he launched into a short speech about the goals of the new independent state of Transdniestria.

'We want independence and peace,' he said. 'Peace with all of our neighbors. But we do not want to be part of Moldova. We are not Moldovans. This is not Moldovan land, and it never has been.'

Nico leaned back and glowered at him with open hostility.

Tiraspol, he said, had been founded by the Russians in 1792, shortly after the Russian victory over Turkey. Catherine the Great had ordered it. Tiraspol had been a planned city, a fortress town built by soldiers; even today its streets ran at right angles to one another, like the streets of Manhattan.

'Before Tiraspol,' he said, 'there was nothing here, nothing at all. No one, no people, no culture, no history. Russia founded Transdniestria.'

Nico sighed ostentatiously.

The press spokesman eyed him.

'My dear man,' he said, 'where are you from?'

'Bucharest,' said Nico.

'Ah,' said the vice-president, and he turned away from Nico and kept speaking to me.

The whole region, he said, had been called Novorossiya, New Russia. Once, Novorossiya stretched all the way from Tiraspol to Kherson, down to Odessa and the Black Sea. It had been a Russian colony, like the Russian colonies in Alaska and California. Catherine the Great herself grew interested in Novorossiya, sent some of her favorite courtiers to become governors. Russian aristocrats came to Novorossiya and began to farm large estates; Russian merchants came to trade; Russians built up the economy from scratch.

'There was nothing here before Russia came, no culture, no history,' he repeated.

It was too much for Nico.

'There were Romanians here,' he said, his voice dark with fury. 'Moldovan princes. An ancient civilization. An ancient language.'

The press spokesman turned to me with a sigh of regret. 'These Romanians, such hotheaded nationalists! Always getting things wrong.' He turned back to Nico.

'A few peasants in a few poor shacks do not make a culture,' he said. 'When the conquistadors came to America, they found Red Indians. When Russians came here, they found Moldovans.'

'Were you born here in Transdniestria?' I asked the press spokesman.

There was a long silence.

'No, not exactly.' He explained, rather weakly, that his father had been a captain in the navy, that his family had moved around.

'And what did you do before coming here?'

The press spokesman began to mumble. His former job, he admitted, had been quite different from his present job. Until recently, he had been a Latin American expert. He had studied Spanish in Moscow, and taught history to Cubans and Nicaraguans at Kishinev University – until the Kishinev authorities closed the department for educating foreign students.

'Silly of them,' he sniffed. 'They could be earning foreign currency with it right now.'

'And how long have you lived here, in Tiraspol?'

'Oh,' he hesitated, 'quite a while now.'

'But when exactly did you come?'

There was another silence.

'Two years ago,' he confessed.

At once the press spokesman's peculiar story fit into a pattern. Like Dobrynin, the odd Pole I had met in Brest, the press spokesman of the president of Transdniestria was almost certainly a spoiler, someone who had been sent to Tiraspol to cause trouble for independent

Moldova. Perhaps he had been planted by someone; perhaps he and his friends, afraid of losing their jobs teaching Cubans and Nicaraguans, had come of their own accord. It was hard to say – so many people might have had an interest in causing trouble for Moldova. A skirmish between local Russians and local Moldovans could do wonders for the morale of the Russian Fourteenth Army, stationed nearby; a bit of trouble could help the cause of Russian nationalists in Moscow. It could even give the new Moldovan government in Kishinev an excuse to arm itself, to rally the population behind it.

From the same distant room came more sounds of clinking glass.

'And how long has the president himself lived here?'

'Same as I,' said the press spokesman. 'Two years.'

'Thank you,' I said.

We left, walking down the stairs and back out to the plaza where Lenin stood. Before returning to Kishinev, we stopped in a sordid, smoky bar and drank a Russian soft drink. It tasted like dirty water with food coloring poured into it.

For a few minutes, Nico worked himself up into a fervor about the iniquities of Russia and loudly advocated the Moldovan character of Transdniestria: 'Transdniestria, our Transdniestria, will belong to Romania one day.' He slammed his fist on the table.

It seemed like too much emotion to expend on grubby, ugly Tiraspol. I eyed Nico, remembered that Russians were not the only ones with agents, and wondered who had sent him to Kishinev.

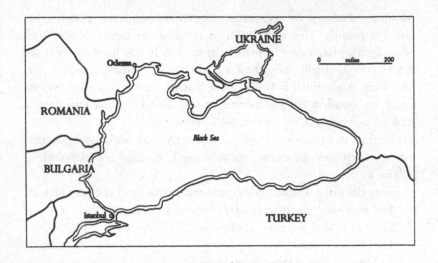

Odessa

I lived then, in Odessa
There the skies are always clear,
There trade is always bustling ...
The tongues of Golden Italy
Resound happily across the pavement
Where haughty Slavs parade, with
French, Spaniards, Armenians, and Greeks,
beside the ponderous Moldovan
and the son of Egyptian soil ...
                    – Pushkin, Eugene Onegin

From the train window, I watched the low Moldovan hills recede behind me. The vineyards gave way to swamp and marsh, the villages gave way to an impoverished urban sprawl. After a while, sprawl gave way to city. Disembarking at the Odessa station, I saw a sailor in a blue uniform and cap walking with his arm around a green-eyed girl. Quite suddenly, the sad tragedy of Transdniestria, the peculiarity of Kishinev, the claustrophobia of Chernivtsi and Kamenets seemed to

274

melt away: I had reached the sea. The early November light was cold and bright, and the wind smelled of salt.

In the city center, people walked quickly while the traffic moved slowly, impeded by broken cobblestones and potholes. The place-names told the city's history: Italianskaya Street, Hevrayokaya Street, Bulgarskaya Street, Grecheskaya Street. There was a 'French Boule-vard' and a Moldovan quarter, a side street named for Odessa's former Albanian colony, and another named for the 'little Russians,' the Ukrainians. Odessa had always possessed an odd population. A nineteenth-century traveler, A. Kuprin, described the city port:

'From the ships to the docks and warehouses and back across the quivering gangways the loaders ran to and fro, Russian tramps in rags, almost naked, with drunken, swollen faces; swarthy Turks in dirty turbans, with large trousers, loose to the knees but tight from there to the ankles; squat, muscular Persians, their hair and nails painted a red-carrot color with quinquina ...'

High, elegant town houses lined the streets. Each facade differed from its neighbor, in the eclectic manner of czarist Russia, in the style that was not really a style. One house might have an Ionic column, a Byzantine arch, and brass knockers on its door; the next house might have high Gothic windows, a round tower with a pointed roof, and a grand staircase. Classicism mixed with the exuberance and color of Ottoman Turkey to produce a jumble of forms and proportions. The resulting buildings were inconsistent, disproportionate, even ugly at times, but in Odessa they seemed right.

It was, in fact, the first beautiful Russian city I had ever seen. Although Odessa is often compared unfavorably with St Petersburg, I much preferred Odessa. While St Petersburg overdressed itself in pal-aces and boulevards and oversized monuments to the czar, Odessa's merchants built their city to a human scale. While St Petersburg strove self-consciously to be a great European capital, Odessa never pretended to be anything but *nouveau riche*. St Petersburg was constructed by slaves, who died by the thousands; Odessa was built by Black Sea mer-chants and traders.

Mark Twain came to Odessa in the nineteenth century and said he felt as if he were home. 'It looked just like an American city,' he wrote:

Fine, broad streets, and straight as well ... a familiar new look about the houses and everything; yes, and a driving and smothering cloud of dust that was so like a message from our own dear native land that we could hardly refrain from shedding a few grateful tears and exe-crations in the old time-honored American way. Look up the street or down the street, this way or that way, we saw only America! There was not one thing to remind us of Russia ...

Twain was right: there was nothing very Russian about Odessa. Until the end of the eighteenth century, a small Turkish fort called Khadzhibei sat on the site. In 1791 the mercenary Don Joseph de Ribas – born in Naples, of Spanish and Irish blood – captured the fort on behalf of Catherine the Great. Because of its deep port, she then declared it should be renamed Odessa, after an ancient Greek fishing village nearby, and made the city the capital of Novorossiya, her new Russian colony on the Black Sea. With the help of a Dutch architect, Franz de Voland, De Ribas began to build.

Foreigners founded the city; foreigners developed it. The first not-able governor of Odessa was Armand-Emmanuel, duc de Richelieu, a grandnephew of the great cardinal and an exile from revolutionary France. He built churches and schools and broad, Parisian boule-vards; later he went back to France and served, twice, as prime minister. The next governor was Count Mikhail Vorontsov, a Russian Anglophile who had attended Cambridge, kept an English secretary and an English butler, gave his orders in English, and lived in what he believed to be English splendor. During his reign, Odessa's streets were paved with tile imported from Trieste.

Odessa grew in the nineteenth century, at the same time as Amer-ica's cities grew, and Odessa was settled by immigrants in an American way: Frenchmen, Spaniards, Polish refugees, Italian sailors, Greek merchants, Turkish traders, and Jews all wanted to live in Russia's only free port. Runaway Russian serfs called 'know-nothings' (if you asked about their ancestry, they would shrug and say 'I don't know') became some of the city's greatest merchants. Odessa was lawless and free, and it acquired the kind of unsafe reputation enjoyed by Missis-sippi river ports like Hannibal, Missouri. It was big and dirty, not the kind of place where an established family would want to live. Smugglers and criminals inhabited its suburbs; sailors and traders filled its cheap hotels. Russian writers and poets went to Odessa when the constraints and the censors in St Petersburg and Moscow grew too harsh. Mickiewicz spent part of his Russian exile in Odessa, and Pushkin served as a state official there until his affair with Countess Vorontsova, the governor general's wife, became too embarrassing for Odessa society. After the Revolution, the city became a haven of sorts. Afraid of the purges in Moscow and Leningrad, the Russian intelligentsia – filmmakers, writers, poets, academics – fled to Odessa. Enough survived to give Odessa the best comic film studio in the Soviet Union, the best poets, and the best musicians.

Once they had arrived, hardly anyone ever left Odessa. Life was easier there. The city's markets were always full of fruits and vegetables. Even in the worst times, tourists from Moscow went home carrying baskets filled with grapes and pomegranates, sweet melons and purple pears. Odessans let vines grow on the roofs of their houses and made their own wine. Odessans sat by the sea in the summer, and in the winter they admired the snow on their beautiful opera house.

Walking around the streets, a phrase lodged itself in my mind: 'the wind of freedom.' In Odessa, one felt as if something like that – the wind of freedom – was in the air. Perhaps it was the presence of the sea, visible from Primorsky Boulevard, the tree-lined promenade that ran along the city's ocean-front. Or perhaps it was that, unlike so many other Russian cities, Odessa had not been built for the sake of a cause.

Peter the Great built St Petersburg to thrust Russia into Europe, and to show the world the extent of his power he insulated the thick walls of the Hermitage with the bodies of the palace builders. Stalin constructed Kaliningrad to erase the memory of Germany, and to discourage the Germans from returning he bombed their monuments and banished their street names. But money – trading money, smuggling money, shipping money – had paid for the carefully laid streets and the orderly parks in Odessa.

Nationalism of any kind was impossible in Odessa, impossible to imagine and impossible to enforce. The Ukrainian national movement had tried to organize demonstrations in the city square and was laughed down. Who spoke Ukrainian in Odessa? Yet even when Russians agitated for the re-creation of Novorossiya, no one cared either. Everyone in Odessa spoke Russian, but what did that mean? Who could be anything at all in Odessa except Odessan?

'Call me Stan,' said Stanislav, 'most English-speakers do.' In a brand-new underground restaurant lit by tall candles, Stan ordered caviar, smoked fish, and white wine. The tables and chairs were made of shiny American plastic, the walls glistened with fresh paint, but the waiter took his time about it.

Stan was the last scion of a long line of Bavarian bakers. His square-jawed ancestors had arrived in Odessa in 1804, attracted by high wages, low taxes, and a concession to bake all the bread for the new city. They had joined the other Germans – the brewers, the butchers, the grocers, the tinsmiths, the ironmongers – in the German district of the city. Together they built red brick churches and solid schools where their children would read Goethe. That lasted until the 1930s, when the Germans of Odessa were packed onto trains and shipped to Kazakhstan. Stan's grandfather spent the rest of his life building the road from Tashkent to Tehran.

In Kazakhstan, Stan's mother had married another Odessa German. Still, she felt a prick of Slavic sentiment when it came to naming her own son. Her first lover, Stanisław, had been a Pole.

'But my father is my father,' said Stan. One could see that it was true: his angular, German face had nothing Slavic about it.

After Stalin died, it seemed natural for Stan's parents to move back to Odessa. Now they lived outside the city, on a road which ran to the coast, and Stan and his father ran a vague sort of business. The business had a post office box and foreign bank accounts: 'We do import-export,' said Stan. The business made it easy to travel. When Stan went abroad he didn't have to carry cash or things to trade, because he could go to any bank when he arrived and get out his own money. Customs officials always searched him, looking for the undeclared currency or the sacks of gold that any normal Russian going abroad would need to survive.

Once, Stan had gone to visit people who he thought were his relatives in Bavaria. When they opened the door and saw Stan, the family were surprised. When they learned who Stan claimed to be, they were cautious, thinking he might want money. When they had compared family trees and birth certificates and legends and discovered that the link was real, they had tears in their eyes.

They were still bakers.

Stan's German relatives begged him to come back. They told him about the right of return: anyone who could prove German ancestry could become a German citizen. They offered to help him. But Stan shook his head.

'I love Odessa,' he told them. 'I am not a German anymore, I am an Odessan.'

Odessa, he told me, was an open city, it might still become anything at all. Bavaria was closed, its history was already written. Stan had no interest in Bavaria. Bavaria seemed to be a step backward.

He smiled, and swept his muscular arm around the restaurant, taking in the dark-skinned men whispering over green bottles, the painted women eyeing their overdressed partners, the slothful waiters, the plates stacked high with food, the glinting cups filled with wine.

'Who could bear to leave this?'

In the afternoon, I went to visit Larisa. Larisa shared her surname with Władysław Sikorski, a famous Polish general, but the family history didn't match. The general's family came from Mazovia, near Warsaw; her family came from Kujawy, in western Poland. But Larisa was certain of the relationship. 'When I was a child,' she told me, 'my father once took me aside, sat me down, and made a drawing of our coat of arms. He told me to look at it carefully; he told me to memorize it; he told me it was the same coat of arms as the general. Then he tore it up into shreds and told me not to tell anyone else.'

She laughed. Larisa spoke her mother's Russian instead of her father's Polish, but the idea of a distant connection to the famous Polish general amused her. One never knew. Someday a relative would turn up with pots of gold and rescue them all.

Larisa and her husband had moved into their apartment several days earlier, but they had not gotten around to unpacking. Bits of antique furniture – tired wooden chairs, a chipped credenza, an unreasonably heavy desk – stood at odd angles to one another around the apartment, unsure of their proper relationships. Unfinished canvases covered with wild, bright colors lay strewn among them. Larisa's husband was a painter, and a musician of sorts. He had long hair and a long mustache. He wrote songs and played them on his guitar. Sometimes he played them for his friends, but never for money; he didn't need money, he said. He told me that Russia's great balladeer Vysotski had stolen his style and his melodies from Odessa.

'Vysotski sings sailors' songs and prison songs,' he said, 'Odessa songs.'

Larisa herself taught architecture at the university. Her colleagues, she said, were in a panic. 'The university is now supposed to be a Ukrainian university, but no one speaks Ukrainian.' She described the old rector rushing about, tearing his hair out, begging for someone to translate his letters to Kiev. 'He was out of his mind,' she said, and began laughing. 'Oh, my,' she said, wiping her eyes, 'it was very funny.'

Larisa yawned and then apologized. She had had to wake up to teach a class early that morning, but tomorrow she would be able to sleep late. 'Laziness,' she told me, 'is my family's curse.' When she had been younger, she had been very ambitious. She had wanted to build houses, to redesign streets, to be a success at the university. But now, why bother? She had plenty of friends, plenty to eat, plenty to drink. Most of the time the weather was good in Odessa.

Politics perplexed her. 'I am Polish, he is Jewish, and we have been living together for thirty years,' Larisa told me, pointing at her husband. 'In all of that time I have never figured out what makes him different from me.'

Ivan lived in Odessa, and spoke perfect, flat, midwestern English.

He appeared not to think much of his achievement. Languages were easy to learn, he said; even a child could speak Russian, Polish, and Ukrainian. But when pressed, he admitted that few others in Odessa could match his accent.

'Those jerks at the polytechnic, they teach theoretical phonetics, theoretical grammar, the history of linguistics, and dialectical materialism, and they can't speak a word of English. I had to quit.'

When pressed, he admitted that he had mastered English by listening night after night to US Armed Forces Radio, back when he was working as a 'Soviet technical assistant' in North Vietnam. Those hours spent over the wireless (you could hardly call it a radio) were the only enjoyable moments of his military service.

Vietnam itself had seemed terrible to him. In the course of fulfilling his internationalist duty, he once had to parachute out of an airplane. He was so frightened that he fainted dead away in the air, and woke up the next morning in a hospital. The nurse told him that he had been discovered hanging from a tree.

Another time he saw American prisoners of war, who begged him to write a letter to the president of the United States. They had stopped dreaming of freedom, and only wanted Ivan to ask the president to ask the Vietnamese to give them more food.

Nowadays Ivan kept his American slang up to date with the help of Frank and Ida, his pen pals. Fred and Ida owned a grocery store somewhere in Pennsylvania and wrote him letters every week. Ivan had also purchased, at great expense, a book titled *American Colloquialisms*. From this, he had learned expressions like 'cool dude' with which he peppered his speech.

Recently he had stopped answering his telephone, although it rang, incessantly. Everyone in Odessa needed something translated these days – a scientific paper or, more likely, a visa application. And in all of Odessa, a city of several hundred thousand, nobody could match Ivan's English.

'I think I know all the Jewish families in Odessa, y'know?' he said. 'I have translated all of their visa applications.'

Ivan could have been a rich man if he wanted to be. They offered him bribes to speed up their visa applications: money, vodka, ham, sausage, even their daughters. Ivan preferred to stay honest. He took everyone in turn and always charged the same fee. He didn't need the money.

'I am not much of a restaurant-goer,' he said.

Stacks of applications to America were piled in a corner of his sitting room. They all said the same things: 'a child teased for being Jewish at school' or 'nasty comments made about Jews at work.' The applicants had to prove that they had been victims of anti-Semitic persecution before America would let them in. Ivan snorted.

'Who wasn't a victim of persecution in the Soviet Union? My father was a victim because he owned too much land, so Stalin sent him to Siberia. I am a victim because I speak English too well, and my colleagues hate me. My wife is a victim because her husband is a private translator, and her colleagues hate her.'

Before, being Jewish was nothing, just like belonging to a large extended family or a club. Now it was something to be used. Ivan was cynical.

'Anyway, the Americans don't really care whether some anti-Semitic bastard threw rocks at your kid. They wanna know how many relatives you have in Brighton Beach, and if your relatives got big bucks, you got a visa.'

America bored him. All of these people so anxious to get there – and then what? 'They all go and live in a part of New York called Little Odessa,' he told me. 'And they try to make everything there the same as it was here.'

Quite suddenly I realized that the weather had turned. Only a few days before, the wind had seemed warm and southerly, a Balkan breeze. Overnight it began to blow cold, and in the morning I could no longer walk comfortably on the street. Taxis were much harder to come by in the changed weather, and the frustration involved in finding one far outweighed the satisfaction of stopping one. The buses were overcrowded; the stuffy air inside the trams smelled of sour, moth-eaten fur. Dust and heat had given way to the sharp smell of burning coal and early darkness. When someone cursed the Soviet Union, when someone else said, 'Things are better in America, are they not?' I found that I no longer had the strength to pretend to disagree.

It was time to go home.

At the Intourist office I was assured that Odessa was virtually impossible to leave. 'There is a train to Bucharest, of course,' said a woman with bright red lipstick and bright red hair to match. She was cheerful, full of advice, and thoroughly incompetent.

'Let's see,' she consulted an ancient timetable, 'that train runs only on Tuesdays and Thursdays, so that means three days from now. You must be at the station at three in the morning. Once you arrive at the border, you must wait fourteen hours, not leaving the station. After Bucharest, the train then goes on to Przemyśl in southern Poland. Then you must wait there for, let me see – four and a half hours while they change the wheels.' As a precaution against rapid invasion, Soviet trains ran on wider tracks than Western trains.

She continued, enjoying the complexities. The Soviet Union had ended; the miseries of Soviet travel had not. 'The train continues to Warsaw after that, but it is only a slow one, I am afraid. You reach Warsaw the following morning. There is a faster one, but you must wait until the following day. And I can only sell you the ticket from here to Bucharest. No farther.'

The Bucharest–Warsaw routes, she said, were famed for their gangs of clever young thieves.

'Perhaps there is an airplane?'

She picked up another worn timetable, this one marked with a barely readable sticker: AEROFLOT. She consulted the back, then the front, then the back again. No one had ever asked her about air-planes before. Finally she concluded: 'There aren't any international flights from Odessa. Perhaps you would like to go to Moscow?'

I shook my head.

She picked up the train schedule again and scanned the table of contents: 'Wait, let me see . . . perhaps you could take the train direct to Warsaw. From Odessa there is direct train, every day, straight to Warsaw and Berlin. Just one night and you're there.'

'Can you sell me a ticket?'

She sighed. 'I am very sorry, I cannot. Our allotment of those tickets has been sold out for the past six months. Why don't you try the railway station?'

But at the railway station, the line for tickets abroad snaked all the way around the central hallway. People had brought pillows and blankets to lie on while they waited two, three, four days.

Three times in three hours I told three different men that I had to have a ticket to Warsaw, I had to go home immediately. The authorities in Moscow and Kiev wanted me to go home, my visa would run out, and the Odessa Railway Administration would be held responsible.

The first man had drooping, doggy eyes, and he told me that he would like to help me, he would love to help me, but he could not help me.

The second man wore a mustache and said it was not his responsibility.

The third man appeared genuinely frightened by the threat of the authorities in Moscow and Kiev, but an hour of telephone calls failed to yield a train ticket. After making the last one, he leaned over and whispered something to me.

'What?'

'The mafia,' he said. 'You will not get a ticket whatever you do.' There was nothing to do but wait until evening and try to bribe your way on, he said. Fifty dollars should do it, and if it didn't work on one day it might work the next. I would have to keep trying.

Furious, I gave up on the Odessa Railway Administration. I left the train station, pushed my way out of its oversized front doors, and walked back down the cobbled streets, past the markets, past the town hall and the statue of Pushkin, down the boulevard, and toward the port.

The sea was cold and gray, the same color as the sky; the gulls shouted their loneliness into the wind. Beside the sagging docks, a gaggle of scrawny fishing boats huddled together for warmth.

Boats. Of course – there was another way to get home.

Epilogue

Weeping, sobbing, pleading, the woman in the customs line begged forgiveness. Just beyond the barrier lay the ship; she could see it, she could practically touch it, but the border guard would not let her through.

'*Nyet!*' he shouted for the third time.

He had discovered dollar bills sewed into one of her bags.

The woman wailed again, opening her mouth wide; she had but a single tooth. Her possessions lay around her in little piles, the washed-up flotsam and jetsam of a Soviet life. She had boxes made of cardboard, tied with frayed, secondhand string, and suitcases so full of old clothes that thick belts had to be buckled around them to prevent the seams from splitting. In one hand she carried a rusty cage; three bedraggled parakeets sat inside. In the other hand she carried a girl child no less frightened than the birds. A frayed scarf wound itself around the woman's neck; another twisted its way around her broad waist.

She had dark hair and deep, dark mascara lines drawn around her eyes. Everyone else in the line looked at her with disgust.

'Gypsy,' whispered someone behind me.

After some time, she gave up pleading and glared at the guard instead. He glared at her back. Finally they reached a truce: he collected her dollars, she was allowed on the boat. Slowly, as if to irritate him and everyone else as much as possible, she gathered her multi-colored belongings and shuffled haughtily onto the boat, dragging her parakeets and her child behind her.

I was next. The guard looked me up and down.

'Going where? Yalta?'

'Istanbul.'

He took my passport out of my hand without asking. He turned it over once, saw that it was American, and immediately lost interest.

'What have you got? One bag? Go ahead.'

Whatever problems foreigners once posed for Soviet border officials have long disappeared. With *glasnost*, the ban on subversive literature ended, and these days foreigners had no limits on the amount of currency they could carry, so foreigners could not be accused of exceeding the limits and foreigners could not be forced to give up their currency to border officials. Ukrainians, on the other hand, could be made to pay.

I caught up to the bedraggled woman. Before stepping on the boat she mumbled a prayer, crossed herself, and made her daughter cross herself, too. Then she turned in the direction of the customs official, mumbled something else – another prayer? a curse? – turned in his direction, and spat.

Someone optimistic had named the ship *Yunost*; it meant *Youth*. In the ticket hall, photographs had shown its gleaming white bow, its polished brass fixtures, its gay red flags, yellow stars, hammers and sickles.

'A very good ship, very high quality,' the ticket girl had said. 'Many foreigners take it. I will give you a ladies' cabin, plenty of space inside, plenty of light.'

But *Youth* had long passed its prime. Its corridors were dark and damp, its decks reeked of sea and old fish. Mold grew on its walls, and the public bathrooms were covered in green slime and black dirt. My cabin contained two bunk beds and nothing else; there was no room for anything else.

The air smelled stale. I put my things on a lower bunk and tried to open the porthole. As I tugged on it, a slovenly woman and a foul-smelling man walked in the door.

'Hey, you,' the woman said. 'Get off that lower bunk.'

I turned to look at them. Her enormous hips drooped over the top of her stretch trousers; his thin hands shook from too much alcohol. Both were sucking on the same brand of cheap cigarette. Their faces were obscured by thick blue smoke.

Pride stirred.

'Why should I?'

'It belongs to us.'

The woman glared at me, her tiny pig eyes narrowing in her fat face, and repeated herself:

'I said, it belongs to us.'

Her husband was already dragging their possessions into the room, seven enormous canvas bags filled with things to trade in Istanbul. I saw why they wanted lower bunks: more storage space underneath.

But the top bunks were hard to climb on to. And I had arrived first.

'No,' I said, looking at the husband. 'I thought this was supposed to be a ladies' cabin.'

'You are wrong,' the woman said. She spun a long tale about ticket numbers.

'Even-numbered tickets get lower bunks, odd-numbered tickets get upper bunks.' It was absurd – there were no numbers written on any of the bunks.

Her husband cursed and lit a cigarette.

'No,' I said again, feeling childish.

'Dirty foreigner,' the woman said, and began throwing her belongings onto my bed.

I threw them back onto the floor.

She threw them back again.

It was too much. Win or lose, I couldn't spend two days with her. I got up, took my bag, and walked down the corridor, knocking on every cabin door, looking for an extra bed.

There was one available, on the lower deck. The room was even smaller than the first, the beds squeezed more tightly together, and there was no chair. But the three Lithuanian ladies who shared it were neat, well-dressed, and disapproving of the other passengers.

'Russians,' they sniffed, when I told them about my previous cabinmates.

But they were smuggling, too. Everyone on the boat was smuggling, except for two prostitutes. The Lithuanian ladies told me that things were getting harder in their country, everything was expensive. Boat trips like this one were still cheap, you could still pay in rubles. They clucked in horror when I told them I had paid $30 for my ticket. The whole trip – train to Odessa, boat to Turkey – was costing them less than $10.

It was worth it, to see Istanbul and make some money on the side.

In the evening, we four dined in the dining room, a low-ceilinged affair without windows. There was a single sullen waitress for fifty passengers. After a long wait, she brought us four thin bowls of sour soup. The Lithuanian ladies tasted it, made faces, and put their spoons to the side. All three of them claimed to be feeling seasick.

'Oh, my stomach.'

'Oh, this terrible food.'

After another long wait, the waitress then brought four pieces of scrawny chicken. The Lithuanian ladies sighed, picked at the chicken, and put their forks down, too.

'Inedible,' one of them said.

'Inedible,' another agreed.

After an even longer wait, the waitress brought a bottle of wine. The Lithuanian ladies stiffened their backs with disapproval.

'I'd drink it if I were you,' said the waitress. 'You won't get another.'

Finally one of them gave in and ate her chicken. The others watched her. 'I'm hungry,' she said plaintively. And she ate the chicken from her two companions' plates as well.

All around us, the other passengers emitted the joyous noises Russians make when released from home. One table opened a bottle of champagne and cheered when it sprayed the table beside it. Nearby, the two prostitutes crossed their legs and giggled when the men beside them told rude jokes. An older woman and her daughter, dressed in identical pink evening dresses, sat alone, distraught. Shiny plastic earrings dangled from their ears. Light blue paint covered their eyelids; their lips and cheeks glowed crimson.

'They told us there would be dancing,' the daughter said forlornly.

All night the boat groaned. It groaned when it hit a wave. It groaned when the wind blew. Sleep was out of the question.

In the morning the air was cold, the sea was gray, and fog shrouded the horizon. Still, outside was better than the stuffy cabins. The Lithuanian ladies wrapped themselves in blankets and lay on old deck chairs. I joined them, and, after a few minutes, another woman did, too.

'May I?'

'Yes, yes,' the Lithuanians said, but looked suspicious.

She quickly won them over. She said that she was from a place I had never heard of: a tiny autonomous republic in the Caucasian Mountains. She was a Russian, but she was married to a local man. She took out a piece of paper and sketched him.

'Like this,' she said, and she drew two slanted lines. Then she drew a picture of her house. It had several layers and a top like a Chinese pagoda.

The Lithuanian ladies oohed and aahed.

She was going to Istanbul to buy a coat for her daughter. There were no coats in the Caucasus, and the coats in Odessa were too expensive. In Istanbul there would be a coat, so she would go to Istanbul and then catch another boat back again across the Black Sea.

She and the Lithuanian ladies spoke about trading in the Istanbul markets. None had done it before. The woman from the tiny autonomous republic felt very confident of her success, because she had brought caviar and gold. Her deep voice boomed across the water.

'Caviar and gold, caviar and gold go a long way anywhere.' The others looked out at the sea. They had brought children's toys, small appliances; they were less confident.

One of the Lithuanian ladies had seen the television on the day before.

'Lithuania has declared independence,' she said.

No one said anything. After a while, all of them got up to go inside.

'Too cold,' they agreed.

I stayed, wrapped the blankets tighter, tried to read, and fell asleep in the fog.

I awoke to feel a damp hand on my arm. I thought it was an insect, slapped it, and looked up. A tall, youngish man was grinning at me. I recognized him – he had opened the champagne bottle in the dining room.

'Come sit with us,' he said. 'It must be boring to sit here all alone.'

His name was Arkady. He and Nikolai, his partner, made the trip from Odessa to Istanbul every month; they were smugglers.

I followed him up to the bar on the top deck. No one seemed to be allowed to sit there except the professionals. They sat at a single round table.

'Ania, meet Nikolai, Dima, Vanya, Alexey, Mitya.'

All six of them wore Italian shoes and expensive, pastel-colored cotton sweaters, the kind one would see in advertisements featuring wealthy blond Bostonians. They had carefully trimmed hair and clean socks – it seemed to be part of the uniform. In Odessa, if you were bright and you wanted to get ahead, you became a smuggler.

In the center of the table stood a bottle of vodka, but Arkady said they could get anything. 'Anything. Anything you want. You want Irish whiskey, you can have Irish whiskey. You want French brandy, you can have French brandy.'

I started to mumble something about not drinking in the morning, but Nikolai interrupted.

'You are a Pole,' he accused me. 'You speak Russian with a Polish accent. You are not an American.'

Nikolai had a long knife scar drawn across his forehead. I showed him my passport.

'Fake,' pronounced Nikolai. His eyes were already unfocused from the drink.

The waitress brought a tray full of drinks: another bottle of vodka for the boys, a bottle of French brandy for me.

'See, I told you so,' Arkady crowed. 'Anything, we can get you anything on this ship. Go ask for it downstairs – they won't have it. Go ask the captain – he won't have it. Ask us, we can get it.'

Dima was perched on the arm of a chair. His torso was slightly swaying, and his pupils were dilated. He disapproved of me. He disapproved of Americans. He disapproved even more when he heard where I had been.

'Vilnius? Minsk? L'viv? Those aren't real cities,' Dima spat over the railing. 'Vilnius – without us, Vilnius would be nothing. Vilnius is a Russian city, Russian. It was built with Russian architects. Nothing Lithuanian about it.'

He was infuriated by the Lithuanian declaration of independence.

'Lithuania, what is it? A Russian colony. We practically invented it. It was hardly a country, no one ever heard of it before.'

Nor was Dima pleased with the idea of me writing a book about my journey.

'What do you know about Russia? You can't write a book about Russia. Why didn't you go to Novgorod? To Sverdlovsk? To Volgograd? Those are real, Russian cities. You can't write a book about Russia if you haven't been there. You know nothing about Russia.'

The book, I said, would not be about Russia.

'What? You write about Lithuania? Ukraine? Those are not real places, those are places we invented. Russians built Lithuania, Russians built Ukraine. Why did you not go to Leningrad? To our Leningrad, to our St Petersburg? It was the greatest city in the world until the Bolsheviks wrecked it. London, Paris – they were nothing beside St Petersburg. People came to St Petersburg to learn how to live. Our literature, it was the greatest literature in the world. Our ruble, it was the strongest currency in the world, much stronger than your dollar,' he pronounced. 'Back then, your dollar was nothing.'

Dima admired the West, he said, but it held nothing for him.

'The West. Nonsense! Do you know who built Oxford University? A Russian prince! And who paid for Heidelberg University, and who paid for the Sorbonne? Russians! All Russians! Russians were your greatest patrons, you in the West. We helped build your civilization, you have become great thanks to our knowledge and our money. Do you know who built your space shuttle? Do you know? Russian scientists! Reagan said so – or maybe it was Bush. Russian scientists!'

'Maybe,' said Nikolai, 'that was why it crashed.'

Everybody laughed except Dima, who slumped back into his chair, furious. A waitress appeared, bringing coffee.

'You want to learn about our country, Anushka?' asked Arkady. This was a Russian gathering, so we were already past first names and on to nicknames.

'Look, there is no coffee on this ship. Everyone has asked for coffee, yet it is not available. The captain cannot get coffee. The crew cannot get coffee. But we can get coffee! This is our system, this is how it works!'

He talked of his country's peculiarities with fondness, as if speaking about an eccentric friend.

'A friend of mine moved to New York. He writes me strange things. He says that when he tries to speak to a pretty girl on the street, she becomes offended and tells him to go away. In Odessa, you can do that – you can go up to a girl, ask her to come and have a coffee, and if she likes your face she will go. If she doesn't, she will tell you so. But she will not be offended. That is how our system works.'

On the other side of the table, the other smugglers traded names of shops in Istanbul.

'Don't go to that one, that one cheats you,' said Mitya.

'Watch out for the customs man in the port, the one with the gold rings,' said Vanya. 'He stole money from me last time around.'

'Go to his office and drink tea,' advised Mitya. 'In Istanbul, just have tea with whoever bothers you. They won't cheat you so badly if they have had tea with you.'

'Not true, not true,' said Vanya. 'You drink tea with them, they cheat you worse.'

I asked Arkady about his visits to Istanbul. He had been there thirty-two times.

'Hagia Sophia?' Arkady twisted his tongue around the name. 'What is that?'

He knew about the Roman Empire in a vague sort of way. But he didn't know where it had been – perhaps in Greece? – or when it had existed or why it had fallen. He had heard the name Constantinople, too, but he was unaware of any connection to Istanbul.

'It's in a song,' I told him.

'They didn't teach us about any of that,' he said. 'We learned about Lenin, and the Revolution, and the Great Patriotic War. We didn't learn about Rome or Constantinople.'

He shrugged. Arkady had discarded the Communist world of his childhood, too, and when that was gone, there was – nothing.

'Sometimes I get so bored,' he told me later, 'sometimes I get so bored I want to die. You cannot imagine how bored. There is nothing to read, nothing to do, nothing to think about. All the time I have to worry about where to buy things, how to buy them, how to sell them. And finally – that is boring, too.'

The boat lurched sideways. The vodka glasses slid. Vanya and Mitya caught them, and proposed a toast to good trading in Istanbul. We all toasted.

'Anushka,' said Nikolai, 'you want to buy a leather coat? A really nice leather coat? In Istanbul you stick with us and we will get you a leather coat, very good price, unbeatable price. We know all the best places. Everyone wants to talk to Russians now, in Istanbul, there are so many of us, they know they will be doing business with us for many years.'

'Anushka,' asked Arkady, 'what is Canada like? My sister has married and moved to Canada. Is Canada the same as America?' The talk of Constantinople and Hagia Sophia had suddenly whetted his appetite for travel.

'Idiot,' jeered Nikolai. 'Canada is not the same as America. It is much smaller.'

'Actually,' I said, 'Canada is bigger.'

The conversation stopped for a bit while the smugglers contemplated a new idea: Canada bigger than America. Did that mean that Canada was more powerful than America? They had been taught that size equaled power.

Arkady and Nikolai fell to talking in admiring tones about the prostitutes. They agreed that the prostitutes were intelligent, well-bred – girls trying to make a living.

'The blond one, she has tried men of every nationality. Every nationality. The worst, she says, are Turks. And the best, she says, are

Russians. She still likes Russian men better than any others,' said Arkady, not without pride.

Somehow inspired by this statement, Dima picked himself up from his slump. He stood up, planting his feet firmly on the ground, and raised his glass to make a toast. Everyone stared at him, waiting.

'To Russia,' he said. 'Russia is the world's most civilized nation. Nobody is more civilized than we Russians. Here's to Russia.' He raised his glass higher:

'To Russia!'

And then he slumped down in his chair. 'We are nothing,' he mourned, 'nothing. We are nothing of what we were.' He fell silent.

'Dima is right,' said Nikolai thoughtfully. 'What is the difference between a peasant on the Volga and man living in an African jungle? Nothing, except that the African has sunlight, fresh air, clean water, and no ice in the winter.'

In the morning the boat was still moving, but the roar of the engine had dulled to a low hum. The voices of the sea gulls filtered through the tiny porthole. One of the Lithuanian women rolled over in her bunk and muttered something incomprehensible. I slipped off the upper bunk, dressed quickly, and walked out onto the deck. The rain had stopped, the cold air was behind us.

We had entered the Bosporus.

'*Prekrasno*,' said Nikolai. 'Wonderful.'

He stood alone on the bow. His eyes were creased with tiny veins, and he seemed to have slept in his clothes. The knife scar on his forehead looked red and angry, but he was smiling. 'I never miss it. I have done this trip maybe fifty, sixty times, but I never miss this sight.'

Silently we passed a Crusader castle, villas, cypress trees, a fishing village. Everything seemed to be made of rich, luxurious materials. The colors glowed: the white houses, green grass, and blue sky were so bright that they seemed to come from a postcard. After so many months of brown and gray it was hard to believe they were real. Bigger boats cruised by us, flying the flags of Britain, Germany, America, and France, emissaries from the wider world. The machinery on their decks seemed rich and shiny, the painted letters on their bows struck me as crisp and clear.

The *Yunost* glided beneath a bridge, and the city drew closer.

'*Prekrasno*,' said Nikolai again.

Ahead of us gleamed the minarets of Istanbul. I was back in the West.

A Note About Spelling

The spelling of place-names in Poland, Lithuania, Belarus, and Ukraine is a source of both endless fascination and endless trouble. Because the cities and towns of the borderlands were ruled by different nations at different times, the question of spelling is also highly politicized. The use of a particular spelling will always please one group at the expense of another.

To keep disputes to a minimum, I have followed a very simple set of rules. If speaking about a place in the past, I use the spelling that was used by the people who ruled at the time; hence the use of Wilno when speaking about Vilnius before the Second World War. If speaking about a place in the present, I use the spelling that the people I am talking to would use. Hence Hermaniszki, Bieniakonie, and Woroniaki (all Polish spellings), as well as L'viv, Chernivtsi, Bukovyna, and Drohobych (Ukrainian spellings) and Kamenets Podolsky (Russian spelling). Occasionally, spellings change within one chapter, most notably between Wilno and Vilnius, depending upon who is speaking.

I have used Belarus instead of Belorussia and Moldova instead of Moldavia, since those are the names that the people who live there prefer, and they are still recognizable to the English-speaking reader. The only exception I have made to this general rule is the decision to use Kishinev (the Russian spelling) instead of Chişinau (the Romanian spelling), because Kishinev is a familiar place to English-speaking readers, and it would not be recognizable at all in such a changed form.

The same rules are followed for names. Russian name spellings are used where people are speaking Russian (Svetlana, Nikolai), but Polish and Ukrainian name spellings are used where people are speaking Polish or Ukrainian (Władek, Liudmyla).

A Note About Sources

Dozens and dozens of books, pamphlets, and essays helped shape my understanding of the borderlands. Among those upon which I drew most substantially were the following. In writing the history of East Prussia, I found Michael Burleigh's essay 'The Knights, Nationalists and the Historians: Images of Medieval Prussia from the Enlightenment to 1945' (*European History Quarterly*, January 1987) to be especially helpful, along with his book *Germany Turns Eastwards* (Cambridge: Cambridge University Press, 1988). I also used Martin Brakas's *Lithuania Minor* (New York: Lithuanian Research Institute, 1976). I have taken quotations from Hans von Lehndorff's *East Prussian Diary* (London: Oswald Wolff, Ltd, 1963) as well as from *Documents on the Expulsion of the German Population from the Territories East of the Oder–Neisse Line* (Vol. I, ed. Theodore Scheider, trans. Dr Vivian Stranders, Bonn: Federal Ministry for Expellees, Refugees, and War Victims, 1958–61) and from Alexander Solzhenitsyn's *Prussian Nights* (trans. Robert Conquest, New York: Farrar, Straus, & Giroux, 1974).

In writing about the history of Poland and Lithuania, I relied upon Norman Davies's two-volume history of Poland, *God's Playground* (Boulder, Colo.: Colorado University Press, 1982), as well as Adam Zamoyski's *The Polish Way* (New York: Hippocrene Books, 1993) and Czesław Miłosz's *Native Realm* (Berkeley, Calif.: University of California Press, 1981). After I had written the chapter on Adam Mickiewicz, I came upon an essay by Miłosz in the September 1991 edition of the Polish émigré magazine *Kultura* that confirmed many of the stories I had heard about Mickiewicz and added some more. A collection of essays edited by Keith Sword, *The Soviet Take-over of the Polish Eastern Provinces* (New York: St Martin's Press, 1991), was also very useful. Quotations from Adam Mickiewicz's poetry come either from George Rapall Noyes's translations (New York: Dover, 1964) or from Kenneth Mackenzie's Polish-English edition of *Pan Tadeusz* (New York: Hippocrene Books, 1992), which was, in fact, the book I carried with me on my travels. Some translations of Mickiewicz and other Polish poets are my own.

In writing about Russia and Ukraine, my most important sources were Orest Subtelny's *Ukraine: A History* (Toronto: University of Toronto Press, 1988), Richard Pipes's *Russia Under the Old Regime* (New York: Scribners, 1976), Hugh Seton-Watson's *The Russian Empire* (New York: Oxford History of Modern Europe Series, 1967), and Robert Conquest's *The Harvest of Sorrow* (New York: Oxford University Press, 1987). Quotations are taken from the Marquis de Custine's *Empire of the Czar* (New York: Doubleday, 1989) and from the new English edition of Henryk Sienkiewicz's *Trilogy* (trans. W. S. Kuniczak, New York: Hippocrene Books, 1991), as well as the sources named above. Quotations from Taras Shevchenko come from *Song Out of Darkness*, Vera Rich's excellent collection of translations (London: Shevchenko Centenary Committee, 1961).

For the chapters on Belarus, I owe special thanks to the proprietors of the Francis Skaryna Library in London, who provided me with much help and advice. There I found a variety of books about the region, including William Coxe's *Travels in Poland, Russia, Sweden and Denmark* (London: T. Cadell and W. Davies in the Strand, 1784), E. Henderson's *Biblical Researches and Travels in Russia* (London: James Nisbet, 1826), W. R. Morfill's *Slavonic Literature* (London: Society for Promoting Christian Knowledge, 1883), and A. MacCallum Scott's *Beyond the Baltic* (London: Thornton Butterworth, Ltd., 1925). The most useful history of Belarus was Nicholas Vakar's *Belorussia: The Making of a Nation* (Cambridge, Mass.: Harvard University Press, 1956).

Acknowledgments

Many people helped me in many ways during my trips to Lithuania, Belarus, Ukraine, and Moldova. But a number of people deserve special mention.

In Lithuania, I want to thank Czesław Okińczyc, Janusz Obłaczynski, and Daiva Nilkelytė, as well as Edita Pukelytė for excellent translations, and Edward Lucas, for advice then and later. In Bieniakonie, Michał Wołoslewicz was a delightful host and gave me permission to use his poetry. In Minsk, Vitaly Zaika helped me with many things, but I want to thank him especially for a lovely afternoon at a Radziwiłł palace that was not, alas, described in this book. In L'viv, Władek and Irena Hrechorowicz were overwhelmingly hospitable, as they always are, and Ilyusha showed me the city, a week before he left for good. Thank you Andrei Markus, Father Andrzej Witek, Dmitri and Elena Apetri, and Stanislav Kislevich.

David Mehnert, Malcolm Gladwell, Terry Martin, and Paul Forty read early versions of this manuscript; Professors Norman Davies and Norman Stone made good suggestions later on, as did Mark Almond, Adam Zamoyski, Timothy Garton Ash, Chrystia Freeland, and Taras Kuzio. Linda Healey was an excellent editor, and Michael Carlisle a helpful agent. The Charles Douglas-Home Trust helped me return to Ukraine. My parents-in-law, Jan and Teresa Sikorski, tolerated long silences while I was writing at Chobielin. Thank you Harvey and Elizabeth Applebaum for moral support over many years; thank you Julie and Kathy Applebaum; thank you Daniel Franklin and Peter David for pretending not to mind my prolonged absences from the *Economist*; thank you Dominic Lawson and Simon Heffer for weeks and weekends away from the *Spectator*. All mistakes, of course, are my own.

GULAG

A History

In this magisterial and acclaimed history, Anne Applebaum offers the first fully documented portrait of the Gulag, from its origins in the Russian Revolution, through its expansion under Stalin, to its collapse in the era of glasnost. The Gulag—a vast array of Soviet concentration camps that held millions of political and criminal prisoners—was a system of repression and punishment that terrorized the entire society, embodying the worst tendencies of Soviet communism. Applebaum intimately re-creates what life was like in the camps and links them to the larger history of the Soviet Union. Immediately recognized as a landmark and long-overdue work of scholarship, *Gulag* is an essential book for anyone who wishes to understand the history of the twentieth century.

History

ANCHOR BOOKS
Available wherever books are sold.
www.anchorbooks.com